CHANGING SCHOOLS

FROM WITHIN

Gordon Wells

Leona Bernard, Mary Ann Gianotti,
Catherine Keating, Christina Konjevic,
Maria Kowal, Ann Maher, Connie Mayer,
Tamara Moscoe, Ewa Orzechowska, Anna
Smieja and Larry Swartz

with a Foreword by
Michael Fullan

CHANGING SCHOOLS

FROM WITHIN

Creating Communities of Inquiry

GORDON WELLS

OISE PRESS
Toronto, Canada

HEINEMANN
Portsmouth, N.H.

The Ontario Institute for Studies in Education has three prime functions: to conduct programs of graduate study in education, to undertake
research in education, and to assist in the implementation of the findings
of educational studies. The Institute is a college chartered by an Act of
the Ontario Legislature in 1965. It is affiliated with the University of
Toronto for graduate studies purposes.

The publications program of the Institute has been established to
make available information and materials arising from studies in education, to foster the spirit of critical inquiry, and to provide a forum for
the exchange of ideas about education. The opinions expressed should be
viewed as those of the contributors.

© The Ontario Institute for Studies in Education 1994
252 Bloor Street West
Toronto, Ontario
M5S 1V6

Canadian Cataloguing in Publication Data
Main entry under title:

Wells, Gordon date
    Changing schools from within : creating communities
of inquiry
Includes bibliographical references.
ISBN 0-7744-0404-3

1. Action research in education. 2. Teaching.
3. Action research in education — Case studies.
4. Teaching — Case Studies. I. Bernard, Leona.
II title.
LB1028.24.W45 1993 371.1'02 C93-095207-3

Library of Congress Cataloging-in-Publication Data

Changing schools from within : creating communities of inquiry /
Gordon Wells . . . [et. al.].
p.   cm.
Includes bibliographical references.
ISBN 0-435-08811-4
1. Action research in education—United States. 2. Educational
change—United States. 3. Classroom management—United States.
4. Education—United States—Aims and objectives. I. Wells, C. Gordon.
LB1028.24.C43 1993
370'.78—dc20   93-33327
                                  CIP

Cover design: TOM SANKEY

ISBN 0-7744-0404-3   Printed in Canada
1 2 3 4 5 6 WC   99 89 79 69 59 49

Contents

vi

Foreword

There is a great deal of rhetoric about teacher-as-researcher, action research, and the like. Much of the literature is *about* teacher as researcher rather than 'inside' it. Proportionately little in-depth work has been written by teachers themselves. *Changing Schools from Within* is an exception. It is solid and exciting, cycling in and out of classrooms. Teachers report on their own action research, focusing on the teaching and learning of language. Students, individual teachers, and groups of teachers become an intertwined community of learners.

The nine middle chapters of the book are written by teachers focusing on their own situations. You won't find in the literature a better set of case studies of teaching inquiry in action. The chapters tell us a great deal about language learning and understanding on the part of children. They tell us even more about how individual teachers can think, inquire, learn and make sense of their own daily work, and more still about how a group of teachers can learn together building a body of knowledge while respecting their own unique situations.

Teaching and learning about teaching become seamless. But it requires deliberately new mind-sets and habits on the part of teachers. This book demonstrates both the process and product of a collective endeavor of a group of teachers and a professor at work in 'real time.' No more are we leaving the classroom to do graduate work. Learning becomes embedded in the teacher as person and the daily responsibilities of teaching and making continuous improvements.

The introductory chapter by Gordon Wells is a stand-alone gem on the topic of teacher research and change. No one has so well critiqued and captured the missing element of teacher-researcher in everyday schools. Wells has written a substantial treatise on the field of teacher-researcher. The need and nature of inquiry, the new roles of teachers — individually and in collaboration — the way in which universities and academics must change are all displayed and clarified. Wells identifies and addresses current criticisms of action research, and shows how the work in this book differs. He holds forth rigorous criteria — deeper understanding of the teacher-learning relationship and the contextual factors affecting it, as a basis for making changes to improve learning opportunities and outcomes.

The teachers' chapters which follow embody the details of individual and joint inquiry into learning and improving the learning situation for all. Wells's concluding chapter, "Watching Ourselves Grow," makes the case that individual and collaborative learning are fundamentally interdependent.

The key to Japan's success in industry and in education, some have argued, is the deeply ingrained values and habits of 'Kaizen.' Kaizen means unending improvements, doing everyday things better by constantly examining them and setting and achieving ever higher standards. In *Changing Schools from Within* one sees the potential power of Kaizen in creating communities of learners. Yet we have a very long way to go.

The learning journey reported in this book occurred despite the system. These teachers had to carve out a learning project in a system not organized to support it. Their work was atypical if not counter-cultural. Imagine the enormous untapped resources that could be unleashed if schools became communities of learners, if administrators and teachers began to redesign their work to incorporate understanding and improvement as unending and organic to their everyday experiences.

Gordon Wells and his colleagues have given us an exciting glimpse of the possible. By what they have already done they challenge us all to create similar learning situations in our own jurisdictions. Such actions by scores of people is the stuff of system change. Schools will never succeed until teachers, individually and collectively, become inquirers, learners and improvers as a normal part of their everyday work. This book represents a significant step in that direction.

— Michael Fullan
University of Toronto

Preface

This book is about change. It is about changing the learning opportunities provided in schools and classrooms so that students are better able to develop the skills, knowledge and understanding needed to live productively and responsibly in the increasingly complex world that we envisage will confront us all in the years ahead. It is also about changing the structures of teacher education and development so that teachers are better able to improve those learning opportunities for the students whom they teach.

In both cases, we are suggesting, changes of this kind can best be brought about through the creation of communities of inquiry, in which knowledge is co-constructed through action, reflection and collaborative talk. This is not just speculation, but a belief that is based on our experiences over the last few years.

The authors of the chapters collected here were all members of a graduate course at the Ontario Institute for Studies in Education, entitled 'Action Research in Language and Learning.' In this community, they met regularly to plan their inquiries and to make sense of the data they were collecting. From this community they also received support for the changes they were making in their ways of teaching, as they explored ways of creating communities of inquiry with their students. But the changes did not stop there. As they talked with their colleagues about what they were doing, other teachers became interested and partnerships began to form. From these beginnings, we hope, further communities of inquiry will develop, in school staffrooms and in Boards and Faculties of Education.

Each of the chapters which follow is the outcome of a personal journey of discovery, starting from a particular teaching-learning situation. But each also contributes to the development of the central themes that are explored throughout this book. Together, they provide convincing evidence that, at all levels of education, the changes that will really make a difference to schools are those that come from teachers and administrators systematically and deliberately inquiring into their own practice and seeking to improve it in the light of the understanding gained in the process. If we want to change schools, they suggest, our efforts will be most fruitful if we, as practitioners, attempt to change them from within.

— *Gordon Wells*
Ontario Institute for Studies in Education. 1993.

Acknowledgments

Every text is the result of many dialogues between the author, whose name appears on the title page, and the many other people who contributed ideas, responses, and suggestions at every stage from the first impulse to write until the final, published version. This is certainly true of all the chapters collected here, and we should like, collectively, to acknowledge our debt to the authors of other texts, to friends and colleagues, and to the editorial team led by Ann Nicholson.

In this context, we should particularly like to thank the two readers of the first draft, Judith Newman and Brent Kilbourn, for their part in bringing this book to fruition. Their enthusiastic response encouraged us to keep working at it, and their helpful comments on individual chapters gave focus to our efforts. From Judith Newman we also received suggestions as to how the collection as a whole might be strengthened, from which we benefited enormously.

Finally, we should like to thank the students with whom we worked, for they continue to be our most important teachers.

1

Introduction: Teacher Research and Educational Change

Gordon Wells

The recognition of the powerful role that practitioners' self-chosen inquiries can play in bringing about educational renewal and change is by no means new. Over the last decade, a number of collections of reports of teachers' inquiries have been published[1] and, going back still further, the idea was already being pioneered in the 1960s in the Humanities Project in Britain under the leadership of Lawrence Stenhouse (Stenhouse, 1975; Elliott, 1990). Nevertheless, despite the growing number of enthusiastic teacher-researchers in many different countries, the idea has been slow to win acceptance in the system at large.

There are two main reasons for this, I believe. The first is that, in valuing the practice-based knowledge and understanding of individual teachers, it challenges the established ways of bringing about educational change. Traditionally, decisions about curriculum, pedagogy and school organization have been made by theorists, researchers and policy-makers, based in universities or ministry offices. Plans for putting these decisions into effect are then drawn up by senior administrators in each jurisdiction, who transmit them to the school administrators who are responsible, in turn, for ensuring that they are implemented. In this hierarchical structure, expertise is equated with power and status, that is to say with those who, at the apex of the pyramid, are furthest removed from the actual sites of learning and teaching. Not surprisingly, therefore, the proposal to democratize the decision-making involved in bringing about educational change by recognizing and drawing upon the very different expertise of inquiring teachers has met with opposition or very limited enthusiasm by many of those who have a vested interest in maintaining the status quo.

The second reason has to do with the nature of teacher research itself. Because of the wide variety of issues that teachers choose to investigate, the inquiries they carry out are very varied in form and often employ methods that have played little or no part in traditional educational research. This makes them difficult to describe in terms that are easily understood by those whose experience and ways of thinking have been shaped by the traditional models of educational research and policy-making. It also means that 'teacher research' cannot readily be reduced to a set procedure or method that can be packaged in a text-book and taught out of the context in which it is to be applied.

Like many complex activities, teacher research is probably best understood through joining a community of practice and working with others who have already acquired some expertise. At present, however, such communities are relatively rare and, like the authors represented here, many of those who are embarking on this form of professional development do so with little idea of the territory to be explored or of the tools and procedures that will be of most use to them. One of the main reasons for publishing the present volume, therefore, is to provide examples of the variety of worthwhile teacher inquiries and to illustrate the range of approaches that have been employed.

As I said earlier, this book grew out of a course in action research, which was offered within the context of graduate studies in education. The course was initially — and still remains — a form of action research in itself, for there are no models on which to base a learning-and-teaching endeavor of this kind. For me, the 'teacher' of the course, as much as for the 'students' who became the authors of the chapters that follow, this has been a voyage of discovery. So, before introducing the individual chapters, I should like to say something about the evolution of my own practice as a teacher and researcher, and about my current understanding of the nature of teacher research and of the conditions necessary for it to flourish.

A Personal Transformation

As a teacher-educator and researcher, I have not always adopted this approach. More recently than I care to remember, I was happy to write reports based on my research in classrooms, which ended with recommendations for the changes that I believed to be implied by my findings. Then, in my role as a teacher of teachers, I would attempt to get my students to put these recommendations into practice. Of course, I expected them to be critical of my suggestions. But it was my agenda that dominated the discussion; I remained the expert who knew what aspects of their teaching they needed to attend to. However, since coming to Canada in 1984, a number of experiences have led me to change my theories about teacher education — and hopefully my practice too.

Learning through Collaboration with Teachers

In 1985, I embarked with a group of colleagues on a new project, investigating language, literacy and learning in schools serving inner-city, multicultural communities. As well as studying the children's development as language and literacy users, our aim was to make our research of use to the teachers in whose classrooms we worked and, hopefully, to embark on collaborative projects with them as well (Wells and Chang-Wells, 1992a; Wells et al., 1992). Quite quickly, I discovered the inappropriateness of the style of classroom research that I had practised in the past and so, abandoning the attempt to be an 'objective' observer in the classroom, I adopted, instead, the role of participant and collaborator. As a result, I came to see the task of teaching in a new light and realised that I had as much to learn from the people with whom I was working, both teachers and students, as they had to learn from me.

Three things, in particular, struck me about those teachers that, from my observations and conversations, I judged to be most effective. First, they behaved like professionals, using their knowledge and experience to make their own judgments about what and how to teach. Not tied to textbooks or preformulated schemes of work, they were willing to assess the needs of the particular students they were teaching and to modify their programs accordingly; they were able, as Atkin (1991) puts it, "to take defensible decisions in concrete situations."

Every class is different from every other in terms of the mix of backgrounds, personalities, and abilities of its members. Individual students each have their own interests, and their strengths and limitations; they also have different contributions to make from their own past experiences, both personal and cultural. Equally, every teacher has a particular style of teaching that is based on personal beliefs, values and past experiences. Together, teacher and students make up a classroom community that is unique, with its own particular potentials and problems. Therefore, teaching can never be a matter of simply 'implementing' packages developed by others, for the generalized curricular guidelines and pedagogical procedures that are thought up by distant experts are rarely appropriate, as they stand, to the needs of particular classrooms.

All teachers adapt and develop the materials and procedures that are recommended to them, but they often do so reluctantly and apologetically, as if such creativity were an indication of failure on their part to do their job properly. However, some of the teachers I met were more confident about experimenting to find the materials and modes of working that best suited their students. In general, these were the classrooms in which students seemed to be most engaged and to be learning most effectively. Clearly, these teachers had developed expertise that needed to be recognized. As professionals with valuable experience, they deserved to be treated as equal partners in decisions about what and how to teach.

A further characteristic I noted about these teachers was that they saw themselves as intentional learners. They actively observed what was happening in their classrooms and were willing to revise their plans and expectations in the light of what they observed. It was this that gave them the confidence to adopt a critical attitude to outside experts, testing proposals against their own beliefs and experience, accepting suggestions that they considered helpful, but rejecting those that they judged to be inappropriate for their own particular circumstances. Not surprisingly, it was these teachers who most effectively encouraged their students to become active, independent learners, since they themselves practised what they preached.

Finally, because they themselves were confident, inquiring learners, they sought out the company of other like-minded colleagues and shared their problems as well as their achievements with them. In this way, they provided and benefited from the mutual support of a community of professionals. In their classrooms, too, they created a similar sense of community, in which individual students learned with and from each other as well as from the teacher.

Reflecting on the Goals of Education

The second important influence on my beliefs about teacher education was also a consequence of my move to Toronto. As a member of the Curriculum Department of an institution in a country very different from the one in which I had lived most of my life, I began to give more thought to the larger goals of education. For most of my career, I had been immersed in questions about language development and about the role of language in learning, but without really concerning myself about what this learning was for. Now, however, I began to question the educational goals I had taken for granted, particularly the emphasis on competitive individual achievement and the segregation of the traditional academic subjects.

Nobody in North America at the end of the twentieth century can fail to be aware of the problems facing humankind — problems that will require more than the knowledge of the traditional academic disciplines for their solution. These range from the inequalities of power and economic well-being between developed and developing nations and within them, and between majority and minority ethnic and cultural groups, to the usurping of minds by the industries of mass entertainment, and the unbridled materialism that is destroying the ecological environment that makes human existence possible. If solutions are to be found to these problems, we need to educate those who will be the decision-makers of tomorrow to understand the need to act differently. Along with the acquisition of subject-based knowledge and skills, therefore, the goals of education must clearly be widened to include a new emphasis on issues of equity and of civic and ecological responsibility.

However, agreement on these goals will not be sufficient without a change in the means we use to bring them into the curriculum. For little will have been achieved if our students merely know what changes in our way of life are necessary, without having also developed the disposition to make those changes that are within their power to effect. A further goal of education must therefore be to develop students who are critical and creative thinkers and problem-solvers, who not only know what needs to be done and why, but who also have the determination to make the necessary changes, both individually and in collaboration with others.

What this calls for, it seems to me, is a radical rethinking, not simply of the content of the school curriculum, but of the manner in which students engage with it. For if we hope that they will manifest independent critical thinking and responsible action in their daily lives after they leave school, these qualities must also be developed and encouraged throughout the course of their education, in all the activities that they undertake. Schools must therefore become places in which students are apprenticed into a way of living — of thinking, feeling and acting — that is informed by these values and which is already being practised by the adult members of the school community.

Once this is accepted, it follows that those who are to be responsible for our students' education must themselves be educated according to the same principles. For we can hardly expect teachers to create the conditions in their classrooms for students to develop these dispositions if the teachers themselves have not had similar formative experiences. Nor can students be expected to develop confidence in their own knowledge and judgment, while recognizing the benefits that are to be gained from collaborating with others, if those who teach them continue to be trained unquestioningly to implement the decisions of others and are given no encouragement to take initiatives in collaboration with their colleagues.

It is clear, therefore, that if we wish to change schools so that they become places in which students acquire the dispositions as well as the knowledge that will enable them to change the societies of which they are members, we must also change the conditions under which their teachers' education and professional development takes place. This includes giving teachers a greater voice in educational decision-making, and encouraging them to develop their own expertise in planning and enacting the curriculum through critical inquiry into their own practice, both individually and in collaboration with their colleagues.

To those tied to traditional modes of teacher education, such a proposal might seem both revolutionary and impossible of achievement. However, my own experiences of working collaboratively with teachers on topics of their own choosing has convinced me that, not only is it desirable, but it is also the only approach that can seriously address the wider goals of education.

Discovering Sociocultural Theory

The third, and perhaps most important, influence on my thinking has been the work of sociocultural theorists, particularly their writings about the activity that Vygotsky, emphasizing its transactional nature, calls learning-and-teaching (Wertsch, 1985). As more of the works of the founding members of this school have been translated into English, I, along with many other educational researchers and writers, have found their ideas particularly valuable in the attempt to construct a theoretical framework within which to make sense of the educational issues that I have outlined above.

In studying children's early language development (Wells, 1985, 1986), I had already been struck by the fact that learning a first language is crucially dependent on the child's opportunities to take part in conversations occurring in the context of purposeful activities, in which the adult — or more expert partner — assists and guides the novice towards full and independent participation. From my research, it seemed clear that those children who learned to talk most readily were, in general, those whose conversational partners were most willing and able to 'lead from behind.'Letting the child take the initiative in selecting which aspect of the task or situation to attend to, these adults seemed intuitively to know how to accept and value the child's contributions and to sustain and extend his or her efforts at meaning-making.Vygotsky (1978) describes this form of teaching as working in the learner's 'zone of proximal development' (ZPD), and argues that it is in this way that the learner is enabled to 'appropriate,' that is to say, take over and make his or her own, not only the language of the culture, but also all the cultural knowledge and procedures that are associated with the activities in which the conversation occurs.

Informed by my reading, I began to see the learning-and-teaching that goes on in classrooms in the same light. Effective teachers, I came to realize, are not those with superb organizational skills and spell-binding powers of presentation — though these qualities are certainly important in the service of enthusing learners and creating the conditions that enable them to engage in individual and collaborative sense-making.What matters more is that teachers be able to observe and listen, as their students engage with the challenges presented, so that they are able to respond in ways that assist the students to solve the problems they meet and, in the process, to encounter and appropriate new cultural knowledge and strategies that can be applied in solving further problems of a similar kind.

Collaborative talk of this kind between teacher and student has not been the norm in most classrooms, although it is, ideally, what the 'writing conference,' pioneered by Graves (1983) and his colleagues, is intended to promote. Unlike most teacher talk, it is responsive rather than directive: it takes its point of departure from the sense the student is making of the task in hand. Unlike casual conversation, on the other hand, it is focused, not diffuse; although the teacher starts where the learner is, she or he intends that, as a result of their collaboration, the student should eventually come to be able to do alone what he or she can now only do with the teacher's help.

However, it is not only with adults that students can learn from collaborative activity and interaction In explaining what he meant by learning and teaching in the zone of proximal development, Vygotsky explicitly stated that the assistance might also come from 'more capable peers' (1978, p.86). And, since the majority of tasks involve a variety of competencies, most members of a group of same-age students will be able to provide assistance on some aspects of a task, and benefit from the expertise of their peers on others. This, too, I observed in those classrooms where teachers provided opportunities for small groups to take responsibility for selecting, planning and carrying out collaborative inquiries within the framework of a whole-class theme or project.

This emphasis on learning through joint activities and interaction with others is of central importance for sociocultural theorists. Like Piaget and other constructivists, they believe that knowledge cannot be transmitted, but must be constructed by each individual learner as he or she makes sense of new information in terms of what is already known. However, for Vygotsky, the source of knowledge — and indeed of the 'higher psychological processes' that are involved in the construction of knowledge — is to be found in the cultural activities in which the learner engages with others, and in the interaction that accompanies, directs and reflects on their shared endeavors. As he puts it:

> The very mechanism underlying higher mental functions is a copy from social interaction; all higher mental functions are internalized social relationships... Even when we turn to mental [internal] processes, their nature remains quasi-social. In their own private sphere, human beings retain the functions of social interaction. (1981, p.164)

However, as Vygotsky also emphasizes, this is not simply a matter of cultural reproduction. It also involves transformation. As the learner appropriates the knowledge and procedures encountered in interaction with others, he or she transforms them, constructing his or her own personal version. But in the process, he or she is also transformed: by taking over the culture's artifacts and practices, and their organizing cognitive structures, the learner modifies his or her own cognitive organization, through which he or she perceives, interprets and organizes the world. Finally, the cycle is completed as the learner externalizes this inner transformation in action. By bringing the newly constructed knowledge to bear on problem situations, he or she may generate new knowledge: by finding new solutions to old problems or even by discovering new problems to be solved.

Thus, just as the learner, by engaging in joint activities and inquiries, is transformed by appropriating the resources of knowledge and problem-solving procedures inherited from the past, so can present activities and inquiries be transformed by the new insights that learners are able to bring to bear on them. In this way, education can function not only as a means of transmitting the achievements of the past, but it can also be a site of cultural renewal and development.

Schools as Centers of Inquiry

As I reflected on these various experiences, I began to form a new image of education. Instead of the traditional model, in which knowledge and expertise are treated as vested in those with power and authority, whose responsibility it is to transmit them to those on lower levels in the hierarchy, I began to imagine a different model, based on communities of action and inquiry. Here, knowledge and expertise are a shared achievement, arising from joint engagement in challenging activities that are personally significant to the participants. In such communities, there is certainly an important place for the ways of acting and thinking that are embodied in the artifacts and practices inherited from the dominant cultural tradition. But these are seen as 'tools,' which are taken over for purposes of action and inquiry; rather than as ends in themselves, they are mastered for their functional utility.

I had already seen such communities coming into existence in some of the classrooms in which I had worked. Here, the teachers no longer assumed an automatic superiority of knowledge — nor attributed it to the texts and other curricular materials they used. Instead, they treated all participants as able to offer new and valuable insights with respect to the issues under consideration. Contributions and suggestions were not judged right or wrong by reference to authority, but rather by whether they helped to advance group or individual understanding, or to facilitate joint action. In these classrooms, too, there was much less emphasis on competition as the spur to individual achievement. Many positive consequences followed from this changed relationship, including a spontaneous willingness to share and collaborate, an increase in self-esteem on the part of the less advanced students, and a greater engagement in learning by all students, with a consequent decrease in the need for the teacher to chivvy them to keep on task.

So, if the 'climate for learning' in the classroom (Torbe and Medway, 1981) could be transformed through the creation of a community of collaborative inquiry and conversation, why not in the staffroom as well? Since the same principles apply to all learners, teachers, too, might welcome the opportunity to become inquirers into their own practice in collaboration with other members of the community of their peers and colleagues. And, if this were true for teachers, why not for administrators, too? And, finally, might these various communities of inquiry not benefit from collaborative links between, as well as within, them?

It was at about this time that I first came across Schaefer's seminal work, 'The School as a Center of Inquiry.' Although published in 1967, its central concept still seems as revolutionary as it doubtless did then. Since it captures so concisely the vision that had been gradually emerging as I reflected on my own experience and reading, I should like to quote a paragraph from the opening chapter.

> By a school organized as a center of inquiry, I imply an institution characterized by a pervasive search for meaning and rationality in its work. Fundamentally, such a school requires that teachers be freed to inquire into the nature of what and how they are teaching. Discovering new knowledge about the instructional process is the distinctive contribution which the lower schools might be expected to provide. As every teacher knows, however, pedagogical strategies cannot be meaningfully separated from content, and there must also be continuing opportunity for the teacher to inquire into the substance of what is being taught. Finally, no school can be reflective about its work or serious in its commitment to learning if students are not similarly encouraged to seek rational purpose in their own studies. (pp. 3-4)

Here, then, was a model for the community of inquiry that I suggested earlier, that would provide both an apprenticeship into creative, critical and responsible thinking and action for its student members and encouragement to its adult members to model those same qualities as they worked together to improve the climate and opportunities for learning that they provided.

The Role of the University

If educational renewal and development are to come from within schools, as teachers and administrators seek to identify those areas in need of improvement and, together, plan and carry out the necessary changes, what is the role of university-based researchers and teacher-educators? Ideally, of course, this question should be one of the major issues addressed within the communities of inquiry that they too should form. Unfortunately, however, just as few schools have, as yet, adopted the vision that I have just described, so have few Faculties and Schools of Education given concerted thought to how best to support this form of educational change and development. Nevertheless, in various parts of the world, increasing numbers of individual faculty members are exploring new ways of contributing to the initial preparation and continuing professional development of teachers and school administrators. They are also developing new forms of educational research, in which they work collaboratively with teachers on issues of mutual interest and concern.

My own first steps in this direction were taken in the context of the 'Language and Learning Project' (Wells et al., 1992), as we invited the teachers we were working with to select topics for inquiry in their own classrooms and attempted to provide them with professional and technical support in planning and carrying out their investigations. Initially, most of these inquiries involved only individual teachers but, by the final year of the project, efforts were being made in one school to build such teacher inquiries into the school's mode of teacher evaluation and staff development. Also, in the context of preparing a conference symposium, a group of four teachers from two of the schools, together with one of the principals and four of the research team, formed a working group to discuss, revise and extend the reports of the inquiries they had conducted (Wells and Chang-Wells, 1992a).

Since then, I have been involved in a variety of collaborative projects with teachers, in capacities ranging from consultant to the Peel Board of Education's 'Talk: A Medium for Learning and Change' (Booth and Thornley-Hall, 1991), to my present role as one of three University-based Principal Investigators in an action-research-based investigation into the role of language in the learning and teaching of science (Wells, 1993). In the former of these projects, genuine school-based communities of inquiry came into existence among the staffs of several of the schools involved and they continued beyond the end of the external support. The same has been true of the district-wide community of teacher-inquirers with whom I worked in Richmond, British Columbia, on the broad theme of active learning in classroom and staffroom.

Inevitably, however, the opportunities for university faculty to contribute in this way to the development of communities of inquiry in individual schools is severely limited. So I began to explore ways of making classroom-based inquiry an integral part of the graduate-level courses I was teaching at the university. To begin with, I encouraged course members to base their major assignment on a practical investigation into an issue of their own choosing related to the content of the course. Then, finding that the vast majority of the teachers taking these courses appreciated the opportunity that such an assignment provided for them to make connections between their daily experiences in the classroom and the readings that I had selected for the weekly meetings, I decided to offer a course exclusively devoted to action research.

Entitled 'Action Research in Language and Learning,' this course was open to educators whose current appointments allowed them to investigate some aspect of their own practice. The reference to language and learning in the title was not intended to limit topics for investigation to a particular area of the curriculum, but rather to indicate that we would be centrally concerned with learning — both our own as well as that of our students — and that language — transcripts of classroom or staffroom talk, samples of students' writing, interview responses, and so on — would be the major source of evidence for whatever topic was chosen for investigation.

In the three years that this course has been offered, its membership has included classroom teachers working with students from kindergarten to grade eight; it has also included school administrators, consultants and advisory teachers, as well as those embarking on a career in teacher education. Despite the diversity of topics selected in each year, however, the common approach of observing, recording and analyzing specific episodes of interaction allowed all of us to learn from each others' investigations and to contribute to one another's inquiries from the insights gained from our own. In our bi-weekly meetings, we thus created another community of inquiry, meeting in the university, but focused on, and intended to support, the development of school-based communities of inquiry through our engagement in action research. The chapters collected in this volume represent the fruits of some of those inquiries.

CHANGING SCHOOLS FROM WITHIN BY CHANGING OUR OWN PRACTICE

The ten inquiries reported here fall naturally into two groups. Chapters two to seven all address issues which arise from the daily practice of teaching elementary age students. Each is concerned with some aspect of literacy learning and with the place that conversations about texts play in the creation of a classroom community of readers and writers. However, within this group, there are three more specific themes. Chapters two and three examine the role of conferencing, both among students and between students and teacher, in grades one and two. Chapters four and five are concerned with ways of providing opportunities for grade four and five students to respond to the books they have been reading. Chapters six and seven explore ways to enable students who are initially excluded from the literacy community to become participating members.

Exploring the Value of Conferencing

The term 'conferencing' was introduced into the professional language of elementary teachers by Donald Graves and his colleagues (Graves, 1983; Calkins, 1983; Atwell, 1987) to describe the talk that occurs around the composition of students' written texts. In the classrooms in which they carried out their research, the new focus on the processes of writing quite spontaneously gave rise to conversations in which the adults asked questions about the student writers' intentions, about the strategies they were using in composing their texts, and about how they felt both about their texts and about themselves as writers. As was quickly discovered, such conversations are not only of value to the researcher; the same questions that help the adult to understand what the child is doing also encourage the child to become more reflective about the relationship between ends and means and to develop the metacognitive skills that are characteristic of more expert writers.

However, a second benefit accrues from questions of this sort. The answers that the children give provide a much firmer basis for the teacher to give them assistance with the problems that they are encountering in a form that is tailored to their current understanding as well as to the goals that they are trying to achieve. The conference is thus a particularly clear instance of what Vygotsky (1978) called learning and teaching 'in the zone of proximal development.'

But perhaps assistance with the task of composing need not be limited to the conferences the young writer has with his or her teacher. In recent years, there has been considerable interest in Vygotsky's suggestion that assistance in the ZPD can also be given by more capable peers and, on this basis, novice writers are encouraged to conference, either formally or informally, with their classmates. As Calkins (1983) writes of the classrooms she observed, "peer conferences occurred throughout the entire writing process" (p.117).

Having read about this research, Mary Ann Gianotti (chapter two) organized her twice-weekly writing workshop in a way that encouraged the children in her combined grade one and two class to conference with each other about their writing whenever they wanted to do so. As a result, their writing was accompanied by a constant buzz of conversation. But, like many other teachers, she was uncertain about the value of all this talk, so she decided to make some systematic observations.

What she found was that the talk was indeed productive, but not entirely in the ways she had expected. However, by looking carefully at the episodes of sharing talk she had transcribed with the aid of ideas gleaned from further reading, she was able to see clear evidence of a number of valuable functions that these child-initiated conversations served. This, in turn, led to a reevaluation of her own role in managing the learning opportunities offered by the writing workshop and of the way she planned the conferences that she herself had with these young writers. Her chapter provides powerful evidence of the value of action research: "I learned many powerful lessons through observing and gathering data about the children that I would not have learned without entering a formal investigation of my classroom teaching practice"(p. 57).

As noted above, the term 'conferencing' came into use to describe the talk that occurs around the composition of a student's written text. However, the practice itself had long been part of some teachers' ways of working, and not only in relation to students' writing. Right across the curriculum, students are often asked to produce representations of what they understand about a topic in the form of drawings, diagrams, models and even 'sums.' When these products are seen as symbolic artifacts, by means of which some meaning is constructed according to cultural proce- dures and conventions, they can be treated in ways analogous to written texts and, like them, form the basis for conferences in which the teacher works with the student in his or her ZPD to assist him or her to gain greater control of the relevant genre and understanding of the meaning that he or she is attempting to represent.

This was the starting point for Tamara Moscoe's inquiry (chapter three). As she states, "some of the most valuable learning seemed to happen as I met with individuals and small groups before, during and after they had completed an activity" (p. 61). And so, like Gianotti, she decided to look more carefully at these conferences to find out what was actually going on.

By carefully documenting with whom she conferenced, how often and for how long, she was able to satisfy herself that her time was equitably distributed. Next she documented what happened during the conferences to find out whether they served the purposes (her own and the students') for which they were held. Here again, she was reassured. However, when she began to examine the conferences more closely, by transcribing selected episodes, she met with a number of surprises. Some of these were positive, revealing learning opportunities that she was unaware of providing. Others were less so, but these, too, were also productive, as they led to modifications in her practice. Moscoe concludes by reaffirming her belief in the importance of talk, but with an added awareness: "It is important to really listen to the talk, not only of the children, but also my own."

For both Gianotti and Moscoe, it was systematic observation — and particularly the practice of transcribing episodes of conversation — that made the difference to their way of being in the classroom. By enabling them to reach a more profound understanding of the opportunities for learning that were occurring (or in some cases were not occurring) in the conferences that formed such an important part of their classroom routines, their inquiries led them to make changes that were based in both theory and practice.

Responding to Literature

Just as the teaching of writing has undergone a radical change as a result of the new focus on the processes of writing instead of only on the finished product, so is the teaching of reading being revolutionized by the research on reader response. In a nutshell, reading, according to this theory, involves a transaction between writer and reader that is mediated by the printed text (Rosenblatt, 1988). Although the writer attempts to convey his or her intentions through the linguistic structure which is the text, the reader's purpose for engaging with the text, and his or her existing knowledge about its content and about the conventions of the genre in which it is written, are as important for the interpretation that he or she constructs as are the cues to meaning that are provided by the text itself.

Reader response thus refers to two conceptually distinct, but inter-related processes. First, as a transaction with the writer through the medium of the printed page, the act of reading involves a response — or series of responses — in which the reader gives meaning to the linguistic cues in the light of the expectations that he or she brings to the text, as these are extended and modified by the interpretation of the text so far. However, since the text is also a message from the writer, reading may well involve a second type of response, which is more akin to the next turn in a conversation (Bakhtin, 1986). In an article in which he contrasts this response-evoking function of a text with what he calls its 'univocal' function (i.e., its function as a conveyor of information) Lotman (1988) argues that it is the former, 'dialogic,' function which enables the text to act as a 'thinking device' for the reader: as he or she thinks about how to respond, the text becomes 'a generator of meaning.' So, by sharing both these types of response with each other, the members of a classroom community — or any other community of readers — can calibrate the interpretations they have made of the text with those of other members, and discover new possibilities that they had not thought of for themselves (Chambers, 1985).

It was in the light of these ideas that Ann Maher reviewed her classroom reading program and found it to be in need of change (chapter four). Her first idea was to allow much more opportunity for her grade four and five students to read books of their own choosing and, instead of engaging in teacher-led discussions of an assigned text, to write their individual responses in journals to which she would personally respond.

As she soon discovered, however, this was not enough. Once given the opportunity, the children had so much to share and so much to teach each other about what books to read and about what made them significant. Dialogue journals shared only with the teacher were not a good medium for this wider conversation; the written exchange was also too infrequent to keep up with their current reading. So Maher made a second change: to a program of independent reading only, accompanied by regular opportunities to talk with others about what they were reading. Both she and the children found the new arrangement much more satisfactory. One of the advantages, as she notes, was that, "relieved from the pressure to plan for reading 'groups,' I now had the opportunity to extend what the students began to call our 'conversations about books'" (p. 88). Another was the increased enthusiasm for reading that she noticed among her students and the evident pleasure they gained from sharing their discoveries with others. Her conclusion, which would be echoed by several of the other contributors, is that, if you want to know what the children think, you only have to listen to what they say.

Interestingly, Larry Swartz (chapter five), also started with a sense of discomfort with his reading program. He had already used dialogue response journals in the previous year, but was disappointed at the paucity of genuine dialogue. At the beginning of the year, however, he was still convinced they could serve a valuable purpose if he could improve his role as dialogue partner. And so, in his inquiry, he planned, through the use of dialogue response journals, "to discover the relationship between the teacher, the text and the learner" (p. 100).

As the term progressed, however, and he systematically noted how the journals were being used and reflected on these observations, he felt a growing sense of dissatisfaction. Despite his efforts, the writing of responses remained an activity carried out mainly to please the teacher and, although he worked hard on his replies, the dialogue never seemed to progress beyond a single exchange. A further problem was that the students did not seem to be making connections between their reading and the important events in their lives outside school.

Two developments were instrumental in leading Swartz to change his strategy. The first was the students' responses to a poem that they read and discussed together. In the oral mode, they were able to draw more freely on personal experiences to tell stories that sparked further stories and to write about them as well. An opportunity to engage in 'booktalk,' it seemed, was an important ingredient in helping students to respond to the literature they encountered.

The second development was one that occurred for Maher as well. Both she and Swartz were given a final nudge by encountering the ideas of other researchers at the point when their observations had convinced them that they needed to revise their current programs. In Swartz's case, the decision to change was the end-point of the inquiry reported here but, as he says, "I have had some questions answered, but I have uncovered many more. I have made some changes; I will certainly be making others" (p. 126). For both Maher and Swartz, action research has become part of their way of teaching, and the initial concern with responding to literature has broadened into a more general concern with providing opportunities for students to make sense of their important experiences by sharing them with others.

Helping Minority Groups Enter the Mainstream Literacy Community

In the last few years, there has been a considerable broadening in the range of studies into the nature and consequences of literacy, as researchers have begun to examine the place and value of literacy in non-mainstream cultures (e.g. Street, 1987), and to document the literate practices through which youngsters in home and school settings are differently inducted into membership of the relevant literacy clubs (e.g. Heath, 1983). As a result of what has been learned, it is increasingly being argued that simply immersing school entrants in mainstream literacy practices, such as shared story reading and writing, is insufficient to ensure that children from non-mainstream cultures will appropriate these practices and gain entrance to the club. More direct instruction in the skills of literacy is the solution advocated by some (Delpit, 1988), while for others it is the cultural relevance of the practices themselves, and of the texts that are used, that needs to be subjected to critical scrutiny (Goodman and Goodman, 1990).

However, for students who are excluded first and foremost by their unfamiliarity with the language that is spoken in the classroom, it seems reasonable to argue that this should be the first focus of attention. In some situations, it has been possible to mount bilingual programs, and often with considerable success. In such cases, the introduction to school literacy takes place largely in the children's first language; being language neutral, it is argued, the important concepts about literacy can best be learned through engagement in literacy practices in a language in which the child is already fluent; once mastered, they are fairly easily transferred to the comparable practices of a second language community (Cummins, 1984). Whether these concepts are indeed comparable across languages for cultural groups with very different literacy practices is more open to question; however, if the practices as well as the language are unfamiliar, the argument for learning to cope with the literacy practices expected in the classroom through the medium of the child's first language seems doubly warranted.

Bilingual programs are not always feasible, however. In cosmopolitan cities such as Toronto, schools serve communities containing families from many different non-English speaking backgrounds. Even if qualified teachers could be found for each of these language groups, the sheer diversity of languages spoken by the children in each classroom would make the mounting of bilingual programs impracticable. In such circumstances, English immersion, supplemented by some form of ESL support, seems to be the only viable solution. However, this is by no means ideal, as there is inevitably a period during which the ESL learner is unable to participate fully in the activities of the classroom community. For some, this exclusion is not just a temporary stage on the way to fluent mastery of the new language; apparently not valued because not heard, the voices of these children remain silenced, and the low self-esteem that this induces leads to school failure and drop-out, which could have been avoided (Cummins, 1984). And even for the majority, who are ultimately successful in becoming full members of the school community (Baird, 1992), total immersion can be a disorienting and frustrating experience, particularly in the early stages.

As Polish immigrants, Ewa Orzechowska and Anna Smieja both underwent this experience themselves and so were perhaps more sensitive than some teachers might be to the plight of non-

English-speaking new arrivals in Canada. Smieja's kindergarten class contained a number of such children, some of them Polish-speaking, and there were others in the grade 2 class in which Orzechowska was a regular visitor. In chapter six, they tell how their inquiry started when they observed the frustration of some new Canadian children during story-sharing time. As yet unable to communicate in the language of the classroom, they were debarred from taking part in the discussion, although they clearly had observations to contribute on the basis of their interpretation of the pictures. Would such children be helped, they wondered, if they were able to discuss the picture story-books that the teacher was reading with an adult who spoke their first language? The answer was clearly in the affirmative, as the transcribed (and translated) excerpts from some of the ensuing discussions show. Not only were they able to join in but, in the discussion, the teacher's attention "could now be given to these students' overall intellectual development, *as well as* to their acquisition of a second language" (p. 149).

On the basis of the evidence that they collected, Orzechowska and Smieja argue strongly for the extension of the sort of support they were able to offer to other areas of the curriculum. They also make some suggestions as to how their 'pilot' project could be built upon in other, similar classrooms. Just as the voices of teachers need to be heard, they conclude, so do the voices of children. For with voice comes power — "the power to use [our] own experience and knowledge and to have them recognized as a valid basis for making meaning" (p. 150).

Another group, who have even more difficulty in gaining entry to the mainstream English-speaking community, are the deaf. Not only do these children have difficulty in communicating with their hearing peers; in many cases, on entry to school, they have developed no systematic language for communicating with others at all. And even when they have become reasonably fluent users of sign language, this does not help them a great deal in learning to read and write English, since there is no equivalent of written English in the medium of sign.

This predicament was the starting point for the writing pro-gram described by Connie Mayer (chapter seven). In collabora-tion with a friend and colleague in the adjoining Public School, she set up an integrated writing workshop, based on the work of Graves and his colleagues (Graves, 1983), in which primary-age deaf and hearing children worked together to learn to communi-cate with each other and their teachers through written English. This chapter offers fascinating glimpses of the operation of this unusual bilingual community and presents some of the wealth of evidence that Mayer and her colleague collected to document the progress of the deaf children in the early stages of learning to write. Despite the different route they were obliged to follow, these children made significant progress in learning the genres of narrative composition and, like their hearing peers, invented systematic ways to represent written words on their way to conventional spelling. Furthermore, as well as learning the value of written communication, both deaf and hearing children learned to understand each other better and, through working together, overcame their initial mistrust of others who were different from themselves.

What is foregrounded in Mayer's chapter, however, is her inquiry into her own development as a teacher. Starting from an educational philosophy that was based on language training through highly structured materials, she learned through her partnership to think of the teaching-learning relationship in very different terms. Although cut off from access to spoken English, deaf children, she discovered, could make significant progress in appropriating the literacy practices of the mainstream community if they were included as co-participants in that community, and received assistance — from peers as well as teachers — that was responsive to their particular needs and given in a form that valued their first language competence as signers as well as the target patterns of written English.

Like several of her fellow teacher-researchers, Mayer found her developing insights were illuminated by ideas from sociocultural theory and, in particular, by Vygotsky's (1978) notion of learning and teaching in the ZPD. However, it was not only her role as a teacher that she came to understand in these terms. As a learner, too, she recognized that she had benefited enormously from her partnership with a trusted colleague who, in their work together, had played the role of the 'more capable peer.' As she looked back over their collaborative action research, several features emerged as critical for its success. However, of these, she concludes, it was their conversations that seemed to be the most important: "Certainly my growth as a teacher in my zone of proximal development came about largely because of my conversations with Evie" (p. 170).

Action Research on Being a Teacher Educator

The remaining four chapters are all concerned with teacher education in one form or another. In each case, the 'students' are other teachers or would-be teachers, and the teacher-researcher's aim is to help them to learn through reflection on their own practice. Simultaneously, however, the teachers are also submitting their own practice to reflective scrutiny as they make it the focus of their own action research.

It is sometimes suggested that, when working with adult learners, different principles apply from those that guide the teacher of school-aged learners. And, to some extent, this is no doubt true. Adults normally undertake further education from choice and with a particular objective in mind. Typically, they also have a greater repertoire of learning strategies than younger students. This means that, in principle, less effort needs to be spent in motivating them and that they are less dependent on the teacher to direct their activities. And, on the opposite side of the coin, they are more ready to express their dissatisfaction if the teacher fails to meet their expectations.

However, what is striking about the chapters brought together in this volume is the similarity in the approach to the teaching-learning relationship that is found right across the spectrum, from kindergarten to graduate studies. This is perhaps not altogether surprising as, in discussing the authors' individual inquiries in our bi-weekly meetings, we were also exploring the relevance of sociocultural theory to the situations they were researching. Nevertheless it is worth pointing out, I believe, that such fundamental principles as the essentially social and constructive nature of learning, the central role of discourse in the learning-teaching transaction, and the applicability of Vygotsky's notion of working in the ZPD, were found to be equally valid at all levels in the educational hierarchy.

Nowhere is this more apparent than in Maria Kowal's account of her work with student teachers (chapter eight). Playing three roles in parallel — classroom teacher, novice teacher-educator and graduate student — she observed the essential similarity between the three communities of which she was a member and exploited her growing understanding of their interconnectedness for the benefit of her student teachers-in-training. As she writes of the beginning of her inquiry: "I was looking for a framework which would allow the student teachers and myself to draw on our practical knowledge, whilst simultaneously causing us to reflect, through discussion, on our teaching performance as we learned about improving our practice" (p. 175).

In chapter nine, we see another configuration of the same three levels — but with a different twist. Leona Bernard was a resource teacher who was responsible for assisting primary teachers who had children in their classrooms who spoke a language other than English at home. Christina Konjevic was just such a teacher; she was concerned that the ESL children in her kindergarten class were not attentive when she was reading a story to the whole class. In part, their chapter is an account of how Bernard helped Konjevic to formulate and test hypotheses about the reason for this unsatisfactory state of affairs and, having arrived at a conclusion, to make changes in her practice to overcome the problem. From this point of view, there are interesting connections to be made with the rather similar situation that formed the point of departure for Orzechowska and Smieja's inquiry (chapter six).

However, the real focus of Bernard and Konjevic's chapter is the story of their developing partnership. As each comes to recognize the limitations of the traditional, hierarchical relationship between consultant and classroom teacher, the purpose of their meetings changes. Instead of being the imparting of knowledge by expert to novice, it becomes a collaborative exploration of the processes of inquiry, and of the role of conversation in advancing their individual inquiries and in creating the sort of supportive yet challenging relationship which enables each to assist the other in learning and growing. Having started separately as members of what each took to be very different communities, together they enter a new and more empowering community — that of teachers who are learners about how to help other teachers to learn and change.

Change in teachers is now recognized to be the prerequisite for bringing about educational change. Traditionally, this has been managed through two complementary activities: teacher training (or retraining) and teacher supervision and evaluation. In recent years, however, educational jurisdictions have begun to experiment with alternative approaches. One such is the 'Supervision for Growth' model that provides the framework for Catherine Keating's inquiry (chapter ten). In this model, a teacher is evaluated in terms of his or her success in working towards learning goals that are negotiated with the school administration. While participation is mandatory, individual teachers have considerable choice as to how they fulfil this requirement, and a substantial effort has been made by the School Board's central administration to present a variety of alternative forms of self-directed professional development, including the option of action research (North York Board of Education, 1991).[2] As the Vice-Principal of an elementary school, it is part of Keating's responsibility to help the teachers on her staff to identify their own learning goals and to develop and implement personal growth plans that will enable them to achieve these goals. As she writes, this requirement "offers a new opportunity for teachers and administrators to work in a collaborative partnership" (p. 218).

In this context, Keating describes her attempt to use dialogue journals with three teachers in her school. From her previous experience of this mode of mentoring with another administrator, she believed that this form of dialogue could be an effective way of establishing a more collegial relationship, in which the teachers would feel able to raise issues that were of concern to them and she would be able to help them to address those issues through practical advice and through encouragement of reflection. This, in fact, proved to be the case: all concerned found the experiment worthwhile and would have welcomed a more frequent exchange than actually occurred. However, as with all the other inquiries, an equally important outcome was the writer's own growth, through her developing understanding of her own role as a teacher educator as well as administrator. Starting with an image of herself as mentor, she came to see that it was even more important to be a learner: "In doing so, I might be better able to help the teachers to perceive themselves as learners as well" (p. 234).

The final chapter (chapter eleven) concerns a different and — at least superficially — more traditional form of teacher education. Where the previous three chapters described various forms of school-based, action-oriented, professional development, the situation described here is a university-based course in a program of graduate studies in education. My problem was how, in a course held in summer when classroom-based inquiry was not practicable, to enable the participants to have an experience of inquiry-based learning that would lead them to want to become action researchers when they returned to their schools and classrooms in the following September. The solution I decided upon was based on Duckworth's (1987) account of her teaching, in which students study a secondary subject and make this experience the material for the primary study of learning and teaching. In our case, we would conduct inquiries into the theme of time and make these the basis for a joint inquiry into the role of talk and texts in our experiences of learning and teaching.

However, there was a further level to our investigation. Like my co-authors, I too adopted the stance of action researcher to my role as teacher, and invited the course members to join with me in exploring the applicability to our work together of ideas found in our readings in sociocultural theory, which formed the third strand of our cross-modal, interdisciplinary investigation. Later, as I reviewed the data I had collected and reflected on the events of the month-long course, I found that many of the issues that I needed to work through in writing my chapter were similar to those discussed by my fellow teacher-researchers. Perhaps this is not surprising, given the many discussions we had had about learning and teaching. However, it did further reinforce my conviction that, although the way in which they are enacted may — and should — vary according to the specifics of each teacher's situation, the underlying principles are robust enough to provide guidance to all, whatever the age or status of the learners they teach and whatever aspect of their practice they choose to investigate.

Themes and Variations

As these brief descriptions make clear, the chapters which follow differ quite considerably in the topics that are addressed and in the roles of those carrying out the inquiries. Yet, from this diversity emerge a number of important commonalities, both in the discoveries that their authors made, and in the conditions and procedures that facilitated their work. In the final section of this introduction, therefore, I should like to comment on what I have learned from our work together about the goals of teachers' action research and about some of the conditions that seem to help it to flourish.

TEACHERS' ACTION RESEARCH AS A MODE OF PROFESSIONAL DEVELOPMENT

Although the number of teachers conducting action research is still very small, relative to the total teacher population, the enthusiasm of its advocates is sufficient to have attracted attention recently from several university researchers — and not always of a positive nature. It seems necessary, therefore, to start by addressing some of the criticisms that have been levelled against this sort of research and to state what I see to be its characteristics and its particular virtues as a *form of professional development*.

The criticisms fall into two broad categories. The first concerns what is seen to be the *ad hoc* and context-bound nature of many of the inquiries that are undertaken. Because they do not meticulously observe the methodological practices required of 'professional' research, it is claimed, such inquiries do not yield valid or replicable findings and, as a result, contribute little of value to the 'knowledge-base' of the discipline (Applebee, 1987). The second main line of criticism is that teacher research is a waste of teachers' professional effort. Since teachers have neither the time nor the resources to carry out 'proper' research, to encourage them to carry out small-scale action research projects, it is argued, is to divert them from their 'real' responsibility, which is to learn more about curriculum, through reading, attending conferences and generally undertaking further training (Glass, 1993). On both counts, therefore, these critics argue, the conduct of educational research should be left to the professionals, meaning those in universities and colleges of education.

In my view, however, such criticisms manifest a misunderstanding of the purpose of teacher inquiry, being based as they are on the traditional model of educational research, of which controlled, experimental intervention studies are the paradigm case. Teachers, on the other hand, are coming to realise more and more that, although such large-scale studies may contribute to knowledge about education at some abstract level, they have little to offer to practitioners working in the specific cultural contexts constituted by the particular children who make up their classes in a particular neighbourhood at a particular moment in history. What teachers are coming to value, by contrast, is research that both grows out of, and has as its purpose to inform, their own classroom practice, and which is rooted in the specific contexts which are relevant to their concerns. In addition, and perhaps more importantly, they are coming to see that, far from being an activity which is only carried out *on* teachers and students by others, research can be an activity that they themselves perform as an integral part of the work of teaching. In so doing, they are also discovering that research is a way of coming to know — that is to say, of learning — which can change the role of the learner from that of passive consumer of other people's ideas to that of agentive constructor of his or her own knowledge and, at the same time, provide a means for the principled modification of professional practice (Atwell, 1991; Duckworth, 1987; Strickland, 1988).

Teacher research can thus be seen to belong to a different paradigm from traditional educational research, both in its objectives and in its underlying ideology. Where traditional research attempted to be objective, value-free, and context-independent, and aimed at the production of generalisable information, teacher research is rooted in the subjective, lived experience of particular classrooms, and intended first and foremost to contribute to the personal and professional growth of the individual teacher-researcher. It is thus its basis in practice that is the defining characteristic of teacher research. Arising from the professional concerns of individual practitioners, or a group of practitioners working collaboratively, the research is undertaken in order that those who conduct it may both improve their practice and increase their understanding of its theoretical underpinnings. Furthermore, unlike most university-based research, teachers' action research does not seek for closure. Instead, its practitioners adopt inquiry as their fundamental stance as, through cycles of observation, reflection and action, they continuously work to develop their understanding and improve their practice.

Of course, as has been frequently observed, effective teachers have always monitored their practice and used their observations as feedback to enable them to take corrective action to maximise the attainment of their objectives. They have also attempted to keep abreast of developments in theory, either through independent reading or by taking professional courses to improve their qualifications, and have then tried to use the theoretical insights gained to modify and improve their teaching practice. Increasingly, too, they are taking time to reflect on their experience in order to arrive at a more conscious and explicit understanding of the bases of their actions (Schön, 1987; Connelly and Clandinnin, 1988). What is different about action research, therefore, is not the attention to theory and practice *per se* but, rather, the creation of a new dialectical relationship between them, as increased understanding is derived from the interpretation of observations of the effect of a deliberately introduced change, and that new understanding is used to plan further change to improve practice, in a never-ending spiral.

At this point, we might try to capture the characteristics of this — admittedly idealized — model of action research in terms of the following component activities:

- Observe: make systematic observations of relevant aspects of the situation to find out what is actually happening.

- Interpret: reflect on the observations to try to understand why things are happening as they are. Where things are working well, what are the factors that seem to make this possible?Where things are not going well, what are the factors that are probably responsible?

- Plan change: in the light of the conclusions drawn about the factors responsible for what is satisfactory/ unsatisfactory about the present situation, construct hypotheses about the changes that would be likely to bring about an improvement. Select one or more of these changes that can feasibly be undertaken and plan how to carry it out.

- Act: put the planned change into operation.

In the idealized situation depicted in this model, the effects of the change would then be systematically observed, the data interpreted, and further appropriate changes planned and carried out. In this way, the research would proceed through cycles of the same component activities in a continuing spiral (Carr and Kemmis, 1986).

However, the four components just listed all belong in the realm of practice. What needs to be added, to complete the model of classroom action research, is the practitioner's personal theory, which informs and is informed by the cycle of action research (Chang, 1990). And it is in making the connections between practice and theory, as this relationship is constructed and made explicit through the cycle of research, that the practitioner adopts the stance of reflectiveness, which is the hallmark of the teacher researcher (Atwell, 1991).

The relationship between these various components can be shown diagrammatically as in Figure 1.

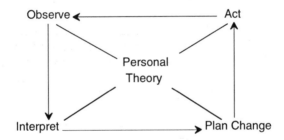

Figure 1. An Idealized Model of the Action Research Cycle

The above figure gives only a skeletal representation of this idealized model of action research. For a more adequate account, it needs to be qualified in two important ways. First, it should be extended to include at least the following dimensions:

- attention to the wider context in which the inquiry is carried out: this is necessary both in order to understand the ways in which what can and cannot be achieved is influenced by contextual factors, and also so that, in reporting the inquiry, the account of what was done and why can be contextualized in ways that will enable others to relate it to their own experience;

- recognition of the importance of reading about other work, both theoretical and practical, that bears on the topic of the inquiry, and of writing about it, both for self and for others;

- engagement in informal, collaborative talk with interested others at every stage in the process.

Secondly, the diagram is inadequate in another way, in that it suggests that, to qualify as action research, a teacher's inquiry must proceed through a fixed sequence of phases. Whilst such a model may come to inform the thinking of the seasoned action researcher, the experience of the authors of the following chapters shows that this is rarely how the activity proceeds in practice, particularly when they are just embarking on action research. To give such a prescriptive interpretation to the model would therefore be doubly unfortunate; for not only would it exclude many worthwhile investigations, but it would also import evaluative criteria which are inappropriate to the goals of this model of action research. Nancie Atwell, a well-known teacher-researcher, is quite explicit about this point: 'There is a danger that we [teacher researchers] could rest content doing something we do not understand. As we continue to consider what teacher research is, we should be aware that it is not theory-stripped, context-stripped method-testing. We need to reject impoverished models that turn classroom inquiry into a pseudo-scientific horse race' (1991, p.16). Or, to put it differently, the doing of action research is more important than having done it, and the searching for routes to the anticipated goal is more important than being able to produce a map which will obviate the need for others to make the journey of exploration.

The distinction that is being made here can be clarified by considering the criteria by which the different types of research should be evaluated. Traditional research, whether quantitative or qualitative, which has as one of its primary goals to advance the field in which it is carried out, is judged in terms of the significance and originality of its contribution and by the generalisability of its findings. By contrast, action research undertaken as a mode of professional development has as its primary goal the personal and professional growth of the practitioner. Its value, therefore, should be judged less in terms of the 'quality' of the 'product' or the rigor of its methodology, and more in terms of the learning that results for the person carrying it out and the improvements that he or she effects in his or her practice as a consequence. In other words, the principle criterion for evaluating a piece of action research is not the significance of its findings for others, but rather the value of the experience of undertaking it for the researcher him/herself. Has it led to a deeper understanding of the teaching-learning relationship and of the contextual factors that impinge on it, such that the teacher-researcher now has a more explicit, principled basis for making changes designed to improve learning opportunities and student out-comes? Has it resulted in more meaningful learning by the students for whom the teacher is responsible?

Key Aspects of Action Research as a Mode of Learning

Earlier, I noted the parallel between practitioners' action re-search and the model of inquiry-oriented, student-directed learn-ing that is being recommended for the classroom. What both have in common is the fundamental premise that understanding grows out of purposeful action and is cumulatively constructed as the learner brings his or her current knowledge to bear on new situations and information in an effort to 'make sense' of them. Here, I want to consider the implications of this parallelism for the expectations that we should have concerning the forms that action research may take and the conditions that enable it to develop. As will be apparent, I owe much of my present under-standing to what I have learned in working with my fellow contributors to this volume.

Individual Journeys

Teachers, like learners in general, start with different reasons for engaging with a topic; they also differ in the nature and extent of the knowledge that they can bring to the inquiry. Differences can also be expected in their preferred ways of working. Not surpris-ingly, therefore, the routes they take and the staging points they pass through in the course of their journey will inevitably be personal and individual.

For some, a question, already clearly formulated, may be what motivates and guides their inquiry from the beginning. But even here, the nature of the question may vary considerably from one that asks essentially 'what's the problem here?' to one that asks about the effects of a proposed new course of action, for example, a new method of grouping or a new way of organizing reading. For others, and probably the majority, the starting point is a much more diffuse interest in a particular area of the curriculum or aspect of student behavior that is perceived as interesting or problematic. And it is often only by beginning to observe closely and systematically an individual child or group at work that the teacher-researcher comes to see what question it is that he or she wants to address. Discovering and refining the question may thus be in itself the major outcome of the first 'cycle' of research.

At one time, I used to think that, where the inquiry did not involve a change undertaken by the teacher in the belief that it would be advantageous for his or her students, the research had failed to be truly action research. But now I recognize that such a judgment may be premature. Simply learning to observe systematically and to interpret what is observed may, in itself, be an important form of action, representing a significant change in the teacher's stance to his or her own working environment. Similarly, choosing to find out more about the area in question through reading books or journal articles in order to make sense of what was observed may also represent an important form of action for someone who has not been in the habit of reading for this purpose. So, also, may be discussing the observations with an interested colleague.

The change that is the goal of practitioners' action research may appear first, therefore, as a change in the teacher as learner as, in one way or another, she or he discovers that the only personally valuable answers to questions about how to be an effective teacher are the ones that one constructs for oneself. Contrary to what is implied in much of the work on effective schooling, there is no single, ideal way of teaching that is universally successful, nor one way of organizing the curriculum such that all students can be guaranteed to learn. To create the conditions that enable students to make their own sense of new information, and thereby to develop understanding which is personally relevant to the world in which they live, requires teachers themselves to be lifelong learners. Not simply about how children, in general, learn, and about the subject matter that is presented to them, but about how the particular children in their own classrooms draw upon their unique personal experiences to make sense of the specific tasks and materials that are presented to them. For many teachers, accustomed to a predominantly transmissional mode of professional training, with its neglect of specific classroom contexts, simply learning to ask their own questions and to be responsible for finding answers through their own inquiries is itself a new mode of action and a worthwhile outcome of their research.

Nevertheless, research that concerns itself only with the exploration of what 'is' in a particular classroom, and stops short of imagining what 'might' be and then tries to achieve it, is still not truly action research in the way in which I have come to understand it. For the goal of action research is not simply to come to know as an end in itself, worthy though that may be, but to use that knowledge to empower others through changing one's teaching so that one's students, in turn, are enabled to become intentional learners. Though the routes taken may be different, and though the rate of advance may vary, only research which has these interrelated objectives of knowing and acting as its ultimate goal is worthy of the name of action research.

Reading and Writing

One of the immediately attractive features of action research for many teachers is that it is directly concerned with what goes on in their own classrooms. Observing children at work, or interviewing them during or after some activity, is so much more concrete than listening to lectures about recommended methods or materials or — still more abstract — reading the conclusions of unknown researchers in distant places or the theories that are erected on their findings. Making first-hand observations and trying to make sense of them is also an important step in becoming an independent problem-solver.

But the sense one can make in this way is only as good as the knowledge one can bring to the data one has collected. Where other people have addressed similar issues, therefore, it often helps to find out how they approached them and what conclusions they drew. There comes a point, then, when the teacher-researcher needs to read about other people's research and about the theories they have used to interpret their data. And it is at this point that suggestions made by somebody who is familiar both with the teacher's topic and with the relevant literature in the field can be most helpful. Now, with a question in mind and observational data that bears on it, those books and articles, that before seemed so remote and irrelevant, suddenly take on a completely different significance. No longer on the receiving end of a transmission line, the teacher-researcher is able to engage with the text with a purpose that makes the reading into a dialogue between fellow researchers. Books that had previously been set aside as too difficult or esoteric are now reread with understanding and enthusiasm because the reader has relevant first-hand experience to bring to the transaction.

Writing, too, has an important role to play in making sense of the information gathered. Solitary reflection certainly leads to a growth in understanding, but writing one's thoughts down makes it possible to revisit them and review them over time. For this reason, many teachers who have, for the first time, started to keep a log or journal have discovered a new purpose for writing. When writing is undertaken to communicate one's understanding to others, however, even more benefit accrues. For, with the requirement to make one's meaning clear and explicit to a real or imagined reader, one is forced to re-examine one's ideas and assumptions in a much more rigorous way than when writing for oneself alone. As a result, one is often pushed into radical rethinking and revision.

Many of the teachers with whom I have worked have made this discovery as, having agreed to make a presentation about their inquiry at a staff meeting or conference, they begin to prepare a script for their talk. At this point, they become much more aware of what they know and what they do not yet know, and this leads either to further analysis, reading and thinking, as part of the process of preparing their presentation or, where this is not possible, to the recognition of the questions that they might address in their next cycle of research. This has certainly been true of all the researchers represented in this volume: working on successive drafts of their original papers has been an important part of the development of the understanding they have achieved.

Collaboration

In my experience, teacher research typically begins with an individual practitioner embarking on a personal inquiry. This is entirely appropriate, as one of the characteristics of this mode of professional development is that it places a high value on teachers taking responsibility for their own development and having ownership of their own inquiries. However, in the longer term, there is a great deal to be gained if such individual initiatives can be linked together in some form of collaborative endeavor.

One way in which this can happen is through the formation of a network of teacher-researchers who meet regularly to discuss their work or, as in the present case, through participation in a university-based course. As individual inquiries proceed, these meetings provide a forum in which members can make reports on their work and receive feedback in a friendly and supportive environment. They also provide an opportunity to pool ideas about workable research techniques and to discuss possible solutions to problems of either a methodological or a substantive nature. But perhaps the most important function of such a group is the mutual support that its members provide for each other. As several individual teacher-researchers have complained, it is difficult to maintain one's enthusiasm when none of one's colleagues is interested in what one is doing and there is nobody with whom to share one's achievements and frustrations. Although the members of a network group or university course may be working in different schools, the fact that all are engaged in action research provides a common interest, and so their meetings serve the very important function of affirming the value of what the individual members are doing.

Thus, whatever form it takes, collaboration with colleagues is an important dimension of teacher research. For, in addition to the need practitioners have for moral support from others who share their commitment to this form of active learning, the very nature of teachers' action research, undertaken as it typically is by individual teachers within their own classrooms, is such as to require opportunities to meet with colleagues to make sense of the research experience by talking it over with others who understand it at first hand.

For this reason, the ideal situation is where a whole school staff, or a majority of its members, together plan and undertake inquiries in relation to an agreed theme, such as the place of writing in the curriculum or the different ways in which talk about books can be encouraged. In addition to the increased collegiality that is created among the staff through engaging in such a meaningful joint activity, the discoveries about learning and teaching made and shared within the group of teacher-researchers can contribute significantly to curriculum policy-making within the school in a way that goes far beyond the specific topics to which the inquiries were directed.

However, if such school-based centres of inquiry, in which teachers conduct action research as part of their professional activities, are our ultimate goal — as I believe they should be — we shall have to look beyond the university classroom or the spontaneously forming network to the institutional context in which teachers work.

The Institutional and Administrative Context

Traditionally, educational jurisdictions have tended to be strongly hierarchical, both in terms of status relations and also of communication (Fullan, 1982). Within this framework, there has been little or no room for individual teacher initiative and neither the resources nor the encouragement necessary for teachers to contribute in a meaningful way to curriculum decision-making, at least officially, at the level at which curriculum is enacted — that is to say in their own schools and classrooms.

These traditional patterns are now beginning to change, however, as can be seen in the various initiatives that are being taken in some educational jurisdictions (e.g., the inclusion of action research as one of the options in the 'Supervision for Growth' model referred to above) or in the provisions for networking in the

'Creating a Culture of Change' project of the Ontario Teacher's Federation (1992).

Nevertheless, these developments are still largely concerned to provide an institutional framework for the encouragement and support of individual teachers' professional development. However, if teacher research is to become more widespread than it is at present, and if it is to become a genuine force in curriculum renewal at the level of individual schools, this can only happen if it is 'institutionalized' *within the school.*

Schaefer was well aware of this when he wrote:

> The principal and the teachers working as colleagues in a particular school must be freed for an independent search for viable patterns. The basic problem is not the control of school faculties, but the deliberate creation of new intellectual outlets for teachers, the development of new work patterns for sustaining imaginative and systematic reflection. (1967, p.41)

The presence of one or two active teacher researchers within a school is probably a valuable first step in this process. But, as experience shows, this is not in itself sufficient to persuade other teachers to become involved in making the whole school turn into a community of inquiry. Two further ingredients seem to be essential. First, the provision of the necessary support — in the form of time and resources — for teachers, working together, to plan and then carry out the inquiries they consider appropriate, to interpret the results, and to determine what changes to make as a consequence; and, second, a new sense of collegial responsibility for decision-making among the staff, that gives purpose to their collective endeavors.

Here the role of the school administrators is clearly crucial, for such changes will not come about without their active leadership and support. At a minimum, they must be ready to value the work of those teachers who are already confident enough to initiate and carry out their own inquiries by, for example, treating their results and their reflections on them as relevant input to curriculum planning and policy-making within the school, and by making it possible for these teachers to present reports of their work to a wider audience at local and national conferences. However, achieving the sort of school-wide commitment to inquiry that Schaefer envisaged will require more from administrators than simply encouragement and moral support. In effect, they will need to develop new ways of thinking about their role as leaders of the school community, seeing it more as one of fellow learner than in terms of supervision and evaluation. For as Barth (1990) suggests, the way in which the school principal relates to other members of staff, and the model of the teacher as learner that he or she provides, will set the pattern for all other relationships within the school. Thus, if the school is to become a community of inquiring learners, the principal must also engage in continuing personal and professional growth, carried out in collaboration with colleagues.

At present, many administrators feel ill-prepared in terms of their previous experience to take on this new and unfamiliar role. There are also many aspects of their administrative responsibilities which may cast them in a conflictual rather than a collaborative role in relation to other personnel within the school. The result, as Barth (op. cit.) notes, is that "seldom do teachers and principals talk openly together about their important work." Indeed, the principal "emerges [as]... all too often part of teachers' problems rather than their solutions" (pp.20-21). One way out of this unwished for impasse may well be for school administrators themselves to undertake inquiries into how best to enact this new role they are being asked to play. Certainly, those who, like Catherine Keating (chapter ten), have undertaken this step have found the experience to be very worthwhile.

One thing is certain: the only way in which all schools will become communities of inquiry, in which all members are committed to life-long learning, is if the impetus for this change develops from within. In bringing this about, therefore, it is those who have already become teacher-researchers who must take the lead: by communicating their enthusiasm and — through publications such as the present — by sharing the insights they have gained. Our hope is that their experiences will inspire others to become inquirers into their own practice and, thereby, to change the schools in which they work.

NOTES

1. See, for example, Atwell (1990), Bissex and Bullock (1987), Goswami and Stillman (1987), Newman (1989) to name but a few.

2. The development of this option and the writing of the relevant part of the Teachers' Handbook was the subject of the inquiry of another member of our action research group (Gordon, 1990). Unfortunately, pressure of work made it impossible for her to rewrite her paper for inclusion in the present volume. Nevertheless, the inquiry itself, and its outcome in the form of the relevant section on the Handbook, is a significant contribution towards the goal of enabling teachers to change schools from within.

2

Moving Between Two Worlds: Talk During Writing Workshop

Mary Ann Gianotti

Formulating Questions

Last September, several of my grade one students announced, "I don't know how to write!" in response to my request that they record information gained from interviewing a partner. This information was to be used to write a story about the interviewee for a class book, our first published text of the year. I was hoping that students in my split grades one and two class would immediately see themselves as communicators of information and meaning, as authors and writers; and I also was hoping they would begin to see that I, as their teacher, believed in their abilities to do so. From the very first day of Writing Workshop in my classroom, there is talk, sharing of ideas, communicating and conferencing with one another and the teacher. This talking with each other and the teacher is an important part of the writing process.

Throughout my formal studies in Education and my teaching career, I have read much about language learning being social. Also, as a learner, I have seen how the "hashing out" of ideas and thoughts with others is an integral part of the learning process. I have, as a result, been interested in the role of talk in my writing program. Stimulated by a language acquisition course in which Vygotsky was studied, I started to think more and more about the writing development of my students and my own personal beliefs about how children learn and develop skills as language users. From my investigation of Vygotsky's theories regarding children's writing development as writers emerged a desire to look at this development more closely in my classroom.

Writing is a complex sign system which initially is a second-order system of symbolism; that is, the written signs are symbols for spoken language, which in turn is a system of signs representing real entities: ideas, feelings, objects. This second-order symbolism gradually changes, and the spoken language that once served as an intermediary link disappears. Written language becomes one of a variety of sign systems that directly signify entities and their relationships (Vygotsky, 1978). The symbolism found in young children in the forms of gesture, play, and drawing eventually influences and leads to the development of writing, another form of symbolism. Vygotsky asserts that "it is on the basis of speech that all other sign systems are created" (1978, p.113). Anne Haas Dyson, a researcher who has produced an extensive two-year classroom-based case study on the writing development of eight children, also speaks of the connection between different forms of symbolism and their influence on the development of writing. She states that "writing as a symbolic and social tool grows directly out of children's experiences with other tools — such as gesture, speech, dramatic play, and drawing — and their relationships with other people" (1989, p.68).

Because written language develops from speech, I decided to look at the speech, or sharing talk, that occurs informally during Writing Workshop time. When I began this study, Writing Workshop took place twice a week for approximately 60-80 minutes a session. During this time we usually gathered as a group for a 'mini-lesson' or discussion about a specific skill or problem that they were encountering as writers, then they had 40 minutes to work on their stories. During this time a space on the carpet was designated for peer conferencing. These conferences occurred when children reached a point in the writing process at which they wanted to share their story with someone else. Informal talk or 'spontaneous conferences' also went on at the tables as children worked on their stories. They were encouraged to ask each other questions and share their ideas. In addition to these activities, children could also sign-up on a chalkboard to conference with me as they needed. These conferences provided an opportunity for the child and me to consider specific issues that arose in their writing. During the writing segment of the period, my time was taken up in these conferences. The writing segment, as one might suspect, was very lively.

Following the 40 minute writing segment was Author's Circle, at which point two or three children had the opportunity to share a piece of writing with the whole group and receive feedback. I have observed that the children in my class have had a very positive attitude toward Writing Workshop, and have looked forward to it, frequently choosing to work on their stories as an activity whenever there has been free choice.

The writing segment of Writing Workshop is bustling with activity and talk, and my questions for inquiry have grown out of a personal curiosity about the sharing talk among children. These questions did not come immediately, but grew slowly as I began to observe the children more closely. I was influenced as well by Vygotsky's (1978) notion of the Zone of Proximal Development, essentially that more-able learners assist less-able learners with tasks until they are ready to take them over completely themselves. Some of the later questions did not form until I began looking at the data I had collected and continued reading professional books that addressed relevant issues.

1. Are there any categories or trends that can be identified regarding children's sharing talk?

2. What do their 'spontaneous' conferences teach them? When are they productive?

3. What is it that children gain from sharing their story-creations with each other?

And later:

4. How is this knowledge useful in influencing my view of the role of talk in my classroom?

5. How will this information influence my role as the teacher?

6. How has classroom research been rewarding and/or problematic for me?

In order to collect data relevant to these questions, I began to observe the students and take notes on their interactions. I also decided to tape record their talk during writing time, using audio and videotape, with a remote microphone attached to one child. I then went back, listened to the audio tapes, watched the videotapes and transcribed pertinent conversations. I chose four students to wear the microphone, although the children with whom they were engaged often varied. I chose children whose writing development had shown significant growth from September to December. Thus my sampling included interactions between grade ones, between grade ones and twos, and between grade twos. I then analyzed the data in an effort to answer the questions listed above. I collected audio and videotapes from January through March, whenever feasible, and I took observational notes from mid-October through March.

The Data and its Significance

As I went over my transcripts and observational notes, I began to see similarities occurring in types of sharing talk. To explore these further, I devised a tentative coding scheme to categorize the episodes of talk. The categories were not exhaustive, by any means, but they included types of sharing talk most prominently exemplified in the transcripts and notes. There was also some overlapping where conversations could be assigned to more than one category. After I had coded the transcripts according to the categories, I tabulated the frequency of each kind of talk to determine which types of talk were occurring most frequently.

Sharing the Text

The first and most frequent type of sharing talk occurred around sharing the text of the story. To identify talk fitting into this category, I looked for instances of a child reading his/her text to others, sometimes overtly seeking feedback and sometimes just to share, i.e., to hear it read. Within the sharing of text, there were two further subdivisions: readings that received feedback and those that did not. I decided to make this division because, initially, my general feeling after listening to/watching numerous tapes was that, in the majority of cases, the children were sharing their texts with others and not receiving feedback. However, to my surprise, I found on closer inspection that, out of the many times children shared their text, on only five occasions did they receive no feedback. I realized that my feeling resulted not from whether or not the writer received feedback, but rather from what I *felt* the writer did as a consequence of the feedback. I also realized that I couldn't necessarily tell if the writer had done anything with the feedback by looking at the transcript alone.

Consider the following text as an example: Lisa, grade two, is sharing a text with Tim, grade one, who is sitting near her. A few minutes prior to the conversation below, Lisa has shared her story with Tim, and then added a new section at the end. She is writing a series of chapters in a book with two classmates about the lives of two characters, Eric and Samantha. The idea for writing stemmed from their new interest in reading chapter books about characters like themselves. Lisa stops writing and says something to Tim and he responds:

1   Tim: Okay read it.

2   Lisa: (reading) "In the summer Eric said, 'Why
              don't we go to Florida?' 'It is nice and hot,'

		said Eric's mother so they all went to the airport and took an 8 o'clock flight."
3	Tim:	That doesn't make sense.
4	Lisa:	Yes it does.
5	Tim:	Oh so what...so...wait let me see, let me see it...read it again.
6	Lisa:	(reads it again slowly)
7	Tim:	Well why don't you put what day they got... what day they decided to go... because you would say ... like I thought you meant that you... like ... it's today and they talk about it <going to Florida> and then they went to the airport THAT DAY?

(Pause while Lisa thinks about it.)

8	Tim:	You don't have to.
9	Lisa:	Well let me finish reading it first. (reads) "Eric was excited to go to Florida. Eric said, 'I can't wait! When are we going to be there?' Right after Eric said that they were swimming in Florida. Eric said, 'I did that with my magical powers.'"
10	Tim:	Well why don't you say that he had magical powers <in the first place>?
11	Lisa:	I already said that before, remember, I told you that? (In their previous conversation, Tim said the same thing and Lisa told him that she had said that in her first chapter. This is her third chapter. She continues reading the new part she has added.) "Eric had so much fun he said, 'The next time we go away why don't we go to Africa?' 'NO, NO, NO!' they all said." (giggling)
12	Tim:	No, no, no! Then you can put (draw) a picture of Africa!
13	Lisa:	No, I'll put a picture of everybody saying, "NO, NO, NO!"

Tim returns to his writing, saying his words out loud as he writes. Lisa reads the last part of her story to a few other people in the background, repeating the last line, "NO, NO, NO!"

When Tim responds in turn seven, he is seeking clarification about the time between Eric's request to go to Florida and their departure from the airport, questioning the possibility of deciding to go on a trip and leaving the same day. In effect, he is seeking to match his known world with the imagined world that Lisa has represented through text. Lisa pauses to consider his point. As a consequence of their discussion, she alters her text at a later time to be more descriptive about this.[1] The kind of sharing talk in which Tim and Lisa were engaged occurred frequently in the transcripts and my observational notes.

The matching or clarifying of the child's experienced, known world with the imaginary, representational world created by text is a challenge. As they are discovering the power and role of written text in their stories, they must come to work among symbolic worlds, and talk is a tool they use to help them with this task. As adult writers, writing a text that articulates one's ideas and thoughts as accurately as possible is also a challenge. We often consult one another, using discussion as a useful tool to check whether our text symbolizes, or captures, our intended meaning for another. In the above episode it was not apparent what Lisa's intent was in sharing her text with Tim, but often the writer would invite someone to listen to the text with a specific purpose in mind. Phrases like, "Does this make sense?" "I'm not sure if this is clear," "Tell me what you think of...," "How would you do <this>?" were common. It was interesting to observe children using the identical phrases that I myself had used when discussing with them ways to conference with another person about their texts. In my own discussions with children, I emphasized clarification of meaning and often said, "Does this make sense?" as an example.

Seeking Affirmation

Seeking affirmation was also a major goal in sharing text. Phrases like "Is this good?" "Does this sound good?" "Do you like this?" were very common in initiating conversation with another child. Affirmation, I believe, is a powerful motivator and confidence builder. I have observed that affirmation statements encourage young authors to confront the challenges they face in creating text-worlds. When they felt their texts were valued by their peers, then they were willing to engage in, and were enthusiastic about, the writing process. I believe this affirmation-seeking is important.

In sharing text, the child also receives ideas from the listener. Often the listener will enter the author's symbolic world, offering suggestions about story-line development. For example:

Bob, Tim, and Eric are waiting to talk to me. Bob, grade one, wants to share his story with me and Tim, grade one, and Eric, grade two, want to tell me about a dispute with another boy. As they are waiting, the following conversation occurs.

1	Tim:	(to Bob, referring to his story) What one is this?
2	Bob:	"The Treasure Chest."
3	Tim:	Can I see it? Can I see your last page? Oh. You only have two pages? I have seven pages.
		(Eric explains what they are waiting to talk to me about)
4	Tim:	Can I read it? (reading from Bob's text) "The Treasure Chest."
5	Bob:	(reading text) "Once a long time ago there was a treasure chest and in that treasure chest there is gold and pirates who wanted it. His name was Jack. He found the island. He saw the 'X.' When he saw the treasure chest a coconut fell on his head and he said, 'OUCH!'"
6	Eric:	That's all? You should make it a continuation...how he finds the treasure chest.
7	Tim:	And he goes back to the town.
		(Hilary interrupts to find out what they're waiting for)
8	Tim:	He goes back to the town.
9	Bob:	(sounding hesitant) I'll have to add...like...a little more on or something.
10	Eric:	I know like he gets lost and then there's another island?
11	Bob:	(getting excited) Yeah, like there's another island that has the real treasure!
12	Eric:	Yeah, then we'll know what happens.
13	Tim:	Yeah, it won't be ending so quickly, and we'll know what happened <to the pirate>.

After his conversation with Eric and Tim, Bob works on the story before sharing it with me. He likes the completed story so much that he chooses it as a story to be published in book form. Eric and Tim enter the world of Bob's text and are dissatisfied with the lack of resolution. They are able to imagine with him what would happen to his pirate. This entering into another's story world also occurred in the next category, that of inquiry.

Inquiring About Another's Work

Inquiry occurred when a child asked others about what they were writing or drawing. Showing interest in another's work was a form of affirmation for the writer, and it provided exposure to styles and genres of writing which the inquirer may not have encountered previously. For example, in science we had studied the "Big Bang" and had written a class book together explaining the organization of the universe. Some time later, Lucy, grade one, decided to write a story about the "Big Bang." The following conversation occurs as she works excitedly next to Karen, grade one. Karen's interest is piqued by observing Lucy get some books from me on the universe to consult while writing her piece.

1	Karen:	What are you writing about?
2	Lucy:	"The Big Bang." I'm going to be a scientist, you know.
3	Karen:	Well, what are you saying? How can you <write about science>?
4	Lucy:	I'm going — I'm telling how the gases collected and how the big explosion made the world and the universe. BANG! ... People didn't live then, you know.
5	Karen:	I know. They would die if they did.
6	Lucy:	Yeah. Well, I'm going to be a scientist.
7	Karen:	Me too.

For the next few Writing Workshop sessions, Karen and Lucy work next to each other, using the books together and discussing their emerging texts. Because of her conversation with Lucy, Karen has embarked on a new task in writing, that of 'content writing.'

At times, inquiry grew into the offering of feedback. As with the feedback when sharing text, it had a lot to do with matching the experienced, known world with the symbolic world of text. In the following episode, we have just returned from Winter Break and many children are writing about experiences over the break. The following conversation occurs between Dan and Eric, two grade 2 boys, who are working at the same table.

1	Dan:	Eric, Eric, what are you writing about?
2	Eric:	Summer vacation. (writing) 'Summer.' How do you spell 'vacation'? Mrs. G., how do you spell 'vacation?'
3	Mrs.G:	V-A-C-A-T-I-O-N.
4	Dan:	(doubtingly) Summer vacation?
5	Eric:	Summer, SUMMER. Not the winter vacation when they let us have a little break.
6	Dan:	You mean before we went back to school? (Dan appears to be confused because it is the middle of January and they have just returned from Winter Break.)
7	Eric:	Yeah, so?
8	Dan:	Well, why are you writing about that? I don't understand.
9	Eric:	Well, I was at Disney World and I haven't had a chance to explain the rides. I'm writing about the rides.
10	Dan:	Well, are you going to talk about all of them?
11	Eric:	No, just my favourites. Have you ever been? What's your favourite <ride>?
12	Dan:	Well, you know the one that goes around? (A discussion ensues about rides and describing them. There is disagreement over which rides they're talking about and if they are indeed ones at Disney World.)
13	Dan:	It's going to be hard for people to know <which ride you're talking about>. Maybe you better draw pictures. I think you were at a different Disney World.
14	Eric:	Yeah. I'm starting with pictures. It'll be easier.

Dan's inquiry not only helps him see that he can write about summer during winter, but it also turns into a conversation about the development of Eric's story and the challenges inherent in describing personal experience so that another can understand.

They are also able to discuss ways of approaching this challenge. For Eric, Dan's inquiry helps in developing his ideas further.

Seeking Ideas

The next major area of talk happened when a child sought ideas for story development or story topics from another child. Comments such as "I don't know what to write about," "What should I put next?" "Should I do/write/draw this?" typified this type of sharing talk. Children have the opportunity to explore styles, methods, and ideas of others; in effect, they are learning from the experiences of another. For example, Mike, grade two, is sitting near Bob, grade one, and begins a story. Mike seeks affirmation frequently, and this time his seeking turns into a request for ideas regarding story beginnings. Joe and Dan, grade two, are sitting near him as well, and they get involved in the conversation.

1	Mike:	Bob, Bob... I just made this story up. It's called "The Adventures."
2	Bob:	The veggies?
3	Mike:	(irritated) The ADVENTURES!
4	Bob:	Why don't you put veggies so then each one would say, "Hi, I'm veggies!"
5	Joe:	No, no.
6	Mike:	What should I start with?
7	Joe:	Something about an adventure.
8	Mike:	Okay. So..."Once upon a time."
9	Dan:	"Once upon a time?" Mike, why "Once upon a time?"
10	Mike:	Because it didn't happen now and it's not true. You know, "Once upon a time?"
11	Dan:	Yeah, but it sounds like a fairy tale, not an adventure.
12	Joe:	No, adventures can start like that.
13	Mike:	Yeah. So... "Once upon a time."
14	Dan:	(unsure) Okay, but I'm not so sure about adventures starting like that ... well, maybe.

15 Mike: I'm just going to try <this beginning> and see.

Bob does not take Mike's request for affirmation seriously, but

Joe and Dan get involved in a discussion with him about the convention "Once upon a time," and its use in adventure writing. Dan tends to separate his experiences into categories and clearly "Once upon a time" goes with fairy tales, not adventures. This division is challenged. The interaction also provides an opportunity for Mike and Joe to consider its use as well. Bob, who is listening to this conversation, is exposed to a discussion about a convention he uses often; perhaps he will re-evaluate his use of it as well.In another instance, Lucy, grade one, presents a problem she has encountered in writing to the children sitting at her table and is offered a variety of resources to use in solving her problem. Lucy has been working on a recipe book for a few days.

1	Lucy:	Is this a good picture of cinnamon toast?
2	Barb:	Uh-huh.
3	Lucy:	I have three recipes, but that's all I know. So I'm crazy.
4	Eric:	Think of some other ones.
5	Barb:	Think of some — like... some cake recipes.
6	Lucy:	I don't know any cake recipes.
7	Diane:	Why don't you go home and look in your cook book?
8	Lucy:	I don't have a cookbook.
9	Diane:	Well your mom might have one.
10	Lucy:	Nancy, Nancy.
11	Trish:	Well go ask Nancy. She might have one and she could give you an idea.
		(No response from Nancy who goes past Lucy and sits down to work.)
12	Lucy:	Diane, do you know any recipes?
13	Diane:	Yeah.
14	Lucy:	What is it?
15	Diane:	I'll say them and you write them.
16	Lucy:	Do you know any with chocolate cake?
17	Diane:	Yeah.
18	Lucy:	Okay. What's that? I'll write the one for chocolate cake. Let me hear the recipe.
		(Lucy writes as Diane tells her the recipe.)

19	Diane:	Butter, eggs, flour.
20	Lucy:	Flour.
21	Diane:	Flour.
22	Joe:	Does this look like a castle on fire?
		(no response)
23	Diane:	Then you mix it.
24	Lucy:	Okay. What else?
25	Diane:	Mix.
26	Lucy:	Mix, mix.
27	Diane:	Then um ...
28	Lucy:	Chocolate?
29	Diane:	Chocolate. Then add chocolate. Then comes sugar.
30	Lucy:	Sugar.
31	Diane:	Then you have to put it in the oven.
32	Lucy:	For how long?
33	Diane:	One hour. Because it has to cook in the night.
34	Lucy:	But the night isn't just one hour.
35	Diane:	Well maybe you put the bell on so it will wake you up.
36	Lucy:	Bell. One hour.
37	Diane:	Put the bell on. Just write "Put bell." There. There's your fourth recipe.
38	Lucy :	Oh this is going to be a good picture. (starts drawing picture of chocolate cake.)

Lucy receives several different options for resolving her problem of not knowing any more recipes: consult a cookbook at home, consult her mother, or ask someone in class. Those listening to and participating in the conversation are also exposed to the idea that, when writing, one can seek out a variety of resources for information. In their discussion, both Lucy and Diane showed their awareness of the genre features used in writing a recipe. Diane's comment in turn 37, "Just write 'Put bell.'" demonstrates her attempt to differentiate between the familiar narrative genre and the genre used when writing a recipe.

Discussing Drawings

The last major category I found in their sharing talk was conversations about drawings. As previously mentioned, drawing (a symbolic tool) precedes and influences writing development. In the developmental space where most of my grade ones and a few grade twos are, the picture is often the most powerful vehicle for conveying the meaning of the story. It serves as a bridge between symbolic worlds — the worlds of drawing and writing. Because of their importance, children took great interest in one another's pictures. Given the variance from child to child within the spectrum of development, the amount of emphasis given to the picture as a vehicle of meaning varied. This made sense. However, I was surprised to discover the large amount of time spent discussing pictures, both during their creation and after their completion. Detail in pictures was very important and a cause for great attention. I had expected the grade twos to be less concerned with the pictures than the grade ones. However, this was not the case, and my discovery forced me to reflect on the amount of emphasis I placed on their pictures in my conferences with children, both grade ones and grade twos.

Often the story-line was developed through discussion about the pictures, and the children offered advice freely about detail that could be included in pictures. They also frequently checked to see if the symbolic drawing matched their known world, just as when considering the written text. Discussing pictures helped develop text, but the results of this discussion were often not incorporated into the written text.

The difficulty of crossing between symbolic worlds is apparent. Quite often a child is so caught up in the task of encoding (transferring oral language to written language) that the full spirit and meaning of the text, evident in the process of drawing, is not successfully realized in the written text. In the following excerpt, Bob, grade one, and Dan, grade two, are sitting near each other. Bob is trying to decode (convert written language into oral language) what he has written on a previous day, and Dan hears him:

1 Bob: (reading from text) "The witch lives in a castle. She has a/s/.../s/...secret force field. She is" um...um...um (stuck on a word)

2 Dan: Where are you?

3 Bob: Here. uh...(trying to figure out text) is.../w/.../w/...witch- rich

4 Dan: "Rich"

5	Bob:	"It. it"

5 Bob: "It. it"

6 Dan: No you have to put a <period>.

7 Bob: (continues trying to figure out text) It is "she?" (realizing that it doesn't make sense)

8 Dan: You better erase that. (tries to help him figure it out) "She does."

9 Bob: Wait. Maybe it's just like this, "it. .. she..." I don't get this (pause) No, I know. (attempts again) "It she dis it." ... "If she dis it?" What's 'dis?' (realizing "if she dis it" is not sensible)

10 Dan: Maybe you better erase this line.

11 Bob: Yeah.

12 Dan: Then you can think of what you want to do.

(Bob erases the line, then looks at what Dan has returned to writing.)

13 Bob: (commenting to Dan) Nice picture! ... I don't know what else to write. Maybe that she is rich?

14 Dan: Why don't you write about that room that... um... she can take her head off and put another head on?

15 Bob: Okay. (starting to write) "She"... How do you spell "she?"

(no response)

"She ... she can ... take... /t/... /a/... /k /... take her" ...

16 Dan: - head off and put another head on.

17 Bob: "She can" — whoops <that is> supposed to be 'C.' "She can take her... /h... /h/head" (stops and looks at Dan's picture) What's this? Is this a pirate ship?

18 Dan: No, a pirate fortress.

(They both return to writing for a few minutes, Dan in silence, Bob saying each word as he writes it.)

19 Bob: "She can take her head... her head... /h.../e/.../ e/... d.../... head... she can take her head off." (to Dan) Is this a pirate ship?

20	Dan:	No, it's a fortress!
21	Bob:	These are cannon balls?
22	Dan:	No, they're cannons.
23	Bob:	What's the difference?
24	Bob:	"She can take her head off." hmm, hmm, hmm. (draws picture)
25	Bob:	Like my picture?
26	Dan:	What is it of?
27	Bob:	That's the evil, evil, EVIL sorceress.
28	Dan:	Sorceress?
29	Bob:	Of the evil, evil witches and she eats children up.
30	Dan:	(laughs)
31	Bob:	And she's so wicked that they chop her head off (voice gets animated and he begins to gesture, as if he's now the characters) Off with her head! Off with her head! And they all go AHHHH! (returns to colouring for a few minutes)
32	Bob:	Dan, if you went to that evil witch you would get destroyed. Would you want that to happen to you?
33	Dan:	Ah, no.
34	Bob:	She is VERY evil.
35	Dan:	I get the picture, Bob.
36	Bob:	Very, very, VERY evil. So evil that you could get your head chopped off.
37	Dan:	I know, you said that already.
38	Bob:	I did? (returns to colouring)

In turns 1-23, Bob demonstrates through talk how all-consuming decoding and encoding can be. Bob struggles first to decode previously written text, and then to encode desired text. With Dan's assistance, he establishes a way of proceeding. Dan, as a more experienced writer, is able to assist Bob in creating his text. This supportive relationship between Bob and Dan is apparent in other transcriptions as well.

In the second part of the transcript, turns 24-38, there is an indication of the life and story contained in Bob's drawing. The story is still developing as he enters his imagined world and attempts to share it with Dan. Dan, who is concerned with his own text, remains on the outside of Bob's imagined world. Bob is not able to capture the energy of his evil sorceress within his written text alone and, to a reader who fails to inquire about his picture, that energy is not apparent. His completed text reads: "Once a long time ago there was a witch. The witch lived in a castle. She has a secret force field. She can take her head off. Her boss is the evil sorceress. She is mean."

The amount of lively discussion around drawing that occurred in the data I collected has left a surprisingly strong impression upon me. Although I had known the importance of drawing as a link to writing, especially for beginning writers, I had underestimated the creative energy children were putting into their drawings and the wealth of meaning the drawings held for young writers. As a result, I see that, during my conferences with students, it will be important to spend more time discussing their pictures. This will be necessary in order to help the children express the story meaning contained in the drawings and to help them capture in their written texts some of the energy symbolized in their pictures. In this way, I hope I shall be better able to help them to connect the symbolic worlds of drawing and writing.

Young Writers Teaching Young Writers

The sharing talk during the 'spontaneous conferences' among children helped them approach some of the challenges writers face in trying to create a meaningful text. Their talk about the symbolic tools of writing and drawing often served the purpose of trying to bridge the gap and clarify the connections between their experienced, known worlds and the imaginary worlds they were creating. The talk helped them to challenge one another as to the accuracy or feasibility of this 'match' occurring. As Ann Haas Dyson has observed:

> children's critiques of each other's stories and pictures often lead to a concern about the relationship between the imaginary and the wider experienced worlds, as they tried to reconcile discrepancies between the two (1989, p.72).

During their sharing talk, students also helped each other with the uses of written language conventions. Inquiry led to exposure to different genres and styles of writing, as previously illustrated in the example of the "Big Bang." There was also frequent talk of literary devices (e.g., "Once upon a time"), play with language, and spelling. Because the composition of my class was half grade one and half grade two students, it provided an excellent setting for the grade ones to learn from watching and interacting with the more experienced grade twos. The supportive relationship between Dan and Bob illustrated this, although it also occurred between students at the same grade level. Often, a child helped another along his/her developmental path, assisting with functions he/she was not able to manage independently. Vygotsky (1978) referred to this as helping the learner in his/her Zone of Proximal Development. Sharing talk in my study has illustrated that such learning occurred among the students. When challenged by a peer regarding the accuracy of a text or the appropriateness of conventions used in expressing meaning, the writer was given an opportunity to reflect upon and consider the issue being contended. As writers, they would wonder together and seek validation for their ideas. When a child's text is responded to by others, the written text may take on new meaning (Dyson, op. cit.). When a child responds to or shows interest in another child's story, the author of the story begins to see the power he/she possesses as a communicator of meaning. This is true of adult writers too. For example, in taking a course on action research with others, I have had the opportunity to share my experiences with them. Their responses have given me new ideas and different perspectives regarding my perceptions of my inquiry.

Sharing Talk as Productive Talk

As a result of considering the question of when this sharing talk is productive, I have made a few discoveries. When I initially listened to the tapes, I was aware of the amount of background noise, and I was uncomfortable with my impression of the frequency of talk unrelated to the writing task. I also noticed that a few children consistently spent the majority of their writing time discussing other's work, but paid little attention to their own.

I presented this dilemma to the children,[2] and we discussed their perceptions of the problem. Several children said they had difficulty in concentrating when there was a lot of noise, and I expressed my concern that some people just weren't getting much done on their own stories. But they were also expressive about how they valued being able to consult with others and to share their stories. As a result of this conversation, we reached a compromise: ten minutes of silent writing and 20-30 minutes of having the choice to share with others while writing. After the first few times of using this structure, the response was very positive. Many children commented on how impressed they were with themselves. They felt they had accomplished more. I was feeling better too. We made this change about half-way through my data collection, and the transcripts from the second-half showed increased evidence of productive sharing talk. The other situation in which I observed a greater amount of productive sharing talk occurred when the entire class was engaged in writing on the same topic or in the same genre. For example, in January, we started corresponding with a grade one class in Washington State. During letter writing time, the focus of the sharing talk was primarily on this specific task, and more children engaged in seeking out the advice of peers — checking meaning, seeking affirmation, sharing ideas for writing, and discussing conventions of spelling and letter writing. A factor that influenced the amount of sharing talk during letter-writing was the knowledge that their texts would be read by an audience beyond the classroom. This focused talk affirmed for me the value of writing within a common framework, a structure I want to use more.

Looking Within/Changing Without: My Role as Teacher

Being engaged in an in-depth study of the writing segment of Writing Workshop this year naturally provided me with the occasion to look at my own behavior as well. For example, the tension I felt around the noise level not only led to a change in the structure of the writing segment, but also to a change in my behavior. A significant incident occurred early on in the study that made me realize I was sending the children mixed messages regarding talk. I discovered, while listening to the tapes, that I would frequently interrupt the entire group to tell them that their talk was too loud, but to keep talking! I realized that I was not dealing with my own tension over the noise level in a satisfying, constructive way — either for the children or for myself. After reflecting on this, I decided on a rather simple solution: in between conferences with children, I would walk around the room and look over shoulders or inquire about the students' progress. This eased my tension with noise because, as I walked around, I could see for myself what was happening, and I was less preoccupied during conferences with individuals. It also led to the children feeling more accountable during the writing segment; thus, my monitoring acted as an incentive for them to stay on task. As I mentioned earlier, my initial impression after listening to the tapes and transcribing key episodes was that children were not sharing their texts or receiving much feedback when they did share their texts. I was dissatisfied with the sharing talk that was occurring. It wasn't until I looked more closely at the transcripts and read the works of other researchers with my own data in mind that I realized I was working with a hidden assumption. Without being aware of it, I had a preconceived notion of what productive sharing talk would sound and look like. The discovery of this assumption enabled me to move beyond it — to look at the talk through broader lenses and see the quality and value of what was actually happening. In turn, this helped me to see more clearly my role as teacher: to provide a stimulating context for the talk and to help the children explore ways of talking with each other about their texts.

As a next step, I changed the format of my conferences. Up to that point, my conferences had been solely with individuals. Now I started conferencing with small groups of children, as well as with individuals. In the small group format, after two or three children had signed up to conference with me, we took turns at listening to each other's stories and responding to them. This gave me an opportunity to model ways in which they could respond to another's text. As mentioned earlier, I was struck by the children's use of phrases identical to the ones I used when talking about peer conferencing, especially "Does this make sense?" I believe I can diversify the way I talk about their texts with them, thus influencing the ways they talk with each other when sharing their texts.

Another turning point for me had to do with observing the children. In October and November, I was engaged in observing and taking notes on the children during writing time. The following is an excerpt from my notes, a reflection upon an incident that occurred in late October with a grade one student. Since September, I had been struggling to help her become confident in her abilities as a writer, as her lack of confidence had been preventing her from attempting to write.

> The next day I watched Karen as I was working with a few other children. And as I glanced at her, it appeared to me that she was stalling, not getting on with her work. It looked as if she was attempting to continue to write on the page, but was doing a lot of looking around, covering her page, and not doing much writing. When the students left to go to Phys Ed, I was surprised to see that she had started a new line in her previous entry — she was not merely 'stalling for time' as I had thought. When the students came back from Phys Ed, I gave them ten more minutes to finish their work. This time I sat at my desk in the corner and really observed Karen without any

distractions. This is something I rarely do because I feel I should be spending that time with students. It was an extremely enlightening experience.

What I observed was similar to what I had noticed when I glanced over from time to time previously, but now I saw it in a different way. She was covering her work, as before, and looking around often to see what others were doing — telling me that she was still feeling very apprehensive about her writing. But what I observed this time was that she was also looking for words on the bulletin board and, as she looked around, she was also sounding out words and recording them. Occasionally she talked to the person next to her.

By sitting and observing her from a distance, I saw things I hadn't realized before. I observed her attempting to get her thoughts down in a variety of ways, and I saw her exhibit signs of her apprehension and concern for being correct. I was surprised by what I discovered about myself and my conceptions: I had rarely taken the time to be an observer in my classroom, but when I did, I was able to see things I wouldn't have seen otherwise.

Marie Clay talks about the importance of such systematic observation and recording by teachers in an article on action research and teacher involvement:

> It was natural to invite teachers...to become careful observers, and even to use some of their busy and precious teaching time for non-teaching observations. I felt that kind of research would lead teachers into new understandings of children (1989, p.38).

Using some of my "busy and precious teaching time" for observing has brought me to new understandings of the individuals in my classroom this year. After my observations of Karen that day, I saw her efforts more clearly and was able to find ways of encouraging her to continue risking, when previously I had not even noticed her real efforts. The same happened with other children through the gathering of audio and videotapes about their sharing talk.

Being Involved in Classroom Research

My involvement in classroom research this year has had many positive consequences for me as a teacher. I believe that teachers generally seek ways to improve their teaching methods, monitoring and observing as they are engaged with children throughout the day. However, this 'instinctive' monitoring is neither systematic nor deliberate. By contrast, classroom research provides a systematic framework within which to monitor and observe. I learned many powerful lessons through observing and gathering data about the children that I would not have learned without engaging in a formal investigation into my classroom teaching practices.

I believe one of the strongest aspects of doing classroom research is reflection. In the course of this project, I was engaged in deliberate reflection in action and, at later times, reflection on action. It is reflection that leads to understanding, growth and change. For example, in taking the time necessary to reflect on my early experiences of observing students this year, I discovered an inaccurate assumption: that I can watch children in a casual way and call it observation. As a result of this discovery, I was able to change my perspective on the role of systematic observation in the classroom and this, in turn, influenced future interactions with my students. Judith Newman wrote an article about this need to be systematic and reflective about our teaching practices:

Our beliefs about learning and teaching are largely tacit. We operate a good deal of the time from an intuitive sense of what is going on without actively reflecting on what our intentions might be and what our actions could be saying to students.

> Our beliefs about learning and teaching can only be uncovered by engaging in systematic self-critical analysis of our current instructional practices (1987, p.727).

But active reflection is not enough. Theory and the reading of what other people — researchers, theorists, other teachers — have to say about pertinent topics is important as well. As I sought to understand Vygotsky's theory of language development, I tried to find a way to connect it to my own experiences of children learning language. As I got more and more involved in critically analyzing my data and returning to Vygotsky and the work of Anne Haas Dyson, I found myself reading the texts in a different way. I probably would have read Anne Haas Dyson's book anyway, because writing development in young children interests me, but I feel that, as a result of my research, I read it, or interacted with it, in a different way. Because I had collected data of my own, I brought things to the text that I wouldn't have otherwise. In other words, I learned from first-hand experience that theory must inform practice, and that practice informs theory. Along with reflecting and reading, discussion with others is a very valuable aspect of action research. As a member of the action research course, I found that presenting my ideas to the others and hearing their responses often influenced my interpretation of things. As well, I have been engaged with a colleague in my school in a more informal investigation of our writing program. The meetings that we have had have been invaluable and have served a number of different purposes. In particular, they have provided us with a chance to share our perceptions, based on systematic observation, and to discuss problems or concerns. It was encouraging to find that, on several occasions, there were similarities between our concerns. We were able to problem solve together. We also engaged in reading professional texts about writing, and we were able to share our ideas about how this reading applied to our unique situations. Current research shows the success of collaboration among students and the value of what they take away from those learning experiences. For teachers, too, I think there is much value in "practising what we preach" and engaging in some collaborative investigations with each other.

The final aspect I would like to mention has to do with how I feel my involvement in action research has influenced my students in a unique way. Throughout the study, my students were aware of what I was investigating. As I developed my perceptions about what was going on in their sharing talk, I shared these with them, listening to their comments and feedback. Near the end of my study, I decided to include the children — to take them on as 'researchers.' I started with a group discussion, after giving them some questions to think about. I was curious to see what they enjoyed about Writing Workshop, why they enjoyed it, if they felt that sharing their stories with someone else helped them and, if so, how, and what they felt I did that helped them. The very things that they enjoyed the most about Writing Workshop were the things I was most concerned about: being able to share their stories when they wanted, with anyone they wanted, (this, of course, affected the noise level) and being able to choose what to write about. When it came to questions about how they helped each other, they had rather few ideas. So I asked them to pay attention to how they helped someone else or how they were helped by another. I shall be interested to see what their perceptions are.

By sharing the process I am going through with the students and actively involving them in the process of inquiry, I have enabled them to take responsibility for Writing Workshop time. Because they have had an influence on the structure of the time (e.g., the decision to have ten minutes of silent writing), I feel the atmosphere has changed. They are being reflective about what they are doing and what they feel enables them to learn and grow. It also makes my own inquiry that much more exciting. By sharing my experiences with them, I have helped them become aware of the value that I place on written language and of my sincere interest in them as language users and learners. This awareness has impact on the value they place on becoming effective language users as well, and it connects us to a common goal. Anne Haas Dyson talks about the effects of such a community:

> In a community that values written language, writing can become an important means for individual reflection and social connection. And it is that feeling of belonging to a community—of connection to other people—that helps make teachers' and children's school lives together personally satisfying and socially meaningful (op.cit. p.xvii).

By investigating the development of written language within the framework of a formal inquiry, I have felt connected to my students' language development in a unique way, and they have been connected to me and to each other as co-investigators. Together we have created a community of language learners.

Notes

1. The new text: "In the summer Eric said, 'Why don't we go to Florida?' 'It is nice and hot,' said Eric's mother. A few days later they all went to the airport and took an 8 o'clock flight."

2. The children were aware of my research from the outset. I had explained that I was interested in what they talked about when they wrote and how they helped each other. To assist me in my research, I explained, different people would be wearing a wireless microphone so that I could record their talk. After the novelty wore off, they seemed to be unaffected by the microphone.

3

Conferences: Planned Transactions

Tamara Moscoe

Asking Questions

Some years ago, when my mode of teaching was largely transmissional, I used to hear phrases like 'child-centred,' 'activity-based' and 'whole language.' I knew that these things were somehow 'right' and what I was doing was suspect. I felt like someone on the fringes of respectable society. Gradually I came to understand how to create activities across the curriculum around a theme, how to introduce children to the activities, and how to ensure that children engaged in certain experiences and had their choice of others. I knew that, as children participated in these activities, they took from them (and from other children) what their level of development allowed them to learn. But as the children worked, what was my role? Surely not simply to organize materials and maintain harmony within the working groups! The more I thought about this question, the more I began to feel that some of the most valuable learning seemed to happen as I met with individuals and small groups before, during, and after they had completed an activity. Or so it seemed. It wasn't until I enroled in Gordon Wells's action research course at The Ontario Institute for Studies in Education that I began to scrutinize these exchanges in an attempt to understand whether they truly had value. When the course first began, the other students and I were casting about for topics to research. After a few false starts, I thought I might look at writing conferences because I had previously written a paper on children's topic selection. As he often did,

Gordon homed in on the key point in my rather vague musings and asked, "Do you have conferences in other subjects besides writing?"'Yes,' I replied, "in just about everything."

I decided that these conferences would be a worthwhile part of my classroom practice to study. After all, I spent much of my day working with children in this way, and it was time to gain more insight into whether this way of working was productive. I had for some time seen references to conferencing in my reading of research on writing (Calkins 1986), and more recently on reading (Graves 1989), but there did not seem to be any literature on conferences as a way of teaching right across the curriculum. I thought about the students who were in my class: twenty-four grade 1 and 2 children in a school with an unusually homogeneous population. All the children spoke English as their first language and came from relatively privileged backgrounds. Even so, their social and intellectual development varied widely. Some children were confident and socially adept, while others found their relationships with other children and adults difficult and unsatisfactory. There were children in both grades who read picture books fluently and who wrote stories of considerable length. On the other hand, there were children in both grades who did not yet understand that print on a page held meaning and who, in their own writing, were at the scribble or random letter stage. I felt, but had not really confirmed, that conferences were a good way of addressing the varying needs of children over a wide range of development. (I suspected that in a class with an even wider range of special needs, such as ESL, for example, a conference approach might be even more useful.) I wondered whether looking at conferences in my class in an organized way would refute or support my theory.

Before I could look at conferences more closely, I needed to come up with a working definition of what they were. Gordon Wells's description of 'collaborative talk' seemed to me to apply to conferences as well:

> [with reference to] teacher-student interaction, using the framework provided by Vygotsky's conception of learning and teaching within the zone of proximal development,...we have argued that, by providing support and suggestions that are contingently responsive to the students' current endeavors and level of competence, the teacher enables them to co-enact and ultimately take over procedures, knowledge and skills that they can apply in future situations (1990, p.1).

I decided that I would keep written records of every conference in which I was involved over a two-month period and would also tape-record as many conferences as was practical. I would then analyze the data in order to try to answer several questions:

1. What areas of study (writing, reading, math, science, social studies) did the conferences address? What areas should they address? Was classifying conferences by subject area consonant with my learning paradigm?

2. How much time did I actually spend on a conference?

3. Although I was holding a large number of conferences, did I actually see each child on a regular basis, or was I giving an inordinate amount of time to certain children? Should or could I be more systematic about dividing my time fairly among all the children?

4. What were my purposes for holding the conferences?

5. What were the child's (or children's) purposes?

6. Were our purposes accomplished?

7. Did learning/teaching occur that I had not anticipated at the beginning of the conference?

As time went by, new questions began to emerge:

8. How did the children feel about the conferences? Did they find them valuable or, at least, enjoyable?

9. What were the difficulties or rewards inherent in doing classroom research?

10. What issues were there for my own professional development?

The Data and What I Learned From It

Time and Frequency

Because of the busy nature of life in the classroom, my attempts to keep track numerically of conferences sometimes fell by the wayside, but the few 'statistics' I came up with did help me get an overview of the scope and frequency of conferences in my class. They also put my mind at rest. I will in the future not feel the compulsion to keep counts and checklists and will therefore be able to use my conference times more productively. In the course of two months there were 34 school days on which I held a total of 245 conferences. This averaged out to about seven conferences a day, but in actual fact the number of conferences per day ranged from a low of 0 to a high of 19. I kept track of roughly how long I spent on most conferences. Of the 194 conferences I timed, 69 were short conferences of under five minutes, 94 were of medium length (five to 15 minutes) and 34 were long conferences of anywhere from 15 to 35 minutes. The difficulty and, in fact, counter-productivity of assigning a subject area to a conference is discussed elsewhere, but to the extent that this could be done, the vast majority of conferences (116) were on writing, 54 were on math, 39 were on social studies and 30 were on reading, while a few were on other topics. I knew that writing conferences, although seemingly over-represented, were often not simply about writing; they just revolved around a piece of writing that related to a social studies, mathematics or science topic. Therefore I was not dissatisfied with these results. Next I wanted to see whether each student was getting a fair share of conference time. The largest number of conferences for a single child in the two-month period was 23, and the smallest number was 12. Interestingly, the 23 conferences were held with a child who frequently demanded time and attention. Each of the three children with whom I held only 12 conferences, on the other hand, were self-reliant, adept at finding things to do that interested them, confident in their own abilities, and often willing to extend an activity beyond what was required. I thought about this and concluded that perhaps it was appropriate, at least some of the time, to give attention to children in response to their own perceived needs.

Seeing that the number of conferences held with each child was somewhat related to the child's needs, I felt it might be worthwhile to see who initiated the conferences. Of the 221 conferences of which I kept track, I found that I initiated 147 and a child or small group of children initiated 74. In the vast majority of cases, my purposes and also the child's stated purposes for the conference were achieved.

Purposes of Conferences

An Opportunity for the Child to Elaborate and Clarify
I usually had several purposes in mind for each conference. First, I felt that looking at the written text of Grade 1 children and many of the Grade 2 children without oral elaboration on the child's part would serve to confuse rather than enlighten me as to the child's achievement and level of understanding. For instance, looking at a sample of Jessica's work might lead me to think that she had used random letters in some parts of her piece, but when she read it to me, I could see that all of her writing was

already at the 'syllabic-alphabetic stage' (Pontecorvo 1990, p. 61). For example, when I had first looked at Jessica's work, I did not know what

vda a sh p a Ba22

said, but when she read it to me, I could see that it was a very good rendering of how she pronounced "vegetables."

Working in the Zone of Proximal Development

The purpose that I recorded most frequently was to build on skills or present concepts in response to something that the child was doing. I didn't have any preconceived notion for what these would be as I went into the conference. For example, I had a little lesson on topic selection with Gary after I asked him to read me the story he had finished. This is what he had written: (translated here into conventional spelling):

The Germans' Revenge of Air Raids

The Germans didn't like the Iraqis, so they decided to try and kill them, but instead of killing them, they almost got killed. After a while of fighting, the Germans decided that they didn't like it.

I felt that this topic was one that six-year-old Gary could not possibly handle in any meaningful way, but I wanted to give him a reason for choosing a different topic that was sincere from my point of view and understandable from his, so I asked him if he knew much about war and Germans, or had any direct experience with this topic.

"Not really," he said. Our conversation continued like this:

T: It's hard to write about something you don't know much about, isn't it? Is there something that you're interested in that you know a lot about?

G: Well, I know about working at an airport.

T: Really? How did you find out about it?

G: My dad used to work there and he took me and showed me around.

T: I think lots of people would want to hear about that. Do you think you'd want to write about working at an airport or maybe your visit there?

G: Yeah....

T: Do you want to find out more first?

G: I could ask my dad.

T: That's a great idea. Maybe you could interview him tonight.

On another occasion, I listened to Becky struggling over a word in her reading because she'd just tuned into 'sounding out.' " Read on and come back. You'll figure it out," I suggested, not wanting her to forget about context as a reading strategy.

In the vast majority of cases, both my and the children's purposes were accomplished, but were there ever unexpected outcomes? Since I seldom had a preconceived notion of what, if any, specific 'teaching,' or learning would take place, just that hopefully some would, I am considering the many 'lessons' that I had with various children in response to things that emerged in the conference as expected outcomes. The range of these 'lessons' was fairly wide, although many of them were related to writing. As I went through my records of conferences, I noted what was accomplished in each one and came up with a list of forty different topics related to revising writing, writing content, editing surface features, reading strategies, math concepts, social studies content and science hypotheses.

I have often considered the argument that it may be a waste of time to teach skills and concepts such as these to single children, since the same lesson may be taught over and over. In fact, when I looked over the times that I recorded each item as having been addressed during a conference, I noted a surprising result: the vast majority of mini-lessons had been taught only once. A very few were taught two, three or four times. Only three items were addressed five times each and that was the highest rate of frequency. Sometimes items were addressed in response to a query from the student. Most often, I made a judgement call, based on evidence in the child's writing, or how she was doing something (and in my discussion with her), that she might be ready to understand a particular concept. I then tried to watch the child's reaction to judge whether I was right. Judith Newman describes this process:

> I recognized many of my moment-to-moment teaching decisions. I was suddenly aware of how I am constantly watching

students' bodies and listening to their voices in order to know how to proceed (1990, p. 20).

This open-ended technique for leading the child just a little beyond where he seems to be does not always work so neatly in some subject areas. In math, more preconceived mini-lessons were taught on topics such as looking for patterns, place value, counting, making change and creating a graph.

I began by saying that I have in the past vacillated, feeling on the one hand that this way of teaching to individuals or very small groups helped me to meet the individual needs of children, but wondering at the same time whether it was an efficient use of time if I was simply teaching the same thing over and over. Systematically keeping and analyzing conference records has shown me that not only is it efficient; it is also logical. It is important for me to have this evidence, not only to justify my practices to myself, but also to others.

Evaluating, Responding and Clarifying

Another important purpose of the conferences was to evaluate a child's progress. When Katie kept looking up at me as she read John Burningham's *The Snow* (1974), I could see that she wasn't very confident. However, I could also see that she was no longer relying only on memory, picture and context clues. She knew a few function words like 'the' by sight and she was using some knowledge of sound-symbol relationships.

The evaluative function of conferences became explicit when I worked on written reports to parents in the middle of the term. As I wrote, I kept my book of anecdotal records close at hand. Most of the comments I was writing on the reports were based on these anecdotal records, and the anecdotal records themselves were largely accounts of what went on during conferences. One example will reveal this close connection between the content of the conferences and the content of the reports. These comments in the language arts section of one child's report were derived almost word-for-word from notes I had made during conferences with her:

- has developed a literary writing style (e.g.,"ventured far into the forest," "came to a clearing");

- sustains mood, plot and genre in a piece of writing; is beginning to use characterization;

- uses dialogue; is working on quotation marks and sentence stops;

- spelling is becoming more conventional; has begun to keep

a list of words that are frequently used and spelled almost correctly in her writing;

- has almost completely overcome a tendency to write letter reversals;

- expressive oral reading suggests good comprehension;

- is making use of all reading strategies; self-corrects to establish meaning in a passage;

- makes insightful observations and connections about literature.

'Simply to respond' (Calkins 1986, p.119) to the child's work in order to celebrate it, or at least support it, was also important. This purpose often manifested itself as help with publishing. As I acted as editor in one after another child's publishing venture, I wondered whether with children who have not yet reached the point where they can recognize areas in their own writing that require revision, there is much point in my helping them to make 'good copies' of their writing, or, where necessary, doing it for them.

However, the children's reactions when their and others' published books appeared in the class library convinced me there is value in this practice. The author and other children would read and reread the books, and isn't that much of the point of being an author, to have an audience for one's writing? Whether there is actual improvement in reading and writing from ending up with a published version of one's work is another question, but I think that, at the very least, it provides a piece of familiar reading for children who are just learning to read.

I could also learn about a child's interests, 'what strikes a child' (Graves 1989, p. 41). In this conversation with Lana, which took place after I had asked her to read to me in order to assess her progress, she helped me learn more about her interests. But she also provided some insights into her self-concept as a reader and she suggested a course of action for me:

T: Do you like reading?

L: Yes.

T: Any particular stories that you've tried lately?

L: I like reading chapter books.

T :   Do you remember any titles that you've liked?

L: Well, I got one from the library and it's called Different

Dragons. It's about a guy who hates dogs and his aunt gets him one for his birthday. And I borrowed it from the Public Library.

T: Oh, great. Do you think we have enough chapter books in the class?

L: Well, there's not very much, I don't think.

T: Maybe we should . . . (get more)

In math, particularly, it was sometimes necessary to clarify an activity for a child or a group. During this conference, Daphne and Rick are using a mat with columns for ones, tens, hundreds and thousands, and plastic counters that can be snapped together. One partner places counters on the mat and, each time counters must be snapped together and moved to a new column, the other partner writes the number that has been reached on a paper that is similarly divided into columns. Then the partners change roles. I met with the children to see whether they were understanding the concept of place value and to offer help and support, as well as to try to take them a little beyond where they now were in their understanding:

T: How many ones do you have, Rick?

R: Zero.

T: Good. So what's the new number?

R: 20 (he writes the number.)

T: Good. Okay, Rick, now you make a number.

R: (counting as he places the counters) 21, 22, 23, 24, 26, 27, 28, 29, 30

T: Is that okay? When you get to 30, can you leave these (counters) on the ones side?

R: No. (Rick snaps together the ten counters and moves them over to the tens side.)

T: How many groups of ten do you have now?

R: Three.

T: Daphne, would you write the new number?

(Daphne writes 30.)

T: Daphne, do you want to take a turn now? (to make a new number with counters)

D: 31, 32, 33, 34, 35, 36, 37, 37, 38, 39, 40.

(As she places the last counter down, she begins to snap together the ten pieces she has put down.)

T: Okay, now would you write the new number? What is the new number, Daphne?

D: 40

T: And 40 means how many groups of ten, Rick?

R: Four.

T: And how many groups of one?

D: None.

T: Okay, let's speed it up a little.

(I help the partners get to 100, so that they can see what happens when 10 groups of 10 counters accumulate in the tens column.)

While my conversation with Rick and Daphne was used mostly to underscore the notion that when ten counters are built up on the ones side, they must be bundled together and moved to the tens, it was also an opportunity to assess how the children cooperated in a shared task. Evaluation of children's ability to work cooperatively in a group took place every time there was a conference with a small group.

Conferences also provided opportunities to gain insights into a child's attitudes or knowledge about a particular topic as we began to study it, so that some comparison could be made with the child's attitudes and store of information at the end of the unit. This purpose was particularly important as we began a unit of study on the Chinese New Year and the Chinese community in Toronto. Jeffrey and Georgie revealed what they knew as they read me what they had written about the Chinese New Year at the beginning of the unit:

J: We didn't get many ideas.

T: Why do you think that is?

J: I guess we don't know very much.

At the end of the unit, I asked them to write down what they knew. This time they made a list. They read their list to me:

Food: rice cakes, spring rolls, noodles, mung beans, stir fried bok choy, water chestnuts, broccoli, fortune cookies

Things that they have and things that they do: kites, lanterns, lion dance, dragons, dragon dance

When I asked them if they wanted to add anything, they continued:

J: Panda bears

G: Chinese hats

T: What kind of hats do you mean?

G: These... uh... weird...

J: You shouldn't say weird. You should say interesting.

The Children's Purposes

In response to a suggestion made by Gordon Wells, I began to document the students' purposes in seeking conferences. Their most frequent purpose was a purely practical one, "to get help with publishing this piece I wrote." At our next meeting, Gordon asked whether I could dig deeper, and an article I read reinforced this idea: "I discovered that children are cognizant of and can articulate what it is they want to learn next about reading and writing" (Siu-Runyan 1991, p. 102).

So I started saying, "Is there anything you'd like to learn about writing; is there anything you've been wondering about?" Most of the children seemed to interpret this question as referring to handwriting, as Daphne does in this exchange that took place when she showed me a description of a dragon that she had written:

T: Is there anything that you've been wondering about writing, maybe that you don't know how to do that you'd like to learn how to do?

D: Sometimes I'd like to learn Chinese writing. I love it.

T: Some kids have done it. They've just chosen to do it. You could choose it if you like.

D: Yeah, sometimes I go down the hall to go to the bath room and I see some kids doing Chinese characters. (A group from another class had been working in the hall.)

T: Fine, you could do it. If you notice, I've put up some work. I think Clara did those. She just chose to do it. But what I'm talking about, when you're writing a story, or writing a description like this, is there any thing that puzzles you about how you do it, that you think I might be able to help you with?

D: No, not really.

T: All right. Maybe you can read your description to me. Maybe I'll find something I can help you with.

D: My dragon looks like this. He has horns coming out of the front of his head. He has... he is green with red stripes. That's what my dragon looks like.

T: I have a question. (pointing to two words in Daphne's text) If that's 'looks,' can that also be 'looks?'

(Daphne shakes her head.)

You know, when I say, "Write it the way you think," I mean write it as close to the real way as you can. But if you know the real way to write something, you might as well do it that way.

I had noticed that Daphne was spelling the word 'looks' conventionally in one place and not in another. I pounced on this as an area for instruction. As I later listened to the tape, I was struck by how dismally I had failed at conveying the message I was trying to convey — that I wanted her to tell me what she wanted to learn. I had dismissed her request to learn how to write Chinese by suggesting that she could choose to do it by herself, but had insisted on talking about maintaining the conventional spelling of a word, a notion she would no doubt have picked up herself eventually, and I had done so before I had even responded to her descriptive piece. Had I handled things differently, perhaps acknowledging that I couldn't teach her to write Chinese because I couldn't do it either, but that she might want to try copying some of the models of Chinese writing that were about the room, she might have gradually over time learned to believe that I really wanted to know what she wanted to learn, and might have become adept at identifying her own needs.

Later in the week, when Andy said, "I'd like to learn how to do cursive writing," and Corey said, "I'd like to know about that little mark you put in words like 'didn't,'" I gave them the help they asked for, even though my own opinion was that there were other elements in their writing that we should have been attending to.

Other purposes that the children sometimes offered were to share a story or poem they'd been reading and had enjoyed, to simply show me a piece of work they'd done and were pleased with, or to get help with reading.

I suspect that the children's inability to articulate their needs might have been due to lack of practice. It was late in the study when I began specifically asking what they would like to learn and it will be interesting to see what happens if I continue to pursue this line of questioning, but do so in a way that shows my sincerity, having learned a lesson from my conversation with Daphne.

Some Surprises

A New Teaching Technique

As I began each conference, I had a general notion of what I expected to achieve, but I was also prepared for the unexpected. Even so, some things I learned surprised me more than others. I'm going to document a sampling of these.

A teacher in my school had told me that she taped children in her class reading aloud at various times of the year in order to have a record of their progress. This seemed like a good idea to me and so I tried it, incidentally using the resulting tapes as additional records of conferences for this chapter. I know that children enjoy hearing themselves on tape, so I asked each child at the end of the reading whether he wanted to hear her or himself. Invariably, the children did want to hear themselves, and they all listened attentively. But Benjie did something the other children had not done: he opened the book he had been reading and followed along. It occurred to me that this would be an excellent technique to help children with their reading, and I had learned it from one of my students!

Learning by Listening

Sacha's writing consisted almost exclusively of a series of x's and o's, so I assumed he could not write and probably could not identify most of the letters of the alphabet. He had, however, been writing his own first name since the beginning of the year, usually reversing the 'S.' I decided to give him a little help with the 'S,' and when he seemed to have no difficulty in writing it the conventional way, I wondered if he knew more than I realized. I asked him if he thought he could make many other letters. "Sure," he said.

"If I say some letters, will you write them for me?"

"Okay," Sacha replied, and proceeded to write correctly all of the upper-case letters except Q, making only a few reversals.

When I asked Sacha why he wasn't using his knowledge of letters in his writing, he said, "I don't know how to spell the words." It turned out that he could write at least the initial consonant in many of the words he wanted to use in his story. I didn't know whether all children go through a stage where they don't use the knowledge that they've newly acquired, or whether Sacha really believed that words had to be spelled for him.

A parent-teacher conference day was coming up and I invited Sacha's parents to attend. In my conversation with his mother it became evident that she hadn't read the missives on the writing process and the stages of writing that I had sent home, and thought that the way to help her child write was to spell things out for him. In case it was this practice that was causing Sacha's reluctance to try out his knowledge, I suggested some alternative strategies to his mother. So far, my mini-lesson has had some effect: Sacha now uses random letters, a stage beyond his x and o period. Of course, it's possible that he might have reached this stage even without my intervention.

Working with Jimmy provided a somewhat different example. He didn't seem very 'with it' most of the time and accomplished very little in a day. Yet, when I worked with him on various mathematical concepts, he showed surprising adeptness and understanding. Had I relied on his written recordings of math activities to assess his progress, instead of conferences, I would have grossly underestimated his level of mathematical understanding.

A Change in Theory Can Lead to a Change in Perception

Georgie has a lot of difficulty getting his ideas out in a logical and coherent way. In fact, he seems much more interested in getting a turn to speak than in conveying information. Sometimes he will tell an anecdote that rambles on and on, and seems not to attend to the listener's reaction.

One day he was about to read me a story he had written. I thought it might be helpful for both him and me if we discussed what the story was about before the reading. Our conversation here may be too brief to convey what I often felt in my talks with Georgie, that there was little common ground between us. But the pattern had become very familiar to me in the two years I had known him.

T: What's this story about?

G: Well, it's about me and my babysitter was at my house because my mum's, um, going away for a little while, up to, um, New Mexico to ski and she was coming over

to see, just to have a little time with us. Last time she
was there, she only had a little bit of time...

T: I see. So what's the story about?

G: The milk, it's about when me and my and my brother
were wrestling in the kitchen and the milk spilled.

T: Oh, I thought you said this was a story about your
babysitter.

G: No, she dumps milk on top of me.

T: Oh, she's in the story.

G: Yeah.

T: Is this a true story or did you make up some parts?

G: It's a true... my babysitter...

T: So this really happened?

G: Yeah, this down here, it's kind of made up. The Milk
Spill. I was wrestling with my brother in the kitchen
with my, oops, I forgot 'my," there was on...

T: I'm sorry? Where are you?

G: We guh, a, got, got the babysitter, the babysitter, I
don't know what that says.

As I listened to the tape of our conversation in order to transcribe
it, I had an image of Georgie in conversation with his mother, who
was a frequent visitor and volunteer in the school. I realized that
this hurried, somewhat incoherent, style of speech was hers too
and that much of her conversation with him was 'testing' and
'teaching' content and skills rather than the sort of relaxed and
natural conversations that other children had about real things
with their parents. Still, even if this impression of mine were
correct, it did not offer much direction for me in helping Georgie.
Reading Wells's description of intersubjectivity gave me some
insight into Georgie's speech patterns:

> In a nutshell, what I want to suggest is that the attempt to
> achieve intersubjectivity in discourse itself entails learning,
> and so an important part of the teacher's role consists in
> establishing and maintaining intersubjectivity with the stu-
> dent in his or her zone of proximal development in relation to
> the agreed upon task or topic (1990, p. 14).

For whatever reason, I and others that I had observed engaging
in discourse with Georgie were failing to establish and maintain
this intersubjectivity, and we would somehow have to learn to do

so if our conversations with him were to become productive. Perhaps all that was needed was time and patience:

> Nevertheless, conversation rarely breaks down completely and, over time, the child gradually appropriates the resources of the culture's language system and learns to use it to achieve his purposes in interaction with those around him. What makes this possible, I want to suggest, is the persistent attempt to achieve intersubjectivity that underpins all communication (Wells, op cit. p.14).

In the following weeks I found that I was less impatient and frustrated by my apparent lack of ability to communicate effectively with Georgie, because I began to understand that our difficulties were not related to a 'defect' on either of our parts, but that achieving intersubjectivity was a developmental process just like learning to read and write.

Developing as a Teacher Through Classroom-Based Research

Looking at Classroom Practices More Critically: Conferences

The act of doing classroom-based research seems to encourage a tendency that teachers already have: to find ways of doing things better. Obviously, I began to look more critically at what I was saying, doing and implying to children during the classroom conferences. Listening to the tapes critically, I identified some problems that I have already described. But there was also something about the management of the conferences that disturbed me, and I found in a survey of the children's perspectives that it was a concern of theirs too. Most of the time I was initiating conferences with children, but sometimes they would come to me and ask whether they could see me. If I wasn't busy with someone else, I complied with their request. If I was busy, I would ask them to come back later.

There were problems with both of these systems. Often, when I asked to see a child, the child would have to leave what she was doing. Or, if the child made the request and I was busy, other things would intervene and I would sometimes not get back to her. I decided to try something that I had done with older children. I made a place on the board where they could sign up for conferences. Sometimes I wouldn't get to a child for quite some time, a couple of days even, but because the topic had been important enough for the child to feel he wanted to sign up, he invariably remembered what he wanted to see me about and the conference proceeded. Probably I will end up with a system that combines signing up with my requesting to see children.

Looking at Basic Assumptions More Critically

In reading the work of researchers such as Calkins and Graves, I was struck by the use of conferences almost exclusively during the writing process. (Of course, that may be simply because writing is what they are researching.) I had, myself, perhaps been influenced by this emphasis for, when I first decided to undertake a study of conferences in my class, I had intended to look at writing conferences only.

Graves himself hints, in *Experiment With Fiction* (1989), that he is moving away from a conferences-for-writing emphasis and beginning to see conferences as an important way of transacting with children in the reading process as well.

I suspect that this seeming isolation of conferences for writing — and perhaps for reading — may be a by-product of a tendency to isolate reading and writing as separate activities in the classrooms where Graves and Calkins did their research. It may also be a by-product of the necessity to offer practical solutions to questions about how writing and reading should be taught in a context where the researchers could not hope to totally revolutionize the philosophy of how children learn and teachers teach.

It seems to me that, when something else — hands-on science or social studies activities, most likely — is the starting point, more meaningful reading and writing take place because there is a real-life context for the reading and writing. Thus, when my class was working on the Chinese New Year-Chinese Community unit, we carried out a variety of activities that certainly involved reading and writing but were actually about things as diverse as running a 'store' with items bought in Chinatown, measuring and sprouting mung beans, cooking, and drama, and therefore the conferences had a focus that went beyond writing and reading.

Putting It All Together

Many of the insights I have described may be only slight modifications of beliefs that may, in turn, lead only to temporary modifications of practice. I have come to feel, however, that most important, long-term changes are merely the sum total of a series of slight or temporary modifications, and that these modifications will only happen under certain conditions. Five important conditions have become evident during the course of this study.

1. Encouraging Talk, Engaging in it Actively, and Listening Both Literally and Figuratively

The importance of talk in classrooms has been stressed for some time and, being a dutiful teacher who tries to follow the dictums of those in the know, I have tried for the past few years to ensure that many of the activities in my class include group work that requires collaboration, that even when children are working alone they feel free to discuss and consult with others, and that much of my day is spent in conferences with children, alone or in small groups. However, I now see that having talk in the classroom is not enough. Jerome Harste (1991) says that "the core of the curriculum has to be conversation, but it has to be substantive conversation." This implies that conferences need to be, to a great extent, 'planned transactions.' But I also think that it is important to really listen to the talk, not only that of the children, but also my own.

This is true both in the literal and figurative sense of listening. When I listened literally to Jimmy, I realized that he understood much more about math than his recording of his work during hands-on activities indicated. While I was talking to Daphne about what she wanted to learn, I was too busy thinking about what I was going to say to attend to Daphne's message in the figurative sense of listening. I did not understand that I was negating what she told me. It was only when I listened reflectively to the tape later on that I became aware of this.

2. Reading Reflectively

Encouraging talk and then really listening are, by themselves, not enough either. I talked with Georgie and I listened reflectively to the tape, but it was not until I reread Wells' article on intersubjectivity that I realized what was missing from our conversations. In other words, reflective listening also needs to be informed by reflective reading of the insights of others and by the application of those insights to one's own situation.

3. Gathering Information Systematically

Thirdly, impressionistic information gathered from casual observations and conversations is not enough. Even keeping careful written records, while it goes a long way, is not enough when it comes to something as ephemeral as talk. Keeping a written record of all my conferences for two months provided data that, in some cases, confirmed what I believed to be happening in my class in regard to conferences but, in other cases, negated it or at least shed new light on it. I learned about the purposes of conferences, whether purposes were fulfilled, what transpired, the efficacy of conferences versus teaching to large groups, their frequency and duration, and students' feelings about them. But some of the insights I gained could not have been achieved if the conversations had not been taped so that I could listen to them later. The demands of dealing with a large number of children are too great to allow teachers to be totally reflective about their conversations while they are going on.

4. Engaging Formally in Action Research

To hope that teachers will engage in action research without any outside impetus is unrealistic, at least at this time, when this type of professional development is largely unknown at the school level. Certainly, taking action research courses was my personal motivation. Perhaps when Boards of Education recognize the value of this kind of research, they will offer extrinsic rewards, that, added to the intrinsic rewards that come from the research itself, will make this kind of project attractive to teachers or will at least give them the courage to get started. Reports from some boards where classroom-based research is officially recognized and supported are encouraging.

Working on such a project in an isolated setting, on the other hand, has some pitfalls. There is no one to 'keep you honest' that is, to react to your observations by questioning them, or, where appropriate, supporting them, although the class at The Ontario Institute for Studies in Education did, to some extent, take on this function. Related to this pitfall is the problem, inherent in writing about one's own practice, of trying to sound objective about oneself. One fears that a certain note of self-righteousness or self-congratulation can creep into the reporting. Or one can take the opposite tack and be ruthlessly self- critical. But this approach might not necessarily be honest or productive either.

For myself, I know I have gained some valuable insights into my students' learning in general and the place of conferences in particular. I am, however, nagged by a certain sense of superficiality. I feel that I have raised a number of issues that I have not fully come to terms with. This would be acceptable if I had firm plans to pursue one or two issues in the future, but I cannot be certain that this will happen. On the positive side, while some of my findings may have been shallow, there is no doubt in my mind that even this limited level of depth and rigor would never have been achieved without the action research project.

5. Placing Data in a Theoretical Framework

Finally, the truth of a notion that certainly did not originate with me, but has often been stated, once again became evident. Experience needs theory and theory needs experience. The many notes and recordings that I collected provided bits of information and fragments of understanding that might have been interesting and even instructive in themselves. But until I placed them within the larger theoretical framework of intersubjectivity, it was difficult to make sense of them, and until I had gathered enough data to see the framework clearly, I had too little experience to fully understand the theory.

4
An Inquiry into Reader Response

Ann Maher

This inquiry developed from my growing discomfort and dissatisfaction with the reading program in my Junior grade 4/5 classroom. Too often it seemed that reading discussions were superfi-
cial; they seldom moved beyond surface features of the text. And
when a meaningful group conversation did begin in one of the
groups, it was often impossible to sustain it because of the
constant interruptions of scheduling demands and the needs of
other students. On the other hand, from my experience of working
in a more open manner in the areas of mathematics and environ-
mental studies, I knew that the students were eager to participate more fully in the work of the classroom. So, when a course I
was taking presented the opportunity to examine some aspect of
my teaching in more detail, I welcomed the challenge with
enthusiasm. The goal I set myself was to create reading experiences that would lead to more satisfactory expressions of personal
response.

The approach to reading that I was following was fairly traditional in its teacher-directed organization. Typically, I would
work with a small group of eight or ten students, reading and
discussing an assigned story, while the rest of the class was busy
with reading activities that I hoped would be creative and challenging. However, in order to make this system work, I had to put
a lot of time and effort into creating meaningful activities; I also
had to spend valuable reading time in discussing, marking and
evaluating the outcomes. As a result, the students spent too little
time reading and I spent far too much time on keeping the system

functioning. In sum, my method of organizing reading was preventing the very activity it was intended to promote.

But it wasn't only more time to read that was required. I had come to see that the students also needed more control over what they read and time and opportunity to respond to their reading in a comfortable and natural manner. Given the opportunity, I was convinced, they were capable of far richer expression of their insights and perceptions than the daily routine was currently allowing them to communicate. My goal, then, would be to provide a wide variety of interesting materials and sufficient time and opportunity to talk about the children's reading experiences.

First Steps

I told my class that I was concerned that they did not have enough time to read and discuss books of their own choice. They agreed. So I explained what I had planned: there would be two periods of independent reading each week, with the other three periods being spent in directed group reading. Then we organized the new daily schedule on a large planning board to help us all keep track of the changed arrangements. However, I was still troubled by a number of questions: When would I find time to hear individual students read? How would I evaluate their reading comprehension? And, most important, how was I going to find time for talking about the books they were reading?

The most manageable method for allowing more reader response, I had decided, was to begin using Reading Journals. "Write to me about your book," I told the children. "I want to know what you think and feel about what you are reading." And it was from reading their weekly journal entries that I began to see further possibilities for changing and improving my reading program.

The following entries from Sophie's journal are typical of those that many students wrote. Here is what she wrote on 5 January.

By Beverly cleary
Thurs, Jan 5, 1989   Otis Spofford

Otis was always geting it to trouble.

He was always triing to stirr

up a little excitment. But it was hard to stirr up anything at home. because the manager, Mrs. Brewster was always watching him.

This is simply a summary of the first part of her novel, Otis Spotford. There is nothing here of her reaction to Otis or the difficulties he had in stirring up excitement. When I read her journal entry, I was surprised at how impersonal it was and I wondered why. So I asked her some questions.

Jan 5

Dear Sophie
Otis sounds like a strange character I want to know more about him.
Does Beverly Cleary make you want to read and read?
If so, how does she do this?
Mrs M.

When Sophie writes again on 16 January, there is a very evident change. Picking up my use of a standard letter form, she starts her entry, 'Dear Mrs Maher' and, in her comments on Henry, the central character in her new novel, her chatty, personal voice begins to come through.

> By BEVERly Cleary
> Mon. Jan, 16, 1989. HENRy and THE Paper Route
> Dear.Mrs. MaHer, I think Henry is the
>
> strangest character. He tries to get a paper
>
> route, I think that Beverly cleary writes
>
> good stories. It always makes me laugh.
>
> But he is to young to get a paper
>
> route. I want to read as much of
> Beverly's books as I can.from Sophie

In the first entry, Sophie is writing with no audience in mind. Using the practical logic of the child, she does not begin the dialogue until she has someone to communicate with. By the second entry, however, she has received my reply. Now she is taking part in a conversation with me and so it is natural for her to talk about her feelings and her plans for future reading. Looking back, I can see my mistake. I had not thought to talk to them, in advance, about the nature and purpose of dialogue journals, assuming that they would understand — even before the dialogue began.

Reading the subsequent entries in Sophie's journal, I become aware of another problem. Many of my questions are failing to evoke a response, although I notice that a comment of mine on 25 January about reading in bed followed by a question about when she likes to read is picked up by Sophie on 8 February, when she remarks that 'sometimes I read the books in bed.' Because the entries are only made once a week, the replies, when they come, are often out of date. Questions about what Sophie was reading when she wrote on 2 February have become irrelevant by her next entry on 8 February, as she has gone on to read a different book. The infrequent exchanges mean that the dialogue lacks the immediacy of true conversation.

But it is also clear to me that the students' comments and opinions deserve a wider audience. I want Sophie to talk to her classmates about what she is discovering about the books she is reading. I want the other students to know that, in all her reading, she never saw a person so strange as Harriet (1 February). Gregory, too, amazes me with his opinion about his 'choose your own adventure' book (9 January). Even though it would be quite fair to describe Greg as a reluctant reader, he is quite able to express his enthusiasm for his adventure story, balanced by his growing literary taste: he dislikes flipping about to different pages. Jason's delightful conviction in his remark that E.B. White 'just makes excellent animal stories' (14/15 January) and Chi's advice to read *Blubber* (13 January) really deserve to be shared with their peers. The children have so much to teach each other; but how can we find ways and means to allow this to happen amidst our busy schedule?

Listening to the Children

While the children and I were beginning to dialogue through the reading journals, I was still continuing to run the guided reading groups as before. However my discomfort with this way of organizing the program continued to grow as I observed and listened to their responses to what they were reading. One extraordinary experience, in particular, stands out in my memory. A group of students were following along in their basal reader as I read aloud a story called 'The Old Man's Mitten.' On the floor beside me were some stuffed animals and a mitten I had gathered with a vague idea of using them to increase their understanding and enjoyment of the story. Just as I finished reading, I was called to the telephone. When I returned, I found to my delight that the children had organized themselves into the roles of the characters and were enthusiastically engrossed in reading and dramatizing the story. Given the appropriate opportunity, I realized, children do respond naturally and sensitively to their reading experiences, and adult intervention can all too often be experienced as interference in the natural flow of events.

I noticed, too, that the children seemed to be talking to me about their books in new and more revealing ways. For example, one morning, in the discussion that followed the group reading of a patterned folk tale, I spent too long on the obvious features of the events in the story and so failed to move the conversation on to a consideration of the nature of the story's characters. A few days later, however, Son, a member of the group, spontaneously offered me his considered and thoughtful opinion of the main characters.

"You know, Mrs Maher, I don't really like that little girl in *The Piney Pedlar*. She's kind of spoiled. She just tells her father to get her a shiny dollar — she doesn't even say please. Her father is foolish to get everything she asks for. My mother doesn't do that. At Christmas I get just one good gift."

As I thought about these events, I remembered something I had recently read in the editorial to Language Matters, 1979 (2).

...we must never underestimate the natural competence of children to use language effectively — when they have something they really want to say and the right person to say it to. In Margaret Donaldson's words, "By the time they come to school, all normal children can show skill as thinkers and language-users to a degree which must compel our respect, so long as they are dealing with 'real-life' meaningful situations in which they have purposes and intentions and in which they can recognize and respond to similar purposes and intentions in others" (1978, p.121).

I was grateful for this reminder, for it helped me to see that, when Son wanted me to know his considered opinion of the story characters, he was assuming that I would be interested to know what he thought — as indeed I was. But Son was not alone in wanting to tell me about his thoughts. And so we began to talk about books during writing time and about what we were writing during reading time. In fact, the conversations continued throughout the day. We were truly becoming a community of readers, writers and thinkers.

Ka Chun's journal entry on 2 February, showed me what changes had already come about as a result of the conversations that were going on. But it also convinced me that more time was needed for reading and talking about books. I could no longer escape the fact that I had to make further changes in my program.

Dear Mrs Maher
The book I'm is encyclopedia Brown it detective book
ten detective stories in the novel. I like the frist
1st story it was favirtie. it call the champoin skier.
it a was about a man called mr. ware got kidnapped by
a man I figure out who was the kidnapper. It Harry Smith
He was one one of Mr. Ware freinds. He brought in a can
ski wax and all the other ones of Mr. Ware freinds
brought in something water and Harry Smith only brought
in ski wax for snow and that's encyclopedia brown the
boy detective slove the mysertry of case of the champoin

skier. This is sort scary in the other chapters. This is
book sort of like sherlock bones. The book has solution
in the end. at the end of chapter it says what page
number to the solution page. I might get out anther books
about encyclopedia brown books. Because it is exciting
book. maybe you may want to read one Mrs. M.
   The end
p.s. Hernani is reading encyclopida brown books too. He
the one that got me into encyclopdia browns books
I wish I can intrest him something.

I wrote my reply to him, then wrote in my personal journal.

Things have been fermenting lately. In the classroom, the
students are very content since the change to the new organization.... I am still unsettled about reader response — I know
they need to read independently more often — but I'm not
ready to move to a complete program of student choice of
books. I've been reading through professional books. Disap-
pointing — discussions are either very general or too directed,
i.e., use regimented responses to books. (7 February)

With this entry — as I can see in retrospect — I was edging still
closer to the changes that, at some level, I already knew were
inevitable; it was also leading to what was to become my statement of inquiry. Finally, two important events gave me the
information and the courage I needed to make the definitive move
to a complete student-based reading program. I heard a speaker
at a reading conference and, at the same conference, I bought a
useful book.

The speaker was Jane Hansen, who talked enthusiastically
about her research in a New Hampshire school. She had just
completed a three-year inquiry into a whole school's conversion to
an independent reading program. Her enthusiasm was conta-
gious and so, when I got home, I immediately settled down to read
the book, *Literature-Based Reading Programs at Work*. Origi-
nally published in Australia, this collection of articles was written by teachers and librarians about their experiences of moving
into more independent reading programs. Each of the articles
provides a well-documented account of personal experience, supported by extensive references to the work of recognized educators. Together, they offer a variety of alternative approaches and
describe stages along the route towards an individualized reading program. At this point, I was ready to articulate my statement
of inquiry. It took the following form:

If I refocus the structure of my reading program from
directed   group work to one that is based on the reading of

books of students' choice, will there be an observable difference in reader response?

Conversations About Books

Although I was eager to get started, it took a few days to work out the essential practical details, such as time-tabling and arranging for the bulk-borrowing of library books. I wanted to help the children make appropriate book choices by preselecting the reading materials that would be available. It was obviously essential to provide books that appealed to a range of tastes, but I also knew that it was my responsibility to gently extend my students' reading habits. Having obtained the books, I planned for what I hoped would be a natural, relaxed and enjoyable reading time: I arranged the books in an inviting manner; prepared a simple record-keeping system, with a page for each student; arranged for weekly individual conferences; and told the children what I had in mind for reading time during the next few weeks.

Then, in mid-February, we began our Independent Reading. We gathered in the carpeted meeting place and I read the first sentence from my detective novel. Immediately, several students volunteered to read from their books. Amy was one of them. As she read the first line, "Marley was dead to begin with," there were startled gasps as students responded to Dickens' powerful opening. Spontaneously, a lively discussion of writers' techniques began. Following this, it was only natural that we should focus on story leads, in the next little while, in our writing as well as our reading. And how easily the reading-writing connections flowed; how the students' interest in reading and writing grew.

I still remember the magic of our first silent reading times. Everyone got comfortable around the room and we all enjoyed the peaceful companionship of reading together. The silence was broken only by Butterscotch, our guinea pig, whose squeal of alarm, I am convinced, was provoked by the unnatural silence! As Amy wrote in her journal on 22 February, "I think we should read silently at the same time every day so Butterscotch would get use to it."

So the new rhythm swung more or less naturally into place and, relieved from the pressure to plan for reading 'groups,' I now had the opportunity to extend what the students began to call our 'conversations about books.' Each day, we began our reading time with a conversation about some aspect of our books. Then followed twenty to thirty minutes of silent reading, during the latter part of which I met with individual students to talk in more detail about their books. The records I made during these meetings also enabled me to keep track of each student's progress. The following is the record of my meetings with Jerome.

Mar 1	*Eating Ice Cream with a Werewolf* 3pp. Doesn't know what it's about - too difficult.
Mar 7	*Frog and Toad All Year* (reading for quite a while) Enjoyment — able to recount small bit. Or r. f. pt. — rereading for meaning — hesitates but shows some measure of understanding.
Mar 8	Finished F & Toad — encouraged him to read.
Mar 14	*Tale of Squirrel Nutkin* begin — too diffic. decided to change.
Mar 28	*Mouse House.* R. Godden — p.6. unable to tell anything about story.
Apr 3	Abandoned M. House - "a little hard." Offered him West of the Moon: A Hungry Thing. Very tired. p.28
Apr 10	Finished A Hungry Thing. Could retell with confidence (voice deeper and louder than usual) Choosing.

By contrast, here is the record of my meetings with Son.

Feb 25	*All About Great Medical Discoveries* — habit. reads non-fict. Avoids fiction. Underst. spotty but does understand bits Ch. Mad Dogs & Sick Sheep — diffic. stating theme — eventually did — fluent or. reading
Mar 2	*Lion, Witch & Wardrobe.* C.S.Lewis - 2 pgs — talk about air raids Interested in magic wardrobe. Used inform. on bk jacket. judge
Mar 10	*Oliver & Co.* Walt Disney P.20 — enjoying — Fagan — dog - oral r. fluent.
Mar 29	*Oliver & Co.* continues to R (slowly) but with consid. enjoyment & underst.

As these records show, each child's reading biography is unique. For some there is what looks like steady progress. For others, the route is more uneven, with quite long level periods, interrupted by moments of insight which mark an abrupt shift to a new level. To enable me to investigate more fully what was happening for individual children, I recorded some of the reading conferences and transcribed parts of them. It is episodes such as the following which, to my mind, provide the most convincing evidence of the value of this type of reading experience.

Teacher:	You're reading 'Walter the Lazy Mouse.'
Marina:	I've finished it.
Teacher:	You've finished it! Oh, gosh, I read your journal last night and I had seen that you were reading it. Can you talk about the ending and what you think of it?
Marina:	(She begins to read from conclusion) "Walter's Mother said, 'Now don't forget us.' Walter waved and waved as his family left for home and he was a very proud and important young mouse, indeed. Good bye."
Teacher:	And all his family went home and he's staying?
Marina:	Uh-huh.
Teacher:	Yes.
Marina:	And it doesn't feel like it's finished yet. He- like it- they-
Teacher:	(getting the drift of her meaning) Marina ... that's terrific!
Marina:	So I think I'll go write it (as she says this she is already off her chair and on her way to carry out her intention).

Marina is proud to have finished reading *Walter the Lazy Mouse*, but not entirely satisfied with E.B. White's ending. Her solution to this dilemma occurs to her as we talk and she doesn't stick around any longer than necessary. In her eagerness to get on with her version of the ending, she is half way across the room as she finishes her sentence.

And so the conversation expands. We have weekly small group meetings to share our reading with each other, at which the children tell about their books, make comparisons, and recommend favourites. They read exciting parts and generally have a wonderful time swapping 'booktalk' (Chambers, 1985). But the conversation is not limited to these meetings, as the dialogue journals make clear. In the children's entries, I read about ideas and suggestions that the children are exchanging among themselves. As I had hoped, they are no longer dependent on me to nudge them into exploring new genres or trying the works of new authors. Here is Nicky's report of the advice she received from her friends, Sophie and Lucy.

The Pinballs

Dear Mrs Maher, I finished reading the Blue Nosed Witch

(finally). I am going to start a book called The Pinballs. I

havent started it yet, but Sophie told me about it and so

did Lucy and Sophie said it's good and Lucy said the

father hits the older sister.

Love Nicky

As the conversations continued in the dialogue journals, understanding deepened and the quality of the response grew richer and more satisfying. I know, for example, that Son has made *The Velveteen Rabbit* his own in a deeply personal way when he writes:

> "It made me feel like I was a toy rabbit and I was loved by someone and they really cared about me and I turned into REAL." (Feb. 2)

And Cyndy's lyrical response to the nudging that she tell me how she felt about *Walter the Lazy Mouse* convinces me that she has learned how to enter the imaginary worlds that authors create:

> "I felt that I was Walter and meeting frogs, and being lazy and being fast again. Oh my, what adventures I had." (March 28)

The threads of the reading-writing connection weave throughout the day. In conversations, the children and I are flowing from one to the other in a most illuminating and natural way. One morning, we were speculating on why the authors of our books decided to write them — what did they want us to know when we finished reading what they had written? As it happened, a newspaper journalist was coming to visit our classroom that day, so we had some fun guessing what the intention of his writing might be. Then we checked out our ideas with him. He told us that he was gathering information for a book about different kinds of schools to show what a difference to children's lives a really good program can make. His point was proved, I felt, when Sophie explained what she felt was the author's intent in the book she was reading, *It's Really Awful in the Sixth Grade:*

> "Some kids were foster children and that was really sad and frightening. But they still had lots of fun when they went to this camp. I think that the author wants you to know about an experience that you might never have. And that, even when it seems really bad sometimes, it can be all right."

Taking Stock: The Children's Views

As these brief glimpses show, the students' response to the new program has been overwhelming. They now ask for extra Silent Reading Time and are disappointed if circumstances force us to miss a scheduled period. Children know what is important about their school experience and, when they share in the responsibility for program planning, their decisions are nearly always well founded. About the value of having more time for self-chosen reading they have no doubts at all. But, perhaps more significantly, they have discovered the added pleasure that comes from sharing their responses with others, both in face-to-face conversation and through the medium of the dialogue journals. This comes over with powerful spontaneity in the small group discussion that I tape recorded on 12 April.

As we get our chairs organized and set up, the conversation begins without me.

Sophie:	I've got number one and two.
Nicky:	You've got the whole collection?
Sophie:	No.
Teacher:	You've got number one and two of what?
Sophie:	Of Lee Valley High.
Teacher:	(turning to the whole class)

	Remember before the March Break I talked to you about how we were going to change our reading program because I was very interested in seeing if we did more reading of books of your own choice to see what it would be like.
Jason:	Reading has been good.
Teacher:	You think it's been good, uh-huh. Has reading changed for you?
Nicky:	I like Independent Reading.
Sophie:	I read more books... more interesting books.
Teacher:	More interesting books. Well...
Nicky:	You get to talk more about my books.
Sophie:	I've really enjoyed that too.
Carolina:	I like people to talk about my books.
Lucy:	'Cause you get to hear what everybody else's... what everybody else's... story is about and everybody gets to hear what your story is....
Nicky:	And then you could try it.
Lucy:	Yeah, yeah then you could try it. And then we have lots more books cause some kids bring some in to share.
Nicky:	And then we had to do lots of things. We had to write about it. And you should make this like a rule. Like it's better.
Cory:	Yeah, you get to learn about more books and read more books and get to find out about more books.
Teacher:	Is that right?
Cory:	Like er- we would read a story and then we'd write about it. Now we read our book and then we write in our journals... to you... and like... like we're- we're far away... and we read a book and then we write a story about it... (inaudible) to you in our journals.
Teacher:	I like reading and writing those letters too. Danny, how's it been for you in the last month or so?
Danny:	Umm...I read books, and write about it er- and if you don't remember about it you can

	look in... in...
Teacher:	Oh into your journal?
Danny:	That means if you want to read it again you could look in your journal...
Teacher:	I suppose so, I suppose so. Interesting, isn't it? Well, that's kind of why I'm taping this conversation so that when I get home and I want to think about why these conversations about books are important to us.
Thao:	I just like reading books...
Lucy:	'Cause we have much more time... er 'cause you can get through a book more faster and and you can get through a book more faster and we have lots of wonderful books in the library from Marion and and...
Cory:	And from kids who bring them in and...
Nicky:	And some people haven't even heard of these books and... they're pretty good!
	(Several students agree. Yeah, yeah.)
Sophie:	It gives you a chance to bring in some of your books for other people to read.
Nicky:	And you need lots of reading for whatever you are going to be because like if you want to be a lawyer... you need to know how to read the cases and stuff and if you want to be a doctor or a math teacher or something you need to know how to read and maybe even if you're ... want to be a aerobics teacher you still need to know how to read..
Cory:	Exercises your brain in a way, Mrs. Maher.
Danny:	Maybe when you grow up... your grandson give you the journal and then they could look at it — the title and then they could read it.
Teacher:	Oh, well...
Cory:	Save- saving your journal...
Teacher:	That — that sounds like the Memory Box, which is the book that you are reading, isn't it, Marina?
Cory:	My Mother still has hers — a couple of her pieces of work.

Danny:	I'm saving — I'm going to save mine.
Teacher:	Oh isn't that lovely!
Lucy:	My sister... she has tons of — she got lots of binders ... with all her work.
Teacher:	Does she?
Sophie:	A time capsule.
Chi:	If you have all the work you do... everything...
Sophie:	I got a reading diary. Every time I read a book I put it in my... er... reading diary.
Teacher:	Do you?
Sophie:	About how I think about it... like a journal...
	(several students chime in on the word 'journal')
Teacher:	So you are keeping your own private journal at home, Sophie? Well that's amazing!
Nicky:	That's good.
Thao:	Interesting.
Teacher:	Well it is.
Nicky:	Then after... after... when you have kids and stuff, right, when you grow up you... you can—Sophie can look into her ... er...reading diary, and she can find out all the books that she read and she can read them to her kids and stuff.
Chi:	You're talking too far away. (laughs)
Teacher:	What do you mean?
Cory:	Chi means he's changing the subject.
Chi	Yeah — No, she's talking about all the way when she gets big and has a child.
Teacher:	Yes, she's looking way into the future, isn't she?

What more needs to be said! If we want to learn about what the children think, we need only ask and then listen with active attention. In their own way, they will tell us what we need to learn.

Taking Stock: What I have Learned

I was launched into this inquiry by my increasing dissatisfaction with the quality and quantity of reader response in my reading program. This led me to re-examine my theory and practice. Recognizing the restrictive nature of my teacher-directed program, I had no choice but to look for a better way. Slowly, I moved to open up my program to allow for the expression of my students' responses to the texts that they were engaged in reading. And out of this has grown our many-faceted conversations about books.

For me, this inquiry has involved a fascinating process of exploring new ways of working with all aspects of language development. For what started as simply a concern with the reading component of my program has naturally spread into all areas of linguistic meaning-making. However, as is often the case with action research, it took me some time to discover the full import of where my inquiry was leading. When I first stated my topic question, its meaning was still somewhat hazy and obscure.

> "If I refocus the structure of my reading program from directed group work to one that is based on the reading of books of student choice, will there be an observable difference in reader response?"

Four months later, I answer "Most definitely!"

But there has been so much more to my learning than that. In the end, it was not just reader response that occupied my attention. More central to my interests became finding a solution to the problem of how to facilitate the students' expression and exchange of their responses. It is clear to me now that what was needed to enliven the reader response in my classroom was a wide variety of well-chosen books, lots of time to read them, and opportunities for continuing conversations, in both oral and written form, about our reading and writing.

As I look back over my learning during the last few months, I understand more fully the significance of what Douglas Barnes (1976) had to say about the difference between knowledge that is given to us by others, because they think it is important, and the knowledge that we construct for ourselves, as we take what we know and put it into action, revising and extending it in the light of our own experience and of the assistance that we receive from others when we are ready to use it.

From the outset of this inquiry, I recognized what the problems were with my reading program. I wanted to give my students the time and opportunity to read more widely and to talk more freely about their books. But, without the practical experience of working in this way, I felt helpless; I did not know how to bring about these changes. As we slowly began to work in new ways, my students' responses encouraged me to make further changes in the structure of my program. In fact, those young students helped me to clarify my understanding of the reading process. Now I see that our conversations about books are an essential component of our experience of literature.

Not only did my young students need the time and opportunity to read and to discuss that reading, but I, too, needed the time and opportunity to experience, first-hand, their responses to these changes. Their genuine interest in, and enthusiasm for, our conversations about books convinced me that my program was becoming more successful. Action research focused my attention and thinking on the issue of reading, enabled me to take some action and, by its very nature, ensured that I examine and re-examine the outcomes. This process, I suspect, will be an ongoing experience in my life in the classroom.

5
Reading Response Journals: One Teacher's Research

Larry Swartz

Introduction

It was clear to me back in September when I began teaching my grade five class, that I was going to investigate the use of reading response journals in my language arts program. Through reading, and with one year's experience of using journals in a junior classroom, I started with some assumptions about the use of journals: a journal helps students to discover and inspect their own thinking and reading processes; a journal assists the teacher to discover and inspect what students' individual strengths and weaknesses are so that he can help them to learn about themselves as readers. Journals, I assumed were a significant medium for helping children to reflect on their life stories.

However, I was also feeling some discomfort about the way I had used journals in the past. I felt uneasy with the stance I had taken to help students understand that their thoughts and feelings were important. I believed that I could do a better job of conducting written conversations (dialogues) with the students. If I improved my role as a trusted audience, a skilful questioner and a model reader, then perhaps the students would be more apt to take risks, venture ideas and make personal meaning.

My intention was to discover what the students were saying in their journals, to explore what influenced their responses, to learn about ten-year-olds as readers and to help them learn about themselves. With a keen interest, with a need to change the way

I used journals, with a good grasp of current response theory, with careful planning and with many questions, I felt prepared and eager to discover the relationship between the teacher, the text and the learner.

That was September. By the final term of school, response journals had been abandoned as a medium for revealing thought in my classroom. Looking back on the year, I am now able to reflect upon why I made this decision, and on how I came to revise my language program. Change was the outcome of raising questions, keeping a journal, reading articles, re-acquainting myself with current reading and writing theory, discussing my concerns with colleagues and mentors, and — most importantly — of meeting a few surprises over the course of the year. In other words, I am better able to assess my teaching as a result of becoming a reflective practitioner, a teacher-researcher.

This chapter is the story of my journey as a teacher-researcher in a grade five classroom. In it I will discuss some assumptions I held about written and oral response, and describe the "critical incidents" (Newman, 1987) that caused my assumptions to be challenged.

Teacher as Researcher

"Teacher-researchers are interested in improving the educational practices within their own settings. They undertake research in order to get a better understanding of events in their particular educational environment."

Strickland, 1988, p. 756

One day as I was driving home from school, I began to think about the conference that Georgette, a student in my class, and I had had that morning about a poem that she had written. When I reconsidered the conversation, I felt a bit dissatisfied with the way I had interfered with Georgette's writing process. Next time I would have Georgette hold the pencil and let her suggest the way she might revise the form of her poem, instead of doing it for her. As I continued to mentally revisit the day, I thought about the drama lesson I had conducted with the students after we finished the novel *Hatchet* by Gary Paulsen: Should I have put them in pairs instead of working in a forum theatre mode? Was the technique of creating the main character's dreams the best way of getting the students to consider the change that the main character went through and the feelings he had about his survival experience? I also remembered how I had assisted Ricky with his research project on "airplanes." I asked myself whether I had given him 'proper' help, whether the activity was meaningful for him, and even whether I should have assigned the project in the first place. As I continued my drive, I thought about a conversation I had had with a parent about a student's behavior; I thought about my failure to get to the heart of the legend that I had read aloud that day; and I also thought about Cindy asking me "Why do you like poetry so much?"

When I drive home from school, I do a lot of thinking about what I have done during the day, how I did it and how I could have done it better. These conversations that I have with myself are not unlike those that any thoughtful teacher has. Being thoughtful, according to Nancie Atwell (1989), is manifested in the careful way that teachers continually examine and analyze their teaching. However, the most thoughtful practitioner, Atwell argues, is the teacher who acts as a researcher.

What separates those teachers who 'look back on the day' from those who are researchers, lies in the notion of change. A researcher considers seriously what he might do differently. Thinking about a writing conference, a drama lesson or a poem I taught is one thing; taking action to improve my practice as a result of this thinking is what raises my role from that of teacher to that of teacher-researcher. Strickland (1988) writes: "Simply stated, teacher-researchers use research to do a better job" (1988, p. 756).

Most teachers are reflective, but in Action Research the reflection is deliberate. Teachers may make changes because an outsider tells them to change or because the children demand a change; or they may change just for the heck of it. Teacher-researchers identify an area of concern — something that they believe is worth knowing about — and take action because it is likely to make an improvement.

> Reflecting deeply on our own experiences and those of our students, we discover that explicating and exploring dilemmas is of itself a way of knowing, a powerful, though often neglected, means of moving beyond, creating, transcending.
>
> Jacobs; Roderick, 1988, p. 650

As a teacher-researcher, I went beyond 'having conversations with myself' about my work in the classroom. Not only did I collaborate with others to make meaning for myself, but I began to question, observe, and reflect upon my teaching. I began a systematic analysis of evidence to promote understanding in order to act with a difference.

In her article "The Teacher as Researcher: Toward the Extended Professional," Dorothy Strickland (1988, p. 760) refers to course materials presented by Judith Green (1987) at Ohio State University. Green suggests a plan consisting of seven phases to help teachers conduct research in their classrooms.

1. Identify an issue, interest or concern;

2. Seek knowledge;

3. Plan an action;

4. Implement an action;

5. Observe the action;

6. Reflect on the observations;

7. Revise the plan.

What isn't mentioned in Green's plan is the role of 'surprise' in uncovering our assumptions. Judith Newman (1987) writes:

> It seems to me the switch into 'researcher' occurs at those moments when the unexpected occurs, when things haven't gone as we thought they should, or when our predictions are disconfirmed and we're forced to see a familiar situation with new eyes. It's generally when I'm unsettled about something that's happened, and reflect on it I become aware of another critical incident. The trick is to become adept at noticing those moments and doing something about them.
> Newman, 1987, p. 736

I will be using Green's plan to provide an overview of the use of Reading Response Journals in my program this year. I have, however, revised Green's plan into an eight-phase framework by recognizing 'Critical Incidents' as Phase 7, and 'Revising the Plan' as Phase 8.

Reading Response Journals: Eight Phases of Research

Phase 1: Identifying an Issue, Interest or Concern

Many contemporary literary critics are shifting attention from the text as an autonomous object, that in itself contains meaning, to what happens in the minds of readers as they actively engage in reading the text. Reading becomes personally significant, they suggest, when the students are encouraged to experience the literary work by allowing it to stimulate image, feelings, associations and thoughts.

At the heart of response theory is the notion that reading is guided by the text and influenced by the personal experience and cultural history of the reader, his or her present representation of the world and the reader conventions that he or she has internalized. Because students come from different backgrounds, have different attitudes, values and circumstances, the variations between them in their responses to a text are inevitable and legitimate.

Teaching is thus a matter of improving the individual reader's capacity to evoke meaning from the text by leading him or her to reflect self-critically on this process. According to Louise Rosenblatt (1976, pp. 26-27), "The teacher's task is to foster fruitful interactions — or more precisely transactions — between individual readers and individual literary works." In order to foster the kind of fruitful interactions that Rosenblatt encourages, journals can be used as a method for developing a literature curriculum based on reader-response theory, as they offer the students an "active and concrete means of participating in the text." (Tashlik, 1987, p. 177)

A reading response journal is a convenient and flexible method for students to reflect on their personal responses to independent reading and stories that are read aloud. Usually kept as a separate notebook or folder, the journal is a medium in which students can communicate their thoughts about reading, encouraging them to engage with the literature they encounter and putting them at the centre of their own learning. Researchers have shown that reading response journals serve learners by having them reflect upon, interact with, and find personal meaning in, works of literature. They encourage comprehension, imagination, narration, speculation, and questioning; they also provide information about thinking and learning for both student as reader and teacher as audience and guide (Atwell, 1987; Fulwiler, 1987; Probst, 1988; Staton, 1988; Thomson, 1987; Wolman-Bonilla, 1989).

Much recent response research describes the young adolescent or teenage student. My intention was to extend this research to the junior learner. I was interested in determining whether grade five students, like the junior high or secondary school students described by Nancie Atwell, Les Parsons, and Jack Thomson, could discover their own routes into reading by establishing the same communication that these researchers discuss in their books. Secondly, I was interested in discovering how a reading teacher could effect change in the response of his students through the medium of a dialogue journal.

The introduction of reading journals to my grade five students raised several issues that warranted systematic research. How might these journals serve as a medium for revelation? What would the students think and write about the books they were reading if they were being encouraged to express themselves freely? If students wrote their responses in a reading journal, would they have a better understanding of the process of reading? And, from reading their entries, what could the researcher, as a teacher who believed that the reader counts for at least as much as the book or poem itself (Rosenblatt, 1976), learn about his students as makers of meaning?

Phase 2: Seeking Knowledge

Over the past few years, the work of three people — Nancie Atwell, Aidan Chambers and Jack Thomson — has influenced my understanding of reading response.

Atwell's article "Building a Dining Room Table: Dialogue Journals About Reading," in her book *In the Middle* (1987, pp. 190-197) is often the prime source that is cited for the use of dialogue journals. Atwell describes how her eighth graders responded to their reading in dialogue journals and this program stimulated my interest in implementing the strategy in my literature curriculum. By having the students write letters to her and by responding to these letters, Atwell established a commu- nication — a dialogue — about books. Aidan Chambers (1985), talks about reading as a three-act drama. "Act One" is about selection. "Act Two" is about reading what we have chosen to read, and "Act Three" is about reconstruction, which means "re- making, re-forming and re-structuring." (p. 125) With his "Tell Me" framework, Chambers (1985, pp. 168-173) identifies the various experiences that a reader has with text. In his book *Understanding Teenagers' Reading: Reading Processes and the Teaching of Literature*, Jack Thomson (1987, pp. 360-361) pres- ents a developmental model for responding to literature:

1.   Unreflective interest in action

2.   Empathising

3.   Analogising

4.   Reflection on the significance of events and behavior

5.   Reviewing the whole work as the author's creation

6.   Understanding of self and one's own reading processes

This framework proved useful to begin categorizing the responses that the students revealed in their journals.

Inspired by the insights of these three individuals, in particular, I intended to create a reading program that would give the children time to read and to make meaning through writing and talking about books.

Phase 3: Planning the Action

Professional reading and one year's experience with reading response journals in the classroom helped to refine my research goals. I generated over 100 questions that concerned me about the function of journals. I drew up a list and, by grouping them together, I arrived at the following three sets:

1. Content:
   What would the students choose to write about? Would they write about their own experiences? Would they comment on the behavior of the characters? Would they comment on what they liked or disliked about a book? Would they write about what was happening in their minds as they read?

2. Process:
   How often would the students use the journals? Would they write in their journals unprompted? Would they write in point form? How long would their entries be? Would they write in their journals both at school and at home?

3. Dialogue:
   Would they respond to the letters I wrote to them? Would they see me as a trusted audience? Would they see the journals as "penalty-free?" Would they ask me questions or seek clarification or information about a book? Would they see the intervention as useful?

By observing and reflecting on the action of using journals, I hoped to discover answers to some of these questions and then, through analysis, to devise a framework to draw some conclusions about students' interactions with text.

Phase 4: Implementing the Action

The setting was a self-contained classroom in an Ontario school, containing a mixed group of twenty-eight grade five students with a wide range of abilities. The core of my daily reading program was twofold: 1) a read-aloud time when the students gathered on the rug to listen to the reading of a picture book, a short story, or an excerpt from a novel. Each day, without fail, we would also read at least one poem; 2) an independent reading time, when the students were allowed to choose to read a book from home, from the public or school library and, in particular, from a large classroom collection of 400 novels and picture books.

On the first morning of school in September, I gave each of my students a yellow notebook and told them to label it their Response Journal. I explained to them that this journal would be used to record any of their thoughts and reactions to the books they would be meeting over the year. (Response journals can be extended to include reactions to classroom discussions, current events, television programs, films, video and theatre presentations but, for my purposes, I was particularly concerned about response to reading.)

I invited the students to record in their journals whatever they wanted to about the books they would be reading. Keeping in mind what Aidan Chambers (1985, pp. 168-173) calls the "Tell me" Framework, I encouraged the students to use their journals to "tell me" what they liked, what they didn't like, what they wondered about, what they were puzzled by, and what they were reminded of, as they encountered literature selections from day to day. In addition, I explained to the students that they might want to record any words, sentences or passages that appealed to them, they might raise questions and hunches about what they read and they might want to discuss any connections between the texts and their own lives. Using Nancie Atwell's model for Dialogue Journals, I suggested that the students set up their reading journals as a series of letters written to me so that they would feel that they had an authentic audience for their written thoughts about books.

From the beginning of the term, everyone was assigned a time to write in his or her journal. This was usually done immediately after a silent reading period of approximately twenty minutes and the routine was scheduled two, or sometimes three, times in a five-day cycle. I had hoped that, as the weeks went by, the students would take the initiative to record in their journals on their own but, for the most part, they seemed to require a set time for the activity and, as I came to discover, they usually required a set of prompts or focus questions to assist them in their writing. At times, I would conference with students as they wrote their journals. Each student's journal was collected at regular intervals so that I could offer comments and questions and write a letter back as a response to the student's entry.

Phase 5: Observing the Action

As I continued to read the students' journals regularly from September to December, I began to collect information and try to make sense of it. The following are some observations that I noted about the use of reading response journals in the first term of my grade five program.

At the beginning of the term, despite the cues that I suggested, the students seldom ventured far from summarizing the plot:

> I have read another chapter of *Borrowed Children* and Mandy's mother almost dies while having the baby. So now Mandy has to quit school and take care of her mother and baby brother. Mandy has to clean, cook and make dinner. In the book Mandy said it's hard work but she can handle it.
> (Miranda)

> In this book it's about a boy how cames from Washington D.C. to a new school and he meets a boy called Bradley and everybody does not like Bradley at all.
> (Cindy)

When asked to talk about their reactions to a book, the students might say "this is a really good book" or "I like it because it's funny." I attempted to stretch their thinking by asking them, in a reading conference, what it was about the book that appealed to them, or how they thought the author made the book funny, suspenseful, sad, or whatever, but many, like Ryan, wrote "I don't know why I liked it. I just did."

During September and October, for the most part, the students continued to re-tell the bits of the story that they had just finished reading. As a result of my invitation to the students to be more specific and explain what they liked or disliked about the text, a few began to offer their opinions and share their feelings:

> I chose *The Boy Who Wanted a Family* because it make you think why can't god give everybody a place to live. That why I choose this because: I want to see how it felt to want a family. I like books that tells about some things that's really going on in the world today. If I was that kid I would think I'm a unwanted foster kid feeling unloved.
> (Shannon)

> I am enjoying the part when they were journeying to Bridgeport. This taught me how somebody would feel if their mother just walked away without a goodbye. Because I would be so so so so so so so sad.
> (Christi)

I am enjoying Park's Quest. I think Park's mom should tell Park about his father. I think he should try and find some relatives other than his mom. He should look for his fathers father or I mean his grandpa. His mom should be more open with him because Park should know what his dad was like before he became a name on the wall.
(Janine)

Although encouraged to discuss how they saw themselves as readers, very few students were able to comment on their reading behaviors, as Shawn and Liza have done:

I am not that big of a reader but on the other hand I like books. When I was in Grades 1 - 3 I use to hate Books. Then I descoved the joy of books. I think of some people who can't read so I want to read when I grow up.
(Shawn)

I love reading and I always will. When I was in grade 1 and 2 I didn't know how to read but in grade 3 4 5 I new how to read. Thank you, Mr. Swartz. Last year I read 30 or 40 books. This year I have read 4 books. I want to read 140 books. Mr. Swartz you were the one who helped me read and so did Johanna and Laurie. Think if it wasn't for you and my mom and dad I would not be in grade 5.
(Liza)

The most insightful entries seemed to be those that were made in response to a poem, picture book, or novel that was read aloud to the whole class. These entries were usually written as a follow-up to a discussion, and the students tended to be more critical than they otherwise were when responding orally, as these responses to *The Wall*, by Eve Bunting (1990), reveal:

If my name was on The Wall I would like the people who visit the wall to think about what I did to put my name on the wall.
(Sunny)

That book was very touching. I am all American and I think the war was to save the country. The book made me want to go back to the U.S. I think my great Uncle fought in that war.
(Matthew)

I didn't really like the book The Wall because I hate hearing about people that have died. I have two questions: How do they know the person's name if he/she is dead? Are girls aloud in the war?
(Miranda)

I think that the Wall is a very emotionally place. How did they get all these peoples names into one place. That's cool. The people who made up the idea of the wall is great. If their was one more Vietnam person from the war I would give them the biggest gold and place it on their heart and say you earned it because they are the one who fight for are country.

(Georgette)

When I responded with comments, opinions and questions, the students (unlike those described in Nancie Atwell's research) were generally reluctant to "dialogue" back. Many times my responses would be much longer than theirs. The students didn't seem to answer my questions. If my comments stimulated a thought, students didn't usually articulate a response to my response. Nevertheless, at times, I observed that they were aware of me as audience.

Mr. Swartz do you think the world was more safe when you where little or when we where little?

(Heidi)

Last time you asked me if I want to go to the future. Yes, I would really want to go for two weeks. P.S. Thank you for introducing me to the book *The White Mountain* and finding the sequel *The City of Gold and Lead* for me.

(Sunny)

Yes, I do like sports Mr. Swartz. I think Matt Christopher books are popular. I don't think girls would read them. I like to read books by different authors.

(Harveen)

Mr. Swartz, sometimes I have a picture in my mind from the story you are reading. I have read *Phantom of Fear, Portal of Evil, Stealer of Souls, Vault of the Vampire, Sword of the Samurai*. I would like you to recommend some more books.

(Robbie)

Mr. Swartz, what is your favourite books these days?

(Lisa)

Often, I encouraged the students to consider what they were reminded of as they read the books. These entries were the ones I particularly looked forward to reading in order to discover if they were making connections from the text to both fictional and real experiences:

Here is something I thought about when I read Dominic today. It remind me of Abel's Island because Dominic had to survive to meet his fortune.

(Alan)

Where The Red Fern Grows made me think about...

1) how a dog is man's best friend
2) how love can be precious
3) how there is always hope for love between friends
4) how hope can provide love
5) how hope can turn into true love

(Sunil)

I like *Tucker Countryside* because it's about friends and it remind me of Johanna and Laurie from last year because they were there when I need someone just like Tucker and Harry and Chester.

(Liza)

When I read Abel's Island it reminded me of a dream I had when I was traped on a iland and there was not boat but some how I think I found a way but but then I woke up. or it reminded me to Tom Swoer when him and his friend took a raft and went to a island.

(Greg)

Sometimes, I would encounter journal entries that weren't about the books. Students might share a reaction or a feeling about something that was going on in the class:

Do you know what's going on? Christi and Charleen are fighting non-stop. First they like each other and then they don't — it's driving me crazy. Next time we change seats can I sit next to Liza.

(Heidi)

Why do you always pick on me Mr. Swartz. When I'm on the carpet and someone else is doing something to me you always pick out my name. And when were doing math you don't come to my end and tell me if that's right or wrong and you say it to other people? And I hate that!

(Georgette)

Occasionally, I came upon some surprises in the journal entries that I read.

Mr. Swartz, I just got a great idea from a book I read. In this books the girls form a book club. Do you think we could form a book club in our class?[1]

(Janine)

I am not in the reading spirit today. Do I have to read?
(Ricky)

But it was Robbie's honest and surprising entry that most challenged me to clarify my rationale for using journals:

I do not understand why we do journals. It does not help me. I am doing better this year with the reading program. I like having adventure. I like reading short parts at a time. I have completed six novels. I enjoy listening to you read.
(Robbie)

I was operating on the assumption that the students would come to understand how journals could function to help them become reflective readers. Perhaps it was an inappropriate assumption, because it seemed that the students weren't doing the journals for themselves, but for me, the teacher. Robbie's entry — a surprise — challenged me to consider the part that the children were playing in the research. Perhaps Robbie was speaking for a number of others in the class when he stated that he didn't understand why we had journals. His comment prompted me to consider not only how to invite the children to share in the learning with me but to help them discover learning for themselves.

Examining the 28 journals from my classroom helped me to better understand the way the journals functioned. It seemed that students seldom wrote spontaneously in their journals without having structured class time to do so. I noticed that most students needed a prompt, or suggested questions, or a mini-conference, before they would write an entry. I also observed that, as the students continued to write in their journals during the term, entries seemed to increase in length, and that in the later part of the term they were beginning to write more and more about episodes from their own lives that the story reminded them of.

These observations suggest that students need a substantial amount of experience of talking and writing about literature in order to gain confidence in themselves and to learn that their ideas mattered and were important. I felt strongly that each entry revealed something about the student as writer and reader, but I was frustrated by the, what I'll call 'ordinary,' responses that the students were giving unless I gave them direction for their entries.

My observations helped me become aware of the discrepancy between what I thought was occurring and my students' perceptions of what was happening. Reflecting on these observations and critical incidents opened up possibilities that I hadn't thought of before.

During a professional development session in late November, I shared these observations with other staff members who were using journals. For myself and my colleagues two main questions remained: 1) How do we get the students to see the value of reading response journals? and 2) In which ways can a teacher use the reading response journal effectively for developing response strategies?

Phase 6: Reflecting on the Observations

I was keeping my own journal to reflect upon my teaching practices during the year. The following excerpts are reflections that reveal some of the concerns I had about reading response journals.

Reflection No. 1: What is the role of talk?

September 20, 1990

During this week's seminar discussion at OISE, Tamara questioned me about the difference between oral responses and written responses. Since the role of 'Talk for Learning' was the issue tonight, I began to wonder about response through 'Booktalk' (Chambers, 1985). Should I be conducting a comparative study exploring response dialogue a) on paper vs. b) out loud.

Reflection No. 2.: Who are the journals for and who do the students think they're for?

September 25, 1990

Lois and I were sitting in the staff room talking about our day. Lois told me that one of her students felt that writing in his response journal interfered with his reading. He wanted to just enjoy his books and not take the time to write about them. Lois asked me for my opinion and I replied by asking her if she thought this student (and others) knew what the function of the response journal was. Did he understand why she was asking him to respond in his journal? What did he think he might learn by writing in his journal? What did she think he might learn by writing in his journal?

Reflection No. 3: What is my role in responding?

September 28, 1990

I received a pile of books to 'mark.' I don't know what I thought I was going to do with them but I stayed at school tonight and spent time with these journals and this time matters. I have begun an interaction with the children. A flaw of journals in the previous year was that I didn't dialogue enough. I looked at the pile on my desk and wondered: How long will I keep this up? Will all my responses be lengthy? How will I know whether my questions and comments are significant?

Reflection No. 4: Why aren't we dialoguing?

October 15, 1990

'Dialoguing' has been very limited and I want to discover how we can have more of a conversation about books. I discovered that very few bothered to answer (my letters). They just continue to retell the story. I discussed my concerns with the kids and told them my expectations. Does it then become my agenda? What I've been considering, therefore, is: Do the kids understand what the journals are about? Do they know what a response journal is? Do they know what a response journal can be?

Reflection No. 5: Why do I want them to write in their journals?

October 26, 1990

The kids in the past two weeks have not used their journals much. The reason, of course, is that I didn't give them time in class to do them. It seems that they'll mainly do them only when time is set aside. Few take the initiative to write in them on their own. So I'm wondering ...How can I get them to take the initiative? Why do I want them to write? Which brings up an interesting point — when I read I don't want to take the time to write about it. I just want to read. I think I'd better have a good reason for wanting kids to write in their journals.

Reflection No. 6: What is the purpose of this research?

November 9, 1990

What learning do I want (expect) to happen? How am I going to get there?

Reflection No. 7: Why not talk instead of writing?

November 10, 1990

I am more interested in booktalk than journal talk. I assume that the teacher can stretch the child by talking about the book and raising questions. The journal doesn't seem to do this. For one thing, it's a matter of time. By the time they've read, written and I've answered, they are on to other parts of the book — other books. Talk is more immediate!

Reflection No. 8: Do the students think the journals are useful?

November 20, 1990

Today Ricky said to me "Mr. Swartz, I've just read the saddest part in the book. I've got to have my journal." The journals are important!!

Reflection No. 9: Why aren't we dialoguing?

November 27, 1990

Why aren't we dialoguing?
- what is dialoguing?
- why do I want them to dialogue?
- how do I help them dialogue?
- do they understand what the function of a dialogue journal is?

Reflection No. 10: They aren't dialogue journals...are they?

December 6, 1990

I was looking at the entries that the teachers/researchers gave in their articles as examples of 'good' book talk in journals. What I discovered —   and it was so obvious, I'm angry that I didn't recognize it earlier — is that in each of the examples in each of the articles (including Atwell's), there   is only one piece of feedback given to a student's entry. The examples   stop there. There are no further answers given by the students to the teacher's responses — THERE IS NO DIALOGUING!!! You tell me something/I'll respond/and then what?... This is not dialogue, certainly not the kind of dialogue we can have in talk situations.

Reflection No. 11: Am I a trusted audience? listener? questioner? model?

December 8, 1990

Today the staff had a teleconference with Donald Graves. Graves said that the most significant step in helping the students become reflective readers/writers is when we show them our own reflective processes. This 'modelling' (of response) has more impact, he claims, than our teaching (of response).

Reflection No. 12: What should I be looking for in the journals?

December 10, 1990

I met with Gordon Wells today. He suggested that I might consider what the most frequent categories are that appear in their journals; which are unique to certain students; what are the surprises. He also asked me: "What do you think about the fact that book talk is different from written 'talk?'"

Reflection No. 13: How can I teach them to be reflective?

January 7, 1991

New questions (after reading Calkins' *Living Between the Lines*). How do reading journals help students reflect upon their lives? How can I prompt them to reveal the things that the text reminds them of?

Reflection No. 14: What if nobody responds to their journals?

January 11, 1991

Some kids were actually disappointed that I didn't answer back in their journals so quickly. How often am I expected to respond? Is my response necessary? (YES!) I have to consider the best system to handle the marking. Funny, I still say I'm going to 'mark' their journals. Why do I say 'mark,' when no marks are given? Do they see it as marking?

Reflection No. 15: Should I keep using journals?

January 15, 1991

Beginning the new term is a convenient opportunity for developing and deepening (changing?) our work with journals. The kids have to be in on this research with me...understand why I might make changes, and what we might learn together.

As the above reflections indicate, many challenges confronted me as I continued to raise questions and contemplate alternative plans for my program. My own journal enabled me to consider and reconsider how I might best implement journals and why I was using them as a vehicle for response to literature. These entries (and others) helped me to assess what was taking place in my classroom. Moreover, they also revealed the doubts and questions I had and led me to a more careful inspection of critical incidents in our journal journey.

Phase 7: Recognizing Critical Incidents

> Critical incidents are those occurrences that let us see with new eyes some aspect of what we do. They make us aware of the beliefs and assumptions that underlie our instructional practices.
>
> Newman, 1990, p. 17

This year I have begun collecting and sharing stories which contributed to my understanding about reading and response. Sometimes the incidents have confirmed what I believed, but more often I have been challenged to reappraise my assumptions. What these critical incidents have revealed is a gap between what I believed about response and what my actions were conveying.

There have been several surprises that come to mind, some of them big, some of them small, ongoing occurrences, all of them providing opportunities for learning: a comment made in a staff room, a statement found in a journal, a question by a student, a parent, the principal, or something that I read. Experiences with specific poems and stories either validated my assumptions or allowed me to disagree with something, or become bothered by some practice and so reconsider my beliefs. Written responses to the poem 'When it is Snowing' by Siv Cedering made me think about planning for better talk experiences. A talk experience with Brian Patten's poem 'There Was Once A Whole World in the Scarecrow' made me think about planning for better collaborative discussion experiences.

But it was the story experience with the memoir *July* that made me think about planning for opportunities that would have the children, as Lucy Calkins (1991) has written, "bring the work of their lives to school with heart and soul." (p. 304) The following critical incident provoked the most thought and subsequently was the impetus for change. Writing about it forced me to engage in analysis and explain the situation to myself in order to come closer to an understanding of the role of response in my program.

James Stevenson's (1989) *July* is a prime example of memoir writing. It therefore seemed a perfect vehicle for stimulating personal narrative in the classroom. In his picture book, the author-illustrator recalls moments and memories of his youth, "when each month was like a glacier slowly melting." The author tells stories of summer months visiting Grandma and Grandpa, spending time visiting friends, and playing on the beach.

> Grandma loved to laugh. She was
> kind too. At night she locked all the
> doors, except one. "In case anybody
> needs to get in," she said.

> I never did get to the top
> of the Moffat's windmill.
> Either I got caught
> near the bottom,
> or I got halfway up,
> got scared,
> and came down.

The following stories are samples from a grade two class that I visit three periods per week. These reminiscences were written after the children listened to *July* and after they discussed some memories stimulated by the book.

> When I was seven my dad and me went to the skydome, to see the Blue Jays vs the Brewers. We had a big mac at the skydome. I was happy because Blue Jays won. We ate popcorn. But...the best thing I liked was my dad going with me.
> (Jeffrey)

> I remember once when we went to wonderland I think my mom went on this thing. It was a big toob with water in it I liked it but my mom didn't She was skared. When she went on it she closed her eyes and at the ending she was still screming. We were wondering what she was doing. Finaly she opened her eyes and it stoped and then we all laghed.
> (Samuel)

> In 1990 I got a new cam corder. It was a srpraise for me and my **GRANDMA**! We tapte things. My sister's birthday party and me oping Christmas presents! Now I can go see my grandma when ever I want too on video.
> (Erica)

> When I was five, I went camping. I remember put mush-
> mellows in a pan. When it is all melted, I put it in a cup and
> drank it. I drink mushmellows and there is a kind of taste
> that I hate. So I change my mind. I camp with a rich kid called
> Eva Ho. She is the coolest kid in the whole class in Hong Kong.
> (Karen)

> When I was six I went swimming. I remember when I drowned.
> (Jonilee)

In these written pieces the students are recalling incidents from
their lives. For Jeffrey, a visit to the ball game was an enjoyable
summer experience, but he goes further to tell about his relationship with his father. Just as Stevenson described his fear of
climbing the Moffat Tower, Samuel recalls a time when his
mother was frightened by a ride at Canada's Wonderland. Erica
talks about her grandmother, writing the word 'GRANDMA' in
large letters, because James Stevenson filled a page with the
single word 'JULY' in large, colourful letters. For Erica, her
'grandma' is just as important as Stevenson's 'July,' so important
that she loves preserving her times with grandma on videotape.
In *July*, Stevenson compares those who like toasting marshmal-
lows lightly to those who like them burnt black. Karen thinks
back to a time she put melted marshmallow in a cup and drank
it. But other narratives lurk in Karen's piece when she talks
about a friendship with a rich kid, and a time she lived in Hong
Kong. Stevenson thought it was more fun swimming underwater
than on top. Jonilee remembers a time when she 'drowned.' Her
single statement recalls the episode but what Jonilee needs is an
interested listener to question her and uncover the details of the
event to explain how she might have drowned.

  With *July*, the children listened to a story, told stories, and
wrote stories. Not only is the reading, writing, speaking connection clarified by this event, but narrative is very much being
nurtured in the classroom.

> When storying becomes overt and is given expression in
> words, the resulting stories are one of the most effective ways
> of making one's own interpretation of events and ideas avail-
> able to others. Through the exchange of stories, therefore,
> teachers and students can share their understandings of a
> topic and bring their mental models of the world into closer
> alignment.
> (Wells, 1986, p. 194)

To enhance my research with written and spoken responses to
literature, I repeated the lesson with my grade five students. One

of my objectives was to promote the same kind of narrative experience that I had had with the grade two class, but a second, more significant, objective was to use the experience to discover — and have the students discover — what happens in their minds as they engage with a text.

Before I read the picture book, I shared with the students some of the assumptions that I held about response. I felt that, because we are human beings, we cannot not respond to a story. As we read or listen to a story, we are often reminded of incidents from our own lives, or from other real or imagined stories that we are familiar with. I had a hunch, I told them, that something was going on inside their heads when they listened to the stories, and I was interested in finding out what that 'something' was. The way for me to discover their inside thoughts and pictures was to have them talk about them, or write about them, or illustrate them. I invited the students into my research and asked them to share some of their thoughts during and after listening to *July*.

Through questioning, I tried to uncover some of the assumptions that the students might have about response but, to begin with, they seemed reluctant to answer my questions. I felt that I could find out better how each student saw himself as a reader through a one-on-one interview situation. Perhaps they would come closer to an understanding about response after the lesson.

To begin, I asked the students to tell me what came to mind when they heard the word "July." The students brainstormed various ideas — "swimming," "summer," "my birthday," "America's birthday," "barbecues," "sweat," "lemonade," "cottages," "the beach," "free time," etc. I drew their attention to the fact that one word can inspire a range of stories, and told them that, together, we could discover a variety of stories we might think of as we listened to James Stevenson's stories.

After I read the story, the students shared some of their own experiences that were inspired by the picture book. In order to preserve these narrative experiences, the discussion was videotaped.

Miranda:	I go to my Grandmother's trailer every summer.
Matthew:	That reminds me of aunt and two cousins going down to the beach to have marshmallows and hot chocolate and s'mores.
James:	When we were at my Cub camp, I roasted a marshmallow and dropped it. I picked it up and later my dad ate it.

Ricky: I've got two stories. One is the boat. When me and my cousin went in a boat, a big boat, it had a thousand horse power or something and the other one was once I went down to the board-walk and I was listening to the radio and they were playing the song 'Down on the Board-walk.'

The discussion carried on for twenty minutes or so. Stories begat stories begat stories.

Cindy: You know the beach in Florida. We went there and I saw a killer whale.

Christi: When we went to New Zealand, a few hours after we came on the beach we saw a whale.

Janine: When we went to Barbados on vacation, we went fishing sort of and my cousin saw some fishees in the water and she got so excited she fell in the water and was splashing around...

Teacher: James, when she said that, I thought of your poem about your dead goldfish, because Jan-ine said 'fishees' too.

Liza: That reminds me of seeing porpoises with my dad.

Georgette: When we went to the beach my uncle... well he was going to teach my aunt how to swim and my aunt said "o.k"...I don't know which beach but it was far far away. He let her go and then she went sailing far far away and she started going like that and she was drowning and my uncle...he started running and my aunt was like yelling "Help! Help!" and me uncle, like he falls and he starts getting up to get her. Finally they grab her by the leg. That was the only part they could get hold of her. So they bring her to shore and she says "That was fun. Let's do it again!"

Teacher: When I think of your story, I remember the time I was in Alaska and I saw a man drown.

Students were then divided into small group clusters, where talk is more apt to happen. I explained that they might begin with an episode from *July* or they might think of something to tell as they listened to the story of a member of the group.

Christi told about the time she put ice cream in the goldfish bowl because she thought the fish were hungry. Greg told about a skinny-dipping experience. Ricky told about a cousin who ran away from home. Miranda then told about the time she got lost in a house because she locked herself in a closet and Sunil told about the time he got lost in a mall. He then went on to reveal a story about his two sisters, who had both died when he was younger.

To conclude the lesson, I asked the students why they thought they had told the stories and asked them to consider what they might learn from the experience. In the following conversation, Georgette, James, Greg, Liza, Christi and Janine articulate the essence of sharing memories:

Teacher:	We've been sharing lots of stories for the last few minutes.... How come we're sharing these stories? Why are we doing that?
Georgette:	It's our memories and thoughts that we thought about the book that we just read.
Teacher:	So how come we're talking about these stories? Where do they come from.
James:	They're there to make people laugh.
Teacher:	Sometimes laugh...Greg?
Greg:	It was part of our life once.
Teacher:	How come these stories about fish, about drownings, about aunts and uncles come out in our discussion?
Christi:	Because this is the time we're going to take them out of our mind...
Liza:	...sharing our life
Janine:	Once somebody starts a story about fishing, we think of another one.
Teacher:	Exactly! I hear the word 'drowning' and I think of a drowning story...and somebody thinks of another one.

After recess, the students were asked to choose one of the episodes that they had shared in the discussion, or another one that came to mind, and write a short personal narrative, as the author James Stevenson had done. Writing personal narratives calls for more than a report of the chronological details of an event. The purpose, it seems, is to explore the significance of those events. Having the students write their stories down would provide a means of recording what they had discovered through reading, talking and listening. I felt that the act of writing would help the students to consciously struggle with their thoughts and words and help them to reflect back on what they had said and what they had meant.

In this anecdote, Ricky talks about a time he went to the movies with his cousin but his yearning for a relationship also comes out in his memoir:

> My cousin Keith and I went to see *Rocky V*. My cousin is 15 and when we got there I wasn't aloud to go see it. We went to see *Quigly Down Under*. Now I hardly see my cousin. Now my cousin has a job. He works at Macdonalds. I wish he had a day off on Saturdays. I really would want to see him alot now. He might have a day off and take me somewhere.
> (Ricky)

James Stevenson's *July* sparks Matthew to write about his love of California and the importance of family:

> This story reminds me of going to California in June-July. California gives me chills. I once threw up because I was so excited. It gives me the best memories. I stopped at L.A.X. I turned on the radio and The Beach Boys were on. The palm trees were waving in the fresh Hollywood. My grandparents' house is the best. Meeting my family is the best feeling.
> (Matthew)

Kuni, an E.S.L. student, talks about a lonely time for him. Maybe it was the friendship in Stevenson's story that stimulated this memory. It is interesting to note the way in which Kuni has written his reminiscence. He has chosen a form that is almost poetic and very much like that found in the picture book. The anecdote was also the longest piece Kuni had written to date, and I have a hunch that that was because he told the story first, before writing it:

> I went to Briarwood
> before I came to
> Queenston drive
> I did not have friends
> at Briarwood
> I felt badly.
> I was a good soccer player
> and that's how I got some friends.

The *July* lesson was a successful learning opportunity for me and the children. For the grade two and five students, it seemed that the experience helped them reread their lives and bring forth a context for written and told stories. For me, the experience confirmed the hypothesis that, if a trusting atmosphere is provided, students will reveal stories drawn from their own experiences. Storying in this way can be an important step to more differentiated modes of knowing.

In my work as a teacher, I value the role of story. However, it wasn't until I watched the students, listened to them, tape-recorded and videotaped them, and reflected on the stories that they told, by connecting to a published source and to each other, that I came to recognize the beginnings of what David Booth (1990) calls a 'story tribe' emerging in the classroom. Research helped me learn about story, rather than prove anything about it. I wasn't surprised by the scores of stories that emerged from *July*. But I did wonder about how I might more effectively build a community of story and meaning makers. Writing in journals didn't seem to be the best medium for achieving this.

Then, in December, I read Lucy McCormick Calkins' (1991) text *Living Between the Lines* and was very much intrigued by Calkins' recent thinking about teaching reading and writing. For me, the heart of her research is found in the following quotation.

> Teachers and children need to bring the great cargoes of our lives to school, because it is by reading and writing and storytelling and musing and painting and sharing that we human beings find meaning. When children bring the work of their lives to school, they will invest themselves heart and soul.
>
> (Calkins, 1991, p. 305)

Because I respect the work of Calkins' Writing Project in New York, her book made me think more critically about reading and writing in my program. I mention this book at this time because, with *July*, the students were beginning to unpack the "cargoes" that Calkins writes about. Moreover, the book seemed to reinforce some of the ideas that I was wrestling with. Specifically, how could I provide more frequent opportunities for the students to unpack their memories as a way of reading and writing the stories of their lives? How could I change my classroom into a community through shared stories? How could I change journals into what Calkins calls "notebooks for living?"

Calkins (1991) writes:

> Ramell and his classmates at P.S. 7 do not keep their reading logs separate from their notebooks. Instead, in their notebooks they move from recording cherished phrases from a book to commenting on their sister, from questioning why an

author wrote a story to recalling a hurt dog they saw in the alley....This juxtaposition is a powerful brew — and a logical one.

Writer Vicki Vinton, who supports this way of physically merging reading and writing, says *"After all, the me who notices something at the Metropolitan Museum isn't any different from the me who notices something in a book or from the me who writes a story or teaches a class."*
(Calkins, 1991, p. 49)

The emphasis in the above quotation is my own. I have high-lighted this passage in two colours in the text, I have xeroxed and glued it in my journal, and I have frequently quoted it to teachers in recent workshops that I have conducted. It is these words that challenged me to find a way of extending the journals beyond responding to text, to a medium that could be used to have the children revisit, retell, relate, reflect, and respond to the "stuff of their lives." (Calkins, 1991)

Since I was contemplating some kind of change in my response program, *July* and *Living Between the Lines* were two incidents that together were critical enough to have me revise my teaching.

Phase 8: Revising the Plan

Through my classroom experience I have come to understand that journals can function as a medium of interaction among teacher, text and learner, and agree with Nancie Atwell, who writes:

> Dialogue journals play an important role in encouraging students to pull up their chairs — to become readers, enter the world of written texts, and make it their own. They allow me to respond pointedly and personally to what my students are doing. Dialogue journals allow me to teach every reader.
> (Atwell, 1987, p. 196)

However, as a teacher-researcher, I began to feel a sense of discomfort with using response journals in my program. This discomfort led to further inquiries and further learning about the medium of journals, the function of response, and the significance of teacher interventions with the students. It also led to setting new goals, collecting and analyzing new data, and working towards further change. I felt that there were possibilities for better learning opportunities, (at least what I thought would be better learning opportunities), and revised my practice with two main concerns in mind.

First, response journals didn't seem to offer the same opportunity for fruitful interactions that conferences and discussions could and so I decided to pay more attention to 'booktalk.' Since I had come to recognize more fully the importance of oracy in the classroom, I wanted to introduce activities that would provide the students with situations, one to one, in small groups, and in the whole class, to reveal their thoughts about books by talking about them rather than by writing about them.

Second, I became more aware of the other kinds of writing that the students were doing in the classroom, and after reading *Living Between the Lines* I became concerned about the need for students to have better ways to share "the great cargoes of their lives." In the second term, therefore, I decided to abandon the response journal in favor of what Calkins calls 'notebooks.' In these, the students were invited to respond, not only to literature, but to everyday events in their own lives.

As a teacher-researcher, I wanted to encourage personal response and to help students to write and read and talk in meaningful ways. Whether notebooks and booktalk would be more favorable than journals for achieving my goals, however, was a question that could only be determined through further plans, observations, reflections and actions, i.e., through further action research. As I start the new cycle, these are the key questions I plan to try to answer:

- How does the notebook serve as a medium for reflection on life experiences in response to literature?

- How does collaborative talk empower the learner and develop the potential for revealing thought?

Conclusion

Engaging in reflective practice, I have discovered, is like using a highlighting marker to bring words and ideas and experiences into sharper focus for scrutiny. To summarize where I have come to on my journey with response, it has been necessary to take a highlighter to bring sharper focus to the comments, quotations, and events, which acted as the critical incidents that led to change in my program over the course of the year.

I had been teaching my class in the best way I knew how, operating a good deal of the time from an intuitive sense of what was going on. I started with a special interest in working with response journals but, along the way, my focus shifted. I became interested in Lucy Calkins' use of notebooks for a much broader range of personal writing in response to events as well as books. I also became interested in paying attention to collaborative booktalk because of the immediacy and depth of response to books that it encourages. Concentrating on one aspect of my language arts program thus led to a changed focus and a changed action. As for my original assumptions, I still believe that journals help students to think about their reading processes. I also believe that journals provide a useful means for the teacher to assess a student's comprehension and thinking abilities. However, some of my other assumptions were challenged by the events I have described.

When I began my investigation, I assumed that journals were the best accountable way of revealing children's responses to literature. But when a colleague observed "they are second best to talk," I questioned why I was using a practice that was only second best. I had also assumed that the students would come to write about their personal experiences and discuss how a particular text reminded them of their own life stories. However, this did not seem to happen in any significant way in their journals, although it was promoted in talk situations.Finally, I had imagined that the students and I would have conversations about books in their journals, but the students didn't seem to respond to my letters by writing back. The notion that 'dialogue' would help deepen their reflection, was not validated for me.

In the end, then, I abandoned journals because I read a new book about teaching, because I invited my students to share some reminiscences, because I used a journal to reflect on the incidents in my classroom, and because I talked with colleagues in the staff room, in the hallways of the school, over the phone, and in a university seminar room. It is the sum total of these experiences — these "critical incidents" — that helped challenge my assumptions and re-shape my teaching, my learning, and my research.

> Transforming teaching into a learning enterprise is a journey without end. Becoming a learning teacher means recognizing that our understanding of what we'd like to have happen in our classroom and our ability to make sense of what students are trying to do will be in need of continuous revision. No sooner will some aspect of our instructional program be sorted out, than something will happen to raise further questions.
> (Newman, 1990, p. 24)

Finally, through my writing about my action research, I have come to the present point in my journey with response journals, collaborative talk, and my own assumptions and uncoverings. I have had some questions answered but I have uncovered many more. I have made some changes; I will certainly be making others.

Note

1. I followed up on Janine's suggestion and a book club of 12 children met weekly to share, criticize and respond to books through talk, drama and art activities.

6

ESL Learners Talking and Thinking in their First Language:

Primary ESL Students Sharing Picture Books with a Bilingual Assistant

Ewa Orzechowska and Anna (Ania) Smieja

Ania's Journal, Junior Kindergarten, February 23, 1991:

> During book sharing time, I read *The Fish Out of Water* to Pedro and two other children. Pedro got totally involved in the story. His whole body wriggled with excitement and it seemed as if he wanted to jump into the story. When I read the words "Little Otto began to grow...," Pedro waved his arms and cried, "And bigger!" I continued: "He grew even more." Pedro pointed excitedly at the picture, "Yeah, yeah, look." I turned the page and read, "So they put him into a pot, but he was too big." "Because look!" Pedro squealed with excitement — the fish's tail was hanging out of the pot. Later in the story, Mr. Carp dove into the pool to get the fish and Pedro waved his arms in a wild breast stroke and imitation dive. "And he go like this, yeah, like this!"

Ewa's Journal, Grade Two, December 6, 1990:

> The grade two teacher finished reading the story of the "Last Supper" to the whole class. She asked, "Why did Jesus have

a special meal with his friends?" Robert's hand shot up almost
before she'd finished speaking. She looked around at the
other raised hands and then back to Robert and smiled encouragingly — "What do you think, Robert?" "Because, because he..." Robert blushed, stammered, sank back into his
seat and muttered, "I know, because..." Another child volunteered the answer and Robert looked dejected.

Introduction

There are many children in Canada's multi-ethnic schools who
are confident speakers of their first language but face a daily
struggle to express themselves in English. Sometimes, like Pedro,
they communicate remarkably well, with the help of eloquent
gestures and a sympathetic teacher's close attention. Too often,
like Robert, they are swamped in a larger group of fluent English
speakers and forced into silence. In neither situation are they
able to share the full extent of their knowledge and understanding. Unlike their English-speaking peers, they are denied the use
of their first language as a means for learning and communicating in school. We can empathise with these children since both of
us, as children of Polish refugees, started school in Britain with
no knowledge of English and were plunged into mainstream
classrooms. Our previous five years, during which we had learnt
to think and communicate in Polish, appeared to count for
nothing. Although we achieved eventual success in the English
school system and became fully bilingual, our early experiences
as ESL learners whose first language competence was ignored,
have left us with memories of painful silences and sometimes,
when we did attempt to speak, of humiliating frustrations.

As teachers of ESL students in British and Canadian schools,
we are aware that large numbers of children suffer similar
experiences to our own. This perception is confirmed in a number
of studies (see for example Ashworth, 1988). While some ESL
students go on to successful social and academic integration,
there are others who never participate fully in English language
classrooms. There are also many children who lose their first
language fluency in the process of acquiring English. Is this
pattern inevitable? Neither of us can accept that it is. Our own
strong foundations in a first language other than English, and an
awareness of the central role it has played in our emotional and
intellectual development, as well as the advantages we have
gained from being bilingual, have always prompted us to value
and encourage our students' L1 use. Graduate studies provided
an opportunity for us to examine this "intuitive" response, by
carrying out action research into some of the theoretical and prac-

tical dimensions of first and second language acquisition and use. Our study focused on the use of students' L1 in the context of book sharing time in two primary classrooms in a Toronto school. Ewa acted as an assistant in Ania's Junior Kindergarten classroom, helping one Polish child, and in a grade 2 classroom, where she worked with a group of nine Polish children. (All of these students were recent immigrants to Canada.) We met regularly to plan the study and to discuss our observations, reading, and reflections, which we recorded on tape and in our journals. We found that given the opportunity, with the help of a bilingual assistant, children in Junior Kindergarten and grade 2 were able to use their L1 to discuss stories which had been read to them in English. The quality and quantity of their participation became similar to that of the English-speaking children. Instead of being restricted to minimal, literal responses, the ESL students, using their L1, were able to engage in a wide range of cognitive activities. In addition, we found that these children were using their L1 as a resource in developing their L2 (English) knowledge. Many teachers of ESL students regard their L1 as irrelevant, or even as an obstacle to English fluency and academic progress. Our own study convinced us that, on the contrary, an ESL student's L1 can be viewed as a positive asset in supporting linguistic and cognitive development and overcoming some of the potential trauma of adjusting to an ESL environment, even when the language of instruction is English.

Limitations on Learning in a Second Language

The perceptions with which we started our research were based on more than just intuition and personal experience. Throughout our teaching careers, we had read professional literature and attended courses pertaining to our interests. Now we returned to some of these sources and also discovered new ones. We found part of the rationale for our project in familiar documents and guidelines from boards of education and from the Ontario Ministry of Education, which describe the kinds of linguistic and intellectual development which teachers should promote in the primary grades. According to a Metro Toronto Board publication, *Observing Children* (1983), children between the ages of four and nine should show increasingly more sophisticated abilities in using language to communicate and to think. They should be able to use language to report on past and present experiences, to reason, to predict, to project and to imagine. This document and other board and Ministry publications also stress the social and affective dimensions of learning. Children need to interact and co-operate with others, to feel secure and liked, and to express their feelings and concerns. Looking at the experience of ESL students in our school, we felt that the latter area was partially addressed by the use of the children's L1 in informal (non-academic) situations. Several members of staff could understand some Polish and made efforts to talk with the Polish children, to make them feel welcome and to show an interest in their lives. There were also Polish-speaking older students whose assistance was sought to explain school routines and clarify misunderstandings. The group of Polish students in Grade 2 were not discouraged from speaking to each other in Polish, and did spend much of their time together, although they were also friendly with other students in their class. A similar approach was taken, where possible, with ESL students from other linguistic minorities in the school. It seemed that the ESL students' L1 was being recognised as helpful in meeting their immediate social and emotional needs. On the other hand, we were aware that languages other than English were largely absent from the classroom instructional context, the context in which formal, intellectual and linguistic development was expected to occur. We wondered how this affected the ESL students' ability to benefit from instruction and to maintain the level of intellectual development expected from their age group. Were they receiving opportunities for the range of language use described in *Observing Children?*

Our initial observations in both classes suggested that the beginning ESL students were not in fact engaging in the full range of age-appropriate linguistic and cognitive behaviour. The extent of the ESL children's involvement in lessons which generally elicited very active participation from English speaking children was very limited. It is clear from this journal entry that neither Daniel nor Pedro were deriving much benefit from the group story sharing.

Ania's Journal, Junior Kindergarten, November 5, 1990:

> Today's story, *Harriet's Hallowe'en Candy* was a big hit with most of the children. They listened intently, and excitedly told me about their own trick-or-treating adventures and the sweets they had got. Daniel sat quietly through a part of the story, then put up his hand and said, "Washroom." This seems to be a frequent story time request! Pedro had been fidgeting at the back and crawling away. By the end of the story, he was doing somersaults and kicking his legs up.

More interest was generated in a lesson designed especially for the Polish students in grade two, but their contribution was still very restricted compared to what one might expect from a group of English L1 students, as one can see in the following journal extract:

Ewa's Journal, Grade two, October 29, 1990:

> It was my second visit to the ESL class today. It coincided with Hallowe'en, so I decided to do a dramatised reading of *Meg and Mog*, complete with witch's hat and black cat puppet to stimulate children's interest and support the English text. The children certainly appeared to enjoy this. They laughed a lot and pointed to the pictures. Their verbal contributions, however, were minimal and consisted mostly of one word answers to my direct questions, as in these examples:
>
> Ewa: Who's this?
>
> Hania: A witch.
>
> Ewa: What is she doing here?
>
> Josef: Sleeping.

Avoiding a Period of 'Silent Reception'

From our conversations with children and their parents in their L1, it was apparent that these students could report, reason, predict, project, imagine and articulate ideas and feelings with the same facility as their English-speaking peers, and regularly did so at home and in other settings where they could speak Polish. However, for them and for many other ESL students with whom we have worked, these abilities seemed to vanish when they entered a mainstream classroom and had to demonstrate them in a much weaker second language. Various writers on second language learning describe a silent receptive period during which children listen to L2 input but do not venture to produce any L2 utterances. As with the acquisition of L1, the ability to understand (receptive skill), generally precedes the ability to create a meaningful utterance (productive skill).

Observing the ESL children in Junior Kindergarten and grade 2, we felt strong reservations about an unqualified acceptance of 'silence.' Certainly, beginning ESL learners are likely to listen more than they speak in English, and their English speech may serve mainly communicative rather than cognitive functions. But does this mean that, until they become fluent in their L2, they can never participate in class activities at the level of intellectual maturity which they have attained through their L1? Surely these children need to be sharing and discussing their ideas and feelings with a teacher and with other children. We felt increasingly disturbed by the thought that children who were active and competent language users at home were spending all of their school day feeling themselves to be inept beginners, or being reduced to silent observers and listeners. From the teacher's point of view, such a situation seemed contrary to the generally accepted principle of building on a child's strengths. If ESL children's main linguistic strengths are in their L1, then there is a need to investigate how these can be utilised in the classroom.

Accessing the Benefits of Shared Reading

We chose the shared reading of picture books as the main context for our inquiry because of its importance in primary classrooms. Its role is well established in the development of first language and L1 literacy, and in cognitive, affective and social growth. Wells (1986) explains the importance of listening to stories. He states that it helps children to become familiar with "the sustained meaning-building organisation of written language and its characteristic rhythms and structures," and makes it possible for them to "extend the range of their experience far beyond the limits of their immediate surroundings" (pp 151-152). A further advantage we have noticed in multi-ethnic classrooms is the way in which a stock of jointly experienced stories provides a common classroom culture. It can unite children from a wide range of backgrounds, giving them an experience of other points of view and providing a shared set of references. We also found support in the literature for the role of stories in ESL development. Heald-Taylor (1986) states that "the use of quality literature in language instruction gives students learning English as a second language opportunities to appreciate English in meaningful contexts, to hear the rhythm and intonation of the language, to become familiar with the syntactical structures while gradually gaining an understanding of the text" (p. 5).

As we saw in Ania's lesson on November 5, it was often difficult for her ESL students to focus their attention on stories read to them in English, especially in a large group. We felt that not only were these children not benefiting from this activity in the ways described by Wells and Heald-Taylor (1986), but they were probably growing to dislike it. As a first step in introducing some L1 support for Daniel, a Polish-speaking child, Ewa joined the class during story time. She sat next to Daniel in the circle of children gathered around the teacher's chair. While Ania read the picture book *Are You My Mother?* to the class, Ewa whispered questions and comments to Daniel in Polish. Although he did not respond verbally, he became more attentive than on previous occasions. A few days later, Ewa, speaking in Polish, invited Daniel to retell the story and prompted him in Polish. Using mainly Polish, he described events in the story and also recalled some of the repetitive English text.

Daniel:	I on idzie tu, tam. Gdzie jest mama? (And he's going here, there. Where's mummy?)
Ewa:	Co on tu mowi? (What is he saying here?)
Daniel:	"Are you my mum?" "No...o...o!" [very expressive] On powiedzial. (He said.)
Ewa:	A co to jest? (And what's this?)
Daniel:	To kot. (It's a cat.) "Are you my mum?" "No...o...o!" [Next page.] Dog! On powiedzial (He said) "Are you my mum?" "No!" [picture of a wrecked car] Ono jechalo, uderzylo kamyki, auto. (It was going along and hit some stones, that car.)

We were surprised at how animated and expressive Daniel had become during this session. Ewa's undivided attention and the possibility of communicating in Polish put him much more at ease than he had previously been in this class. Ewa's second session with the Grade two class was also planned to observe the effect of introducing some L1 use. The children listened to the story *Curious George* read in English, and then were asked to explain and predict various events. They were encouraged to respond in Polish if they felt unable to answer in English. The positive results of this initiative can be seen in this example:

Ewa:	What do you think George is going to do now?
Peter:	Maybe he...I don't know.
Ewa:	Powiedz po polsku. (Say it in Polish.)
Peter:	On chyba zje te ciasto i pani bedzie sie gniewac na niego. (He'll probably eat the cake and the lady will be angry with him.)
Christina:	Albo sie zchowa gdzies. (Or he'll hide somewhere.)
Beata:	Eat. He eat cake.

In many of these exchanges during this session, students claimed that they did not know what to say, until Ewa told them that they could use Polish. It then became clear that they had understood much of the English text and were using personal experiences as well as making inferences from text and pictures to develop logical ideas which they could express coherently in their L1.

L1 Use: A Hindrance or an Asset?

Our preliminary observations, and our reading and reflection had reinforced our desire to investigate the positive use of ESL students' L1 in a mainstream classroom. However, we were aware that many parents and educators are concerned by the use of children's L1 in schools. A widely held view is that use of the L1 will slow down or impede the development of the L2, and a great deal of second language teaching is based upon the assumption that the more L2 students are exposed to, the faster they will learn it. First language skills are often regarded as irrelevant or as an actual hindrance to the development of L2 proficiency. These assumptions appear to be supported by the observation that many ESL students, when placed in monolingual English environments, soon become fluent in everyday social communication. Nevertheless, the eventual school achievement of ESL students is often below that of their first language peers. This discrepancy needs to be understood to allay the fears about L1 use of those who see English immersion as the common sense approach for ESL students.

Cummins (1984) provides a clear explanation of the relationship between L1 and L2 acquisition, and academic achievement. He conceptualises two major dimensions of language proficiency. Children readily acquire the easiest aspect of second language use: the basic interpersonal communicative skills (BICS), because most face-to-face communication is both context-embedded and cognitively undemanding. In casual conversation, therefore, children may soon appear to be reasonably fluent. By contrast, they have much greater difficulty with the cognitive academic language proficiency (CALP), which is needed for them to succeed in school. This is because many academic activities depend on "linguistic cues to meaning" and involve manipulation of language for thinking, which is difficult to achieve in a second language. We were aware of this difference in our group of ESL students, some of whom readily made friends with English-speaking children and could play with them, using very few English words, long before they could take part in the same class work as their English-speaking peers.

Another challenge to monolingual L2 instruction comes from Skinner (1985). He points out that L2 learners who are totally immersed in the second language are having to function at a level far below the cognitive level which they are capable of achieving in their L1. Having only a few words and restricted meanings in the L2, beginning second language learners are unable to connect concepts and words, and are limited in the full development of their thoughts. These intellectual restrictions imposed on second language learners were quite obvious when we listened to our ESL students.

Ania's Journal, Junior Kindergarten, December 5, 1990:

> During book sharing time, I was reading with a small group of   children. Pedro was nearby looking at *Spot's Word Book*, a class favourite. He got my attention and pointed at a picture of   Spot and his friends in the garden. He then pointed to the shed and said, "Blue." "Yes, that's a blue shed," I said and continued to read to the others. Pedro was not put off. "Green!" he exclaimed, pointing to an alligator.

> For several days Pedro has been reciting colors during book time. He was able to interact with me the way a two-year-old might, who points to pictures and gives one-word labels. Yet Pedro's drawings are vivid and detailed. In Spanish, he dictates stories about witches eating children and many-legged spiders. In English he was only able to engage in a much less cognitively sophisticated task — the calling out of colors.

Cummins (1989), Skinner (1985) and others strongly question the effectiveness of monolingual second language programs for developing the academic skills of minority students. They suggest that better results can be obtained if the students' first language is actively employed as a medium for learning in school. Cummins (1984, Cummins and Swain, 1986) documents the success of bilingual programs in which part of the school curriculum is conducted through the L1 and part through the L2. Many such programs have shown that students who spend less time in the second language context and use the first language for academic purposes acquire a higher level of proficiency in the L2, while retaining fluency in their L1. They also have better overall academic results than children in monolingual L2 programs. Cummins (1984) explains these results by reference to a "common underlying proficiency," which is shared by all languages. Although the surface features of languages are clearly different, these are based on a deeper level of interdependent conceptual and linguistic proficiency. From this perspective, if students improve their academic skills in one language, they are able to transfer them relatively easily to the second language.

A Practical Alternative to Bilingual Programs

Although the literature appears to justify the extensive use of ESL students' L1 across the curriculum, a fully bilingual program is not always feasible. The existence of several different linguistic minorities as well as English L1 students in one classroom or one school is a common phenomenon in Canada. Under these circumstances, the only place in which the L1 has an official role may be a heritage language class. Thus, the ESL children have to cope with academic learning in all areas of the curriculum in their weaker second language, even at the beginning stages of learning English. We felt that it might be possible to create a middle ground between official bilingual programs and a monolingual English classroom. In many schools, it might be possible to provide for bilingual assistants, or parent and older student volunteers, to work with ESL children in the mainstream classroom. They could enable the children to make sense of the activities and contribute their input, through their L1.

Our research question was formulated to investigate this possibility: Can a bilingual assistant share English language picture books with ESL children, using their L1 to promote the cognitive, linguistic, emotional and social development for which this activity is designed? Without a control group and formal testing, we would not be able to claim proof of the positive effects of L1 use. However, we felt it would be useful, for us and for other teachers, to describe some of the ways in which children responded to this opportunity. On the basis of our reading and experience, we felt that we would be able to make an informed judgement as to the validity of our observations.

From studying our tapes and transcriptions, we found four areas which seemed particularly important for the older grade two students — interaction and engagement with the story, collaborative talk, re-telling, and the use of bilingual language strategies. The junior kindergarten children showed instances of similar behavior, though not as highly developed nor as frequent. However, we would also expect a similar difference between four and eight-year-olds who are learning in their L1.

I. Interaction and Engagement

Good readers are actively involved in their reading. They relate the substance of the text and pictures to their previous experiences. They also make predictions, infer meaning, ask questions and make evaluations. But ESL students soon discover that much of what they have learnt in their first years of life cannot be expressed and applied in the shared reading process, when it is conducted solely in English. This situation was dramatically altered when we encouraged children to use their L1. They revealed themselves to be active, meaning-oriented readers, engaging with stories in four distinct ways. They reported on past experiences, both real and imaginary, commented, questioned and made inferences.

1) Personal Experience

When Ewa read *The Tomten and the Fox,* she found the children very keen to share experiences which related to the story. She chose this story because the setting, an old farm in winter, might be familiar, and the troll which guards the farm closely resembles the Polish "krasnoludek." Upon seeing the pictures, Peter, one of the children, became very excited and made the following comments:

Peter:	To jak u mego wujka, tak samo, tak samo wyglada! (That's like my uncle's place, it looks the same!)
Peter:	Ten lis, on chce do kornika sie dobrac, alekrasnoludek mu nie da chyba. (That fox wants to get in the chicken house, but the troll probably won't let him.)

2) Questions

The use of questions to clarify meaning or to discover more detail increases with a child's cognitive development. Questioning techniques were beginning to emerge within the JK class, but were much more apparent among the fluent English speakers who were better able to manipulate the language and had more opportunity to do so. Pedro's main form of inquiry was "But why, teacher?" as he tried to understand the text of an English story or interpret an illustration.

We took it as a sign of active interest and involvement in the story when children asked questions. Some were directly relevant to an understanding of the story, as in the following example *The Story of Ferdinand* with the grade two group, where Josef was able to help Hania understand the change in Ferdinand's appearance:

Hania:	Pani Ewo, ale kto to jest? (But Miss Ewa, who is that?) [looking at a picture of the adult bull standing next to his growth chart]
Marek:	Fernando (Ferdinand)

Hania:	Ale on taki duzy! (But he's so big!)
Josef:	Bo on urosl (Because he's grown)
Ewa:	Yes, he's grown much bigger.

3) Comments on Text/Pictures

Children often commented on the story, on the picture and on their attitudes and feelings towards characters and events. While re-telling the story of *The Wild Washerwomen* in English, Beata switched into Polish to comment on a character's appearance and to express disapproval of the character's behavior.

Beata:	Ale ona tu jest gruba! (She's so fat here!)
Magda:	Now they go and they happy.
Ewa:	Why are they happy?
Beata:	They like that, throwing everything and play-ing. Ale one nie powinne tak robic w kosciele, sie bawic, prawda? (But they shouldn't do that in church, they shouldn't play, right?) [the washerwomen are swinging on the church bellropes]
Ewa:	No, I don't think people would like it if some-one really played in church like that.

It was interesting to note Beata's switch from English to Polish in her second contribution. The initial description in English seems to be a simpler task than the value judgement which she makes in Polish. Beata probably had the appropriate English vocabulary in her receptive L2 knowledge, but was not able to use it at the productive level.

Both Pedro's and Daniel's speech and interaction with us in the JK class were far more expressive in their L1. They dramatised their voices and used a range of 'sound effects.' When one of us read one-to-one with them, they sometimes interjected comments about the story, and more frequently about the pictures. Ewa read the story *David's Father* with Daniel, and afterwards discussed the cover picture, guessing who might eat with the giant cutlery in the picture:

Ewa:	Czy ten pan moze jesc tym widelcem? (Can this man eat with this fork?)
Daniel:	Nie! Duze ludzie. (No! Big people.)
Ewa:	Duze? (Big?)

Daniel:	Giant.
Ewa:	A czy ty sie jego bojisz? (Are you afraid of him?)
Daniel:	Tak! (Yes!)
Ewa:	A myslisz ze on jest naprawde zly? (Do you think he is really bad?)
Daniel:	Troszeczke dobry. Troszeczke. (A little bit good. A little.)

Daniel understood the new concept of 'giant' and was able to put together the idea of size and appearance (he was fearsome and enormous) with the kindness which the giant showed to the children.

4) Inferences

Making inferences from information in a text or picture combined with prior knowledge of possibilities is essential for meaningful reading. In the following exchange, Marek expressed his thoughtful disagreement with the illustrator's/author's placement of Baby Bear's bed *(The Three Bears)*. This stimulated Christina to make an inference based on her observation of the details (Papa Bear snoring), in the picture.

Marek:	Prosze pani! Ale to dziecko powinno byc po srodku bo zeby sie nie balo. (Excuse me, Miss! But that child should be in the middle so he won't be afraid.) [the beds are arranged in order: Papa, Mama, Baby]
Ewa:	Oh, you think the baby should be in the middle because then he wouldn't be frightened?
Christina:	Ale dlatego tak to jest bo ten Tata tak chrapie i on by nie mogl zasnac. (But that's why he's there, because Papa snores so much that he wouldn't be able to sleep.)
Ewa:	Oh, that's a good idea too. Christina says Baby is here because Papa is snoring.
Christina:	I dlatego Mama nie moze uspac. (And that's why Mama can't get to sleep.)
Ewa:	And it's too noisy for the baby and that's why Mama can't sleep.

Robert: I mama sie za uszy trzyma.
           (And Mama is holding her ears.)

II. Collaborative Talk

The role of student talk in learning is recognised in the efforts which teachers put into establishing co-operative group work. Through talking with each other in the context of shared activities, children are able to refine their ideas and solve problems. There were several occasions on which the grade two students engaged in collaborative talk in Polish, as they tried to construct a description or understand a difficult part of a story. In the following exchange, they arrived at a more complete assessment of Ferdinand's character *(The Story of Ferdinand)* as they built on each other's ideas. Ewa had asked them to tell her about Ferdinand in the bull ring, where he is sitting down, refusing to fight, while the crowds cheer him on.

Magda: They think he very good.

Josef: But he no good.

Christina: On tylko tak wyglada grozny ale on naprawde
            jest spokojny. (He just looks mean like that,
            but he's really peaceful.)

Hania: On teraz jest smutny. (Now he's sad.)

Josef: He no want fight.

Magda: Just smell flowers. On chce wachac kwiatki.
            (He wants to smell flowers.)

It is clear in this example that allowing the children to use Polish did not prevent them from also using English when they felt confident of their ability to do so. Magda's translation of her own English contribution into Polish was perhaps stimulated by Ewa's doing this as a regular part of their book sharing. She may also have wanted to help Hania whose English skills were much weaker.

During Polish retelling of *The Wild Washerwomen*, a disagreement arose, based on Magda's misunderstanding of the English text. The children were able to resolve this for themselves with reference to the meanings of English words. Beata showed explicit grammatical knowledge of English pronouns, which she had not been directly taught.

Ewa: Czy mozecie mi cos o tym panu powiedziec?
           (Can you tell me something about this man?)

Magda: No on byl smutny. (Well, he was sad.)

Christina: Nie, on byl zly, niedobry. (No, he was mean.)

Ewa: Dlaczego niedobry? (Why mean?)

Christina: Bo on kazal im prac duzo.
             (Because he made them do a lot of washing.)

Magda: Nie, tam bylo "sad" to znaczy smutny.
             (No, it said "sad," that means sad.)

Ewa: Poczekajcie. Ja wam te stronice przeczytam.
             (Wait. I'll read that page to you.)
             "They were the best washerwomen for miles,
             but they were not happy. The owner of the
             laundry, Mr. Balthazar Tight, was a very
             mean little man, and he kept them working
             from morning to night."

Magda: Widzisz! "Not happy." (See! "Not happy.")

Christina: Ale to one byly, nie on, prawda?
             (But it was them not him, right?)

Ewa: Co ty myslisz Beata? (What do you think
             Beata?)

Beata: Ja mysle ze to one bo tam bylo " they not
             happy." (I think that it was them because it
             said "they not happy.")

Christina: A on byl niedobry. (And he was mean.)

Ewa: Czy wiecie jak tam bylo po angielsku nap-
             isane o nim?
             (Do you know what it said there in English
             about him?)

Magda: "Very mean"... niedobry, o...o! ("Very mean"...
             mean, oh...oh!)

We also observed instances of collaborative talk among the
English-speaking students in the junior kindergarten class during personal book sharing time. They gathered together in groups,
discussed the pictures and told each other stories. They sometimes debated over the details of familiar stories. Children also
helped one another when dictating personal stories about pictures. The ESL children did not join in these activities. If there
had been pairs or groups of children with a shared L1 other than
English, we would have encouraged them to do so. As it was,
Daniel and Pedro were excluded from much of the helpful,
literacy-related conversations with peers in the classroom.

III. Retelling

The retelling of stories is a frequent follow-up to the sharing of picture books in primary classrooms. It helps children to organise story sequence, identify main ideas, select details, and elaborate their own interpretations. It also provides teachers with information on the children's understanding of the story. As the stories we were sharing were in the children's L2, it was especially important for us to know the extent of their comprehension.

From the grade two children's interactions during book sharing with Ewa, it seemed that they were making sense of the stories but, to check this, she asked two or three children each time to retell the story a few days after the session. First they retold it in Polish, taking turns to tell a part, and then they discussed it with Ewa in Polish. Next, they retold the story in English. The children enjoyed this additional challenge. It seems possible that the Polish retelling, during which they could readily engage in the cognitive activities of recall, extracting main ideas and details, and sequencing, did make it easier for them to 'translate' their organised thoughts into English. With the opportunity to consult with each other and the teacher in Polish, they were also able to obtain the new English vocabulary which they needed at the point where it became important to them. Vygotsky (1962) suggests that learning takes place in the "zone of proximal development," when a teacher can help children to move just beyond what they can do alone and unassisted.

The following retellings of *The Rainbow Crow*, show the contrast between the two languages. They also underscore the extent to which ESL children may be being 'silenced' in a monolingual English environment.

[Polish retelling]

Robert:	Dawno temu bylo slonce w lasach, bylo duzo zwierzat i bylo im bardzo fajnie. Wylegiwaly sie i bawily sie. (Long, long ago, there was sun in the forest, there were many animals and they were happy. They relaxed and played.)
Adam:	I sie zaczela zima i bylo im bardzo zimno i snieg zaczal padac i zwierzetom bylo smutno. (And winter started and it was cold and the snow started to fall and the animals were sad.)
Robert:	I niektore male zwiezatka, naprzyklad zajac, one sie tak zakopaly ze im tylko bylo uszy

widac i niektore wchodzily na drzewo i szukaly jedzenia bo byly glodne i bylo zimno. I mysz sie zakopala i chcialy zeby jakies zwierze polecialo do...do teczy? (And some of the small animals, for example the hare, they were buried so deep that you could only see their ears and some climbed the trees and they looked for food because they were hungry. And the mouse got buried. And they wanted one animal to fly to...to the rainbow?)

Adam: I oni mowili...kto teraz poleci do Boga?
(And they said...who will fly to God?)

Robert: Great Spirit.

Adam: I oni mowili kto pojdzie do Great Spirit?
(And they said, "Who will go to the Great Spirit?")

Robert: I najpierw chcial pojsc racoon. Ale zwierzeta powiedzialy, "Raccoon nie idz. Jak tam dojdziesz? Przeciez ty nie umiesz latac." I sowa powiedziala, "Ja pojde do Wielkiego Ducha."
(First, the racoon wanted to go, but the animals said, "Don't go, racoon. How will you get there. You don't know how to fly." And the owl said, "I'll go to the Great Spirit.")

Adam: Ale sowa nie poszla bo lis powiedzial "Ty nie widzisz w dzien."
(But the owl didn't go because the fox said, "You can't see in the day time.")

[English retelling]

Ewa: Robert, what time of year was it at the beginning of the story?

Robert: It sunny.

Adam: Sum...

Ewa: Summer, lato. Or spring, wiosna.

Robert: They happy.

Adam: The snow is fall and it not fine.

Robert: Is cold.

Ewa: So what did the animals want to do?

Adam: Want one animal to go to Great Spirit... but...racoon cannot fly and owl cannot see.

IV. Comparing, Contrasting, Translating and 'Bridging'

Support for the use of the L1 in second language development comes from Dodson (1983), who looks at the natural language acquisition of bilingual children. He notes that bilingual children actively use the two languages to support the learning of each one, by comparing and contrasting them. They do this in addition to the language play activities of monolingual children. They also seek definitions of words in one language through the medium of the other language. A bilingual child "uses one language at his disposal as a tool for meaning acquisition in the other" (p. 140). Dodson also points out that monolingual speakers, when they cannot think of a word to use, substitute phrases like "that thing" or "you know what I mean." Bilingual speakers have the option of using a word from their other language.'Code switching,' as this is called, seems to some to indicate an inability to speak either language correctly.

However, we know from personal experience that it enriches our communication with those of similar backgrounds by providing us with expanded nuances of meaning.

When discussing mother bear's porridge *(The Three Bears)* with the grade two group, Ewa heard Beata repeating paired words, the Polish one and its English equivalent, apparently to herself. It was something heard often among the children.

Ewa:	It was too...
Josef:	Hot.
Marek:	No, no, cold.
Ewa:	Right, it was too cold.
Beata:	Zimne, cold, zimne, cold.

The children were quick to notice similarities in sound between Polish and English words, whether they were similar in meaning or not. In this case, Christina was quicker to do this than her teachers while talking about Goldilocks' name.

Ewa:	Locks means hair that goes like this.
ESL teacher:	Curls.
Christina:	Loki, loki, to samo! (Locks, locks, that's the same!)

The children frequently translated words back and forth as Ewa talked about the story in English. Most often, they would help each other by supplying a word when someone was stuck or else they would ask each other.

The practice of using a word from the other language in a basically L1 or L2 utterance was a common one. It helped to 'bridge' the children's different level of skill in the two languages. When children substituted a Polish word for an unknown English one, the flow of communication was not impeded. When they used an English one in Polish speech, it was generally one they had recently learnt. In the next example, the word 'fire' is first introduced in Polish by two children, translated into English by two others and finally, Marek incorporates it into his Polish explanation of events in the story of *The Rainbow Crow*:

> Ewa: "...and the Great Spirit said, 'I can't stop the snow, but I can give you something which will help you to stop the snow.'"
>
> Peter: Ogien. (Fire.)
>
> Hania: Ogien. (Fire.)
>
> Magda: Fire.
>
> Marek: Fire.
>
> [Later, the crow has been burned while carrying the fire]
>
> Marek: Dlatego ze ten fire to jest i od tego fire jest, bo od tego zawsze czarne.
> (Because it's that fire, it's from that, from that fire because from that it's always black.)

Very young children appear to be unaware that they are using two separate languages, even when they know which one to use for a specific context. In the following examples, Daniel used a number of bilingual strategies. He translated his own statements, as in this excerpt from a discussion about *Bones, Bones, Dinosaur Bones*, and gave the Polish version an expanded meaning:

> Daniel: All them digging. Oni juz kopali te.
> (They already dug these.)

Daniel regularly used the 'bridging' strategy, incorporating English words and phrases into L1 utterances. In talking about *David's Father*, he always used the English word 'giant,' even in Polish statements.

> Daniel: Tu ten giant. (Here's that giant)

He slipped easily in and out of English and Polish, as in these comments when looking at *Bones, Bones, Dinosaur Bones*:

Daniel: Moze bite me i wezmie mnie i on zje tych ludzi.
           (Maybe he'll bite me and he'll eat these people.)

Ewa: On zje tych ludzi? (He'll eat these people?)

Daniel: Beda w srodku ludzie i bedzie dark.
           (The people will be inside and it will be dark.

We felt that this use of English helped Daniel to communicate, as well as providing him with practice in using new L2 vocabulary in a known, L1 context.

Conclusion

The following journal entries were made in the final days of our study. We could not have wished for a better finale.

Ania's Journal, Junior Kindergarten, April 26, 1991:

> Today was Monika's first day in my class. She came in holding her daddy's hand, clutching her school bag and looking rather apprehensive. Her mother has recently died and she and her father arrived from Poland only five days ago. When I spoke to them in Polish, both father and daughter visibly relaxed, and Monika went happily to explore the classroom. Daniel arrived, and I assured Monika that he also spoke Polish. During personal book sharing time, Monika told me that she already knows how to read in Polish, and I invited her to bring books from home. As I read the story *No Dinosaurs in the Park*, Monika looked at the first few pictures, and then began to look around the class. As soon as I started to translate the main ideas of the text into Polish, she started to listen again, and eagerly contributed comments. The other children seemed quite comfortable with this and it was possible to integrate it smoothly into the session. The rest of the day passed by pleasantly, and Monika went home with a smile on her face. On her first day in a Canadian school she had been able to demonstrate the range of her skills, and had been an active participant in her class.

Ewa's Journal, Grade Two, April 11,1991:

> It was my last visit to the school today. I took some books to read to the whole of the grade two class, rather than just to the Polish ESL children. I was not at all sure how this would work out. I was afraid that the Polish children might not feel able to participate in the mixed-group setting. In the event, I was thrilled by their response. They carried on in the way that we had established in the ESL class. They commented, asked questions, made predictions, and inferences in both

Polish and English. The children who do not speak Polish were interested in   hearing my translations of their friends' contributions. Some of the more advanced Polish students also volunteered to translate. There was no difference in the quantity or quality of participation between ESL children and the English-speakers. The Polish children were able to take part in the class on an equal footing with the English-speaking students.

In these two sessions we witnessed the empowering potential of ESL students' first language. At the beginning of the project, we had been observing children who were unable to speak English, a characteristic which set them apart and at a disadvantage in relation to their English-speaking peers.   But this difference became far less significant once the ESL students' first language was introduced as a legitimate resource in the classroom.   We were now seeing children who, like their classmates, were able to use their own experiences, ideas and feelings as a basis for comprehension and learning and, in the process, they were also becoming bilingual.

The ESL students seemed to welcome this change in status. They certainly had no desire to remain as silent observers if they could be vocal participants in their lessons. From a teacher's perspective, introduction of the ESL students' L1 encouraged a change in focus. Attention could now be given to these students' overall intellectual and linguistic development as well as to their acquisition of a second language. The bilingual assistant, accepting both L1 and L2 responses, ensured that students demonstrated and practised all of their skills in thinking and communicating, including strategies unique to bilingual learners.

Although we made our observations in the specific context of shared reading, we believe that the use of ESL students' L1 could be equally valid, if not more so, in other areas of the curriculum. For example, in Math and Science, the formation of new concepts could be facilitated by allowing children to make sense of them through their L1, before trying to express them in English.

We do not underestimate the practical difficulties of providing the kind of language support which we advocate for ESL students.   However, even a monolingual class teacher without a bilingual assistant can find ways of incorporating ESL students' L1 into some learning activities. The students can be paired up or grouped, and encouraged to work through problems and share ideas in their L1, before trying to do so in English. More advanced ESL learners can be assigned to work with beginners in their L1. Heritage language teachers are an undervalued resource in the schools. Working together with classroom teachers, they could provide L1 input through integrated units, rather than isolating the teaching of L1 from the rest of the curriculum. The crucial step is for educators to acknowledge ESL students' need and right to use their L1 for academic learning. When this idea becomes accepted, then the appropriate means of implementing bilingual support will be investigated by boards of education and schools.

We close this report with some personal reflections:

Ania

Collaborating with Ewa on this research project has provided me with support for my ideas, as well as a new perspective on the subject of L1 use with ESL students. As a classroom teacher, I felt at times isolated from other like-minded educators, and saw that my incorporation of L1 was viewed with scepticism by some of my colleagues. As the project evolved, Ewa and I shared not only our experiences, but also our understanding of research and theory. As we challenged each others' ideas and interpretations, I began to consolidate the rationale for my practice. I also had the chance to stand back and analyze in a systematic manner the strategies I was using, and decide which were the most effective for my students.

Ewa

I have returned to my work as a consultant to ESL teachers with new confidence. My 'professional judgement' is no longer a nebulous concept. It can rest on the firm foundation of observations and data gathered during my own work with students, linked to an understanding of theory, gained through reading and discussion. Action research has given me the kind of power that I want to return to ESL students — the power to use my own experience and knowledge and to have them recognised as a valid basis for making meaning.

7

Action Research: The Story of a Partnership

Connie Mayer

THE SPARK

"I just need a little spark to get me thinking in new directions."

A wise teacher and friend of mine wrote these words in her journal as she reflected on her own teaching. Now they come to my mind as I set out to write the story of the partnership that was to form between myself and the teacher who had penned this line.

The spark that ignited my own thinking occurred one day when I arrived home from school and found this note beside the telephone.

I located the author — my six-year-old son — and asked for clarification. He promptly read the note and explained that he had been writing at school for a long time. I was fascinated! A six-year-old child writing with such assurance was something new to me. How had he developed the confidence to attempt spelling all those words? Certainly the deaf students in my school were not writing in this way. What had his teacher been doing?

As a teacher of deaf children, my training had been centred in the area of special education. There had been virtually no exposure to current theories and research in the area of language development. The work of Graves, Calkins, Giacobbe and Goodman was almost totally foreign to me. I suppose the assumption underlying my teacher training was that deaf children were so different and so language delayed, a unique and specialized way to teach them was required. The strategies used in regular classrooms were not deemed to apply. Instead, the use of structured and programmed materials and a very linear curriculum was advocated.

As I began to teach my own class, I instinctively felt there was something wrong with this approach. I was especially unhappy with the writing (or lack of it!) going on in my classroom.

This concern was not unique to my situation. The difficulties deaf students have with writing are well documented. 'The evidence suggests that the problems deaf children face in mastering written English are more formidable than those they face in developing reading skills. A deaf person can resort to compensatory strategies to understand a message when grammar and vocabulary skills are limited. It is much more difficult to express oneself clearly in writing in the face of such limitations' (Moores, 1987, p.281).

Quigley and Paul (1990) point out that most deaf students have not developed an internal representation of English and cannot even express their thoughts in English in a primary mode such as speech or signing. It is therefore highly unlikely that they will be able to express themselves adequately in writing.

Given my experience with the deaf children, I began to wonder how it was that my six year old son was already able to use writing to communicate effectively. Did it have something to do with what his classroom teacher was doing at school? Were deaf students' writing difficulties in part stemming from the approach used in the classroom?

Wilbur (1987) blames a flawed instructional system for certain chronic errors in the writing of deaf students, asserting that the prevalence of grammar drills in educating the deaf has led to a set of non-standard, but well-learned, grammatical generalizations that are applied with a minimal draw on attention. He argues that deaf students who develop written language competence do so in spite of the methodology used and not because of it. Were the deaf students in my class failing to develop an ability to use written language because of something I was or was not doing? I wanted to find out.

The very next day I met with my son's teacher, Evie. I told her the story about the note and tried to explain some of my dissatisfaction with current programming for the deaf. To my delight and surprise she understood everything I was saying. She told me about her own growth as a teacher and her "discovery" of invented spelling. She empathized with my frustration. She shared my enthusiasm. I didn't know it at the time, but this would be only the first of many conversations we would have on the topic of children and their writing.

Forming a Partnership

For about six months it seemed that all we did was talk about writing and how to help our students become confident writers. Our conversations most often took place over lunch. We chatted very informally and swapped 'teacher stories' about the children we were working with and the different things we were trying in the classroom. I can remember how much I laughed when she told me stories about her first years of teaching in a small town school and about how shocked she was when she moved from there to teaching in an inner-city school in Toronto.

She showed me the published books from her classroom writing program and she shared some of her professional reference materials with me. She encouraged me to read Lucy Calkins' book *The Art of Teaching Writing* (Calkins, 1986). I, in turn, familiarized her with the curriculum used in our language arts program and showed her examples of writing that my students had done.

We began to swap articles and clippings regularly. I can recall going to the office one day just before lunch and finding a Peanuts cartoon in my mailbox. It showed Sally and Charlie Brown treating revising as being done only to satisfy the teacher. This jibe not only provided me with a much appreciated chuckle, it also sparked our lunch-hour conversation on the difficulties of pupil-teacher conferencing.

During this time Evie also shared with me a journal she had kept while taking her first 'whole language' course. This was my first experience with the notion of keeping a journal to record observations and feelings about one's own teaching. I had only been schooled in the ways of daybooks and lesson plans.

Several entries from her journal struck a special chord with me. They made me realize that the challenges and frustrations I faced in developing written language with deaf children, although unique, were not so far removed from those facing all teachers. On trying a new writing activity that 'didn't work,' she wrote, "I suppose no harm was done but I felt somewhat disorganized and pressured — applied only by E. Moskos and no else to blame — a fault I find throughout the year. I always have the feeling I should be doing more."

After attempting some pupil-teacher conferencing, she made these comments, "I need to give them time to talk — something I think we often foul up. Sometimes the quieter ones need that opportunity to express themselves and we rush them rather than make them comfortable."

I also gained a vivid picture of the growth Evie herself had experienced as she changed directions in her own thinking and teaching. Early in her journal she wrote, "Must get to the library and read the stuff on invented spelling by Glenda Bissex. I do want to know more about it and would like to try it. I am also wondering if the 'Big Books' program is something that I could do as part of the integrated class." It was reassuring to me to read that at one time Evie was as unfamiliar with these ideas and terms as I was now.

Near the end of her journal, Evie reflects, "Assuming the power to change is always the scary thing. Some of the things that have been discussed and suggested in this course, I've done, thank goodness — somehow, just out of instinct, because it felt right. The more I see of younger children, the more I feel we teach almost nothing but we're there to guide and expand — particularly when it comes to reading and writing. This whole process of growing — walking and talking (or talking and walking?) and reading and writing (or is it writing and reading?) — makes me wonder what we really know for sure!"

Reading this journal entry helped give me the confidence and assurance not only to rethink my teaching practice but to begin to make changes as well. It was comforting to think that a teacher could trust her instincts when it came time to make changes in the classroom. I began to believe I should trust my own instincts about changing the way I 'taught' writing to deaf students. My instincts also told me one other thing for sure. I wanted to work more closely with Evie.

Six months of dialogue had led Evie and me to believe we shared a common vision of what a reading-writing classroom should look like. We decided that we wanted to put some of our 'talk' into practice. Our main goal was to provide, for both hearing and deaf students, a fully integrated, process approach to writing. We believed that a fragmented approach to the teaching of writing inhibited the purpose of language, 'the communication of meaning.' (Goodman, 1988, p.8). We wanted our students to come to see writing as a powerful tool for communication.

We also believed that writing could empower our students. It would help them develop the ability to see and make choices and to exercise some control over their own lives. It would inform their own thinking.

We also hoped that by working together in a meaningful enterprise, our deaf and hearing students would come to a better understanding of each other and begin to recognize and accept their similarities as well as their differences.

These shared goals provided the foundation for our partnership and we became committed to the idea of working together. After six months of talk, we were ready for action. As Eleanor Duckworth (1987) would say, "We had our wonderful idea!"

Our Action

At that time Evie was teaching a grade 1-2 class in an inner-city Toronto public school. I was working as a resource leader at a school for the deaf. Because our schools were housed in the same building, it made the logistics of planning our integrated program easier. With the support of our respective principals, we began almost immediately.

Our plan was to integrate four to five deaf students into Evie's existing process writing program on a daily basis. The two of us would team teach the class. I would serve as interpreter for the deaf students who relied almost exclusively on sign language for communication. Evie took the lead in actually running the writing program.

The program for our integrated class was patterned after one described by Mary Ellen Giacobbe in a workshop Evie had attended. The class began with a time we called the 'writing workshop.' Individual students would be working at various stages of the writing process. Some were writing first drafts, some were doing revisions and others were illustrating published pieces. The atmosphere was informal, with students working at their desks, on the carpet or at large tables. Evie and I would circulate around the room monitoring progress by asking questions such as "What are you working on today?" and "How's it going?"

After recess, more formal teacher-pupil conferences would occur. These conferences focused on either the content or form of the piece. Content refers to the ideas the children are trying to communicate through their writing whereas form refers to the mechanics of putting these ideas on paper. Elements such as grammar and spelling would be dealt with at a conference for form. At this same time some students, through peer conferencing, could share their writing with classmates.

Each session concluded with a class conference. One student would take the author's chair and read an unpublished piece to the class. The classroom audience would provide feedback to the author. Evie and I became part of the audience and asked questions as well. Often we found the student's questions were paralleling those we asked during teacher-pupil conferences.

Occasionally we would have a 'mini-lesson.' This was a brief teacher-directed activity addressing areas we felt were of common concern to all our students. Topics included things like eliminating repetitive words, writing good leads and choosing appropriate titles.

The first year of the program seemed to fly by and we had no hesitation about beginning a second one. As we became more comfortable with the routine of the program and with each other, we started to examine more closely the progress of our students and our own thinking as well.

Our Research

We started by carefully examining the voluminous writing folders the children had produced. As we talked and looked at samples of student's work, we were struck by the growth evidenced by both the hearing and deaf students.

We were also struck by the similarities between the two groups of writers. Evie might make a comment about a particular topic a hearing child had chosen to write about and inevitably there would be a deaf student who had chosen something similar. Common problems surfaced. If hearing children had trouble staying on topic in their stories, so did the deaf. If the deaf children had problems figuring out how to put periods at the end of sentences, so did the hearing.

In her notes from a presentation we gave, Evie phrased it this way. "For each developmental level, for each behavior, for each personality, Connie and I have been able to find a hearing and deaf counterpart. I'd say, 'Look at what Erika's doing,' and Connie would say Janice had done the same thing. It was amazing!"

These points are best illustrated by looking at actual samples of the writing that the children produced.

The pieces in Figure 1 were both written by six-year-old students. Both pieces are short, include little detail and do not develop a topic. They are untitled, unedited and use no punctuation. Spelling is at the initial and final consonant stage and dashes are used as markers for unknown words. Both students are using a simple sentence to label a picture.

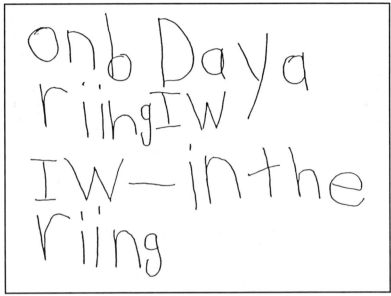

Figure 1 A / One day it was raining. I was walking in the rain.

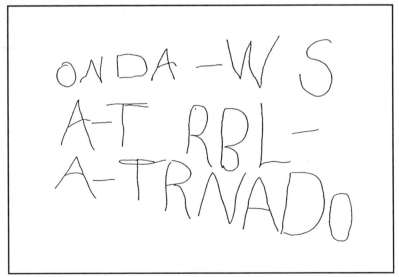

Figure 1B / One day there was a terrible tornado.

Figure 1A was written by a deaf child and Figure 1B by a hearing student.

Figure 2 shows pieces done by these same two students about one year later when they were both seven years of age. The gains made by both children are obvious. A narrative style has emerged, more details are included and characters are named. Punctuation is used and spelling is beginning to approach standard form. Both students have titled their pieces and done some editing. Both of them have relied on the text rather than the picture to carry the bulk of the meaning. Figure 2A is by the deaf student and 2B is by the hearing student.

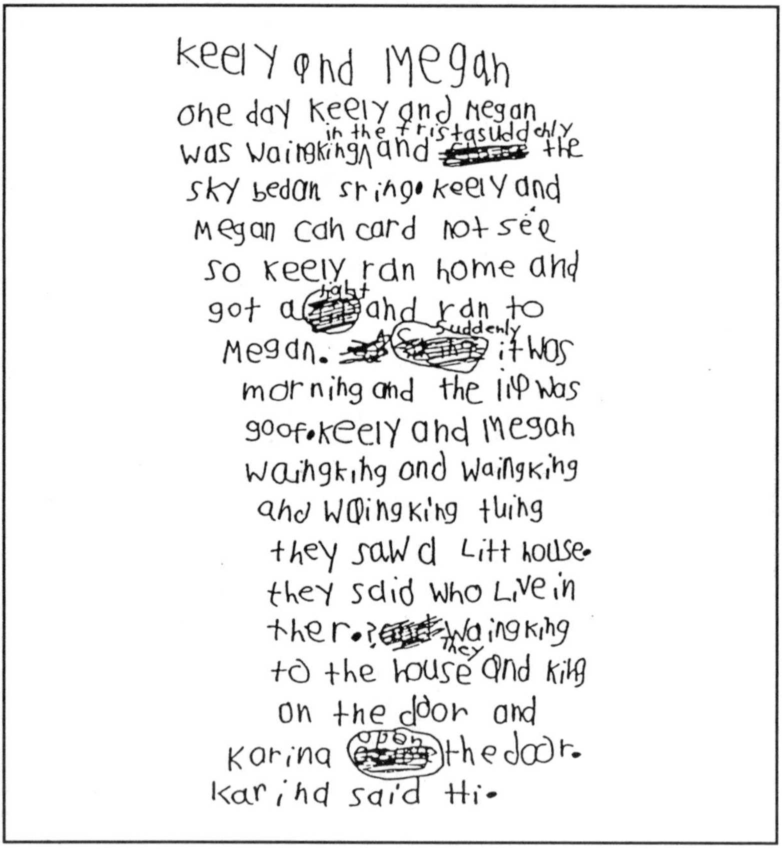

keely and Megah

ohe day keely and negan
was waingking and in the frist asuddchly the
sky bedan sring keely and
Megan cah card not see
so keely rdn home and
got a light ahd rdn to
Megan. suddenly it was
morning and the lip was
goof. keely and Megah
waingking ond waingking
ahd Waingking thing
they saw d litt house.
they sdid who live in
ther. waingking they
to the house and kilg
on the door and
Karina opeh the door.
kar ihd said Hi.

Figure 2A / Keely and Megan

One day Keely and Megan were walking in the forest and suddenly the sky became dark. Keely and Megan could not see so Keely ran home and got a light and ran to Megan. Suddenly it was morning and the light was gone. Keely and Megan walked and walked and walked until they saw a little house. They said, "Who lives in there?" They walked to the house and knocked on the door and Karina opened the door. Karina said, "Hi."

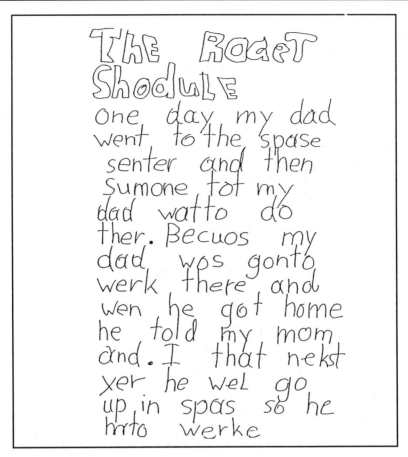

The Rocet Shodule
One day my dad went to the spase senter and then Sumone tot my dad watto do ther. Becuos my dad wos gonto werk there and wen he got home he told my mom and. I that nekst yer he wel go up in spas so he hrto werke

Figure 2B / The Rocket Schedule
One day my Dad went to the space centre and then someone told him what to do there. Because my Dad was going to work there and when he got home he told my Mom and I that next year he will go up in space so he has to work.

It was probably the similarities Evie and I noticed in the area of invented spelling that surprised us most. We had been concerned that the use of invented spelling would be especially difficult for the deaf students. How could we expect them to create spellings when they could not hear? We had assumed that sound-symbol association was necessary to 'invent' a spelling. The deaf children quickly proved us wrong. They invented not only spellings but new strategies for creating these spellings as well.

As we examined the writing folders with regard to spelling, we began to see that the developmental steps through which the deaf children moved paralleled those of the hearing children.

As our program progressed, both deaf and hearing student

writers developed 'spelling consciousness — a sensitivity to the appearance of the written word' (Hodges, 1981, p.21). They were well aware when a word was spelled correctly and when it was not. Although to a casual observer the spelling of the deaf children might look confusing, Evie and I were able, through pupil-teacher conferencing to ascertain that there was method and logic in the spelling decisions that they made.

It was gratifying for us to see the growth that all the students had made and it was a pleasant surprise to find that our anticipated misgivings about invented spelling never materialized. We were both excited about what we were seeing. However, there were still some questions to be answered.

Did adopting a process writing model effect a positive change in the attitude deaf children had towards print? Past experiences had taught me that deaf students tended to view writing as an exercise to fill the page and please the teacher. They did not see it as a meaningful form of communication. The piece in Figure 3A was written by a seven year old deaf student on his first day in our program. It is typical of the compositions done by deaf students who have only been exposed to a very structured approach to the teaching of writing. As the student was composing this piece, he wrote all the 'the's in a vertical line first, followed by the blanks and then the remaining sentence items. He did not write from right to left and it was clear that he equated writing with an exercise in a workbook. This piece is certainly not an expression of personal voice.

The writing in Figure 3B was done by the same student seven months later. This piece has a sense of purpose and has been written for a specific audience. The author is relating an incident that has personal relevance and he has come to realize that writing down such an experience is a powerful way to share it with others. Although many problems remain with regard to English syntax and form, this student has come to see writing as a meaningful way to communicate.

We had also been concerned about the social aspect of integrating deaf and hearing students. Before we began our program, we had separate sessions with the deaf and hearing children. Both groups of children expressed reservations and were wary about working together on a daily basis. They were worried about how they would communicate because the hearing children did not sign and the deaf children did not have intelligible speech.

They were afraid of each other. The hearing children said that the deaf children made 'weird' noises and it upset them. They didn't like the deaf children touching them so much. The deaf children felt that the hearing children would laugh at them and

Figure 3A

Figure 3B / Mama, Asha and I Go to the Store

I said "I want a transformer toy." I said to Mama, "I am happy. I love you." Mama said, " I love you." I said. "Yes or no?" Mama said, "OK. Yes." I said, "Oh, Oh. I love Mama." Mama said, "I love you." I ate supper and had a good sleep.

I went to school and played. Raheel said, "What is that?" I said, "It is a transformer toy." I said to Raheel, "We can share it."

call them 'stupid' because they were not as 'smart' in English.

As part of our program, Evie and I instituted a number of features that we hoped would help alleviate these concerns. I acted as interpreter for the class so the children could interact more easily. This allowed the deaf and hearing children to have peer and class conferences together. What follows is a transcription of a videotape we made during one of our class conferences. The student in the author's chair is deaf. She has just finished reading her piece (Figure 4) to the class and is now accepting questions. (K = Student Author; DS = Deaf Student; HS = Hearing Student; T = Teacher)

Figure 4 /My Bad Baby

On Sunday my baby brother was in his walker and walked in the bedroom downstairs and pulled the pretty flowers. And my Mommy said to him, "No. Don't pull the flowers." My baby brother thought the flowers were something to eat. But the baby still pulled the flowers and my Mom slapped him on the hand. And he started crying. Then he stopped crying. The End (notice how the writer uses a "star" to edit in new information.

DS: Do you have any pictures?

K: Just look. Do you see where the flowers are?

DS: Do you plan to publish this?

K: Yes. Remember I told you — on the back. I showed you. I told you that already.

DS: Did you number the pages?

K: No.

HS: How did you think of the idea?

K: Because it was a true story and a wonderful idea!

T: Does your baby brother do other bad things?

K: No. Just the one bad thing.

T: Most of the time is he a good baby?

K: Yes, most of the time.

HS: What is the baby's name?

K: Christopher. C-H-R-I-S-T-O-P-H-E-R.

HS: Will you add more to your story?

K: No, I already added to it — the part with the star.

HS: How old is your baby?

K: About eight-and-a-half-months.

HS: Why did you turn the paper over to read it?

K: Because I had a star on my page.

HS: What kind of flowers were they?

K: Artificial.

T: I'm curious about the star in your story. Why did you have a star in your story?

K: Because there wasn't enough room for adding.

T: So you used the star to add something in?

K: It means there wasn't enough room to write.

HS: Who gave the flowers to your Mom?

K: Oh, I don't know.

We incorporated a 'See, Say, Spell, and Sign' element to our class conferences. Each day the author, after sharing her or his piece, would choose two words from their text that we would write on a chart. We would then say, spell and learn the signs for these two words. This became a very popular part of the program and the hearing children began to try and sign with the deaf. The deaf children became the experts on sign language in the classroom and this made them feel 'smart.' All of the hearing children were given name signs by the deaf students.

At the end of the first year of the program, we again had separate classroom discussions with the students. The opinion was unanimous — the students enjoyed working together. One boy summed it up very well when he said. "You know what I've learned in writing time this year. I've learned that the deaf kids are just like me except they don't hear so good." When we asked the children if they wanted to work together again the following year, they all said yes.

Evie and I agreed. We wanted to keep working together too!

Reflecting Together

Evie and I continued to collect writing samples and discuss them throughout our second year of working together. Sometime during this year our principals suggested to us that we might like to conduct a workshop and talk about our program at an upcoming conference. It had never really occurred to us that were doing anything innovative. Who would want to hear the two of us at a conference?

After some discussion, we agreed to give it a try. In order to present at a conference we felt it would be necessary to put some of our thoughts and observations on paper.We also felt that writing things down would provide us with a concrete means of sharing our work with others.

But so much more happened as we began to write. Through the process of writing we were able to clarify many issues. Our ideas, thoughts, assumptions and observations became explicit when we confronted them in black and white. Writing forced us to outline clearly what we had been doing and to evaluate and assess the outcomes.

We wondered if anyone else in the field of deaf education was doing what we were doing. And we began not only to write but also to read. We scoured books and journals for any information relevant to our program. The more we read, the more we became convinced that what we were doing was genuinely innovative. Many others had written about the problems deaf students had with written language but few had chosen to tackle the problem in the way that Evie and I had. We found only few references to programs for the deaf that were using an integrated process writing approach similar to our own.

Evie and I were so nervous before we presented our first workshop. We were full of doubts. Maybe our program was nothing so special after all. Was it really worth sharing with other teachers? We rehearsed our presentation many times. We even had our 'scripts' written down on three by five inch index cards! But it was only about five minutes into our presentation before our nerves seemed to vanish and we barely glanced at our 'cue cards.' It was so easy to talk to people about something that we felt so strongly about. In addition, we had each other there for moral support.

After the workshop, over coffee and doughnuts, Evie and I talked about how exciting it was to share our ideas with others. We felt energized by the positive response of the audience. We were eager to talk with more teachers about our ideas.

During the third year of our partnership, we presented at several more conferences and other teachers at both of our schools began to express an interest in adopting some of our ideas. What a pat on the back that was! It made us feel like the 'experts' on this particular topic in the school.   It also made us realize how empowered students must feel when they take ownership of an idea and become classroom experts on that topic.

In our fourth year together, Evie and I signed up for an ESL short course offered by our school board. Guest speakers were a featured part of this course. One of them happened to be Gordon Wells. During his presentation he introduced us to the concept of 'action research.' Neither Evie nor I had ever heard this term before but it seemed to describe very well the work we had been doing.

Our discussions took a new direction. We began to frame thoughts about our program under the umbrella of action research. We agreed that we needed to do more documenting in print and on videotape to provide more data for our research. As well as tracking the progress of our students, we wondered about keeping personal journals that would reflect our own thinking as we continued working in our program.

The more we discussed and reflected, the more convinced we became that our idea was truly 'wonderful.' Neither of us had ever thought before that we would be capable of doing research or that we would actually find it exciting!

In June of this fourth year together, we applied to present at an International Reading Association conference in Sweden in July of the following year. We rewrote our conference proposal many times before we mailed it away. We believed our chances of being accepted were remote but were hoping for the best. Imagine our excitement when we received a letter of acceptance when we returned to school that fall. We were doubly pleased because our board was willing to provide us with financial support to attend this conference. A letter of support from my superintendent touched both of us. The following is an excerpt from this letter.

> I am delighted for both of you in that you have worked long and hard at showing what wonderful growth children are capable of in an atmosphere that values each contribution, builds on strengths, and is coupled with sound teaching strategies. Hats off to both of you and best luck in your future endeavors.

While in the midst of all these plans, tragedy struck. The news made all other considerations fade into unimportance. During the summer Evie had received news that she was ill — very ill. That fall she was too sick to come back to school on a regular basis, although she still managed to come to our integrated class three times a week. That spoke volumes to me as to how much she valued and cared about this program and our work together. Evie worked with the supply teacher (who was unfamiliar with process writing) to help her become an effective part of our team.

We carried on as best we could. Evie, ever positive and forward-looking, made attending the conference in Sweden a goal for herself. She so much wanted to go. However, this was not to be. In March of that school year Evie died.

Her death was a huge personal loss. She was a dear and valued friend and I missed her deeply. But up until that moment, I don't think I realized how much I depended on her. It was not only her presence in the classroom but the countless hours of conversation that I missed. Although there was another teacher in the classroom eager to work with me, somehow it just wasn't the same.

What was the point in continuing? What should I do now? I decided to do what Evie and I had done so often together. I took some time to think.

Reflecting Alone

Judith Newman (1987) contends that we are often forced to see a situation with new eyes when things haven't gone as we thought they should. These unsettling critical incidents spark reflections. The realization that the support, guidance and friendship of my colleague were forever lost to me was my critical moment.

During four and a half years of partnership, Evie and I had thought a lot about our program. We had constantly observed, evaluated, reflected and modified. It occurred to me that most of our thinking had revolved around our students, their writing and our interactions with them. The time had come for me to focus my attention on our partnership. What had I learned as a teacher and how had I learned it? What role had Evie played in my learning?

There was no question in my mind that I had learned a great deal. I began by knowing almost nothing about process writing and the philosophies of the whole language advocates. I had done little reading in the area and was not even sure exactly what to read anyway. After four years I considered myself reasonably knowledgeable in the field. I had given workshops and other teachers were coming to me for advice. Although I had never been consciously aware of being taught, I had learned much. I began to reflect on how this growth had come about.

Because Evie and I had constantly documented our work in papers, in our journals and on videotape, I was able to critically examine what we had done. It seemed to fit the description of what I had learned to call 'action research.' Carr and Kemis state that there are :

> three conditions individually necessary and jointly sufficient for action research to be said to exist. First, a project takes as its subject-matter a social practice, regarding it as a form of strategic action susceptible of improvement; secondly, the project proceeds through a spiral of cycles of planning, acting, observing,and reflecting, with each of these activities being systematically and self-critically implemented and interrelated; and thirdly, the project involves those responsible for the practice in each of the moments of the activity, widening participation in the project gradually to include others affected by the practice, and maintaining collaborative control of the process. (1986, p. 165-166).

Evie and I had looked at the writing of deaf students and decided this was an area in need of improvement. After devising a plan of action, we had continued to observe, replan, act and reflect. The two of us controlled the inquiry which eventually involved other educators with similar interests. Unbeknown to us, what we had been doing was action research.

After experiencing this process, I concur with Nancie Atwell (1992) when she says: 'the most thoughtful practitioner is the teacher who acts as a researcher.' I would go further and say teacher-researchers ultimately change not only their thoughts but their actions as well. Goswami and Stillman (1987) observed that teachers involved in research are transformed. They become theorists, articulating their intentions, testing their assumptions, and finding connections with practice. Certainly our action research (although undertaken unknowingly) was a key factor in my growth as a teacher.

However I was still puzzled. We had conducted an inquiry and felt very positive about it. Why did I now feel confused when confronted with the prospect of carrying on the program with a new partner? If I was to work successfully with a new teacher, it was necessary for me to examine what elements had made our action research work.

I believe a necessary component for any collaborative action research is a joint understanding of the concern to be addressed. From the start, Evie and I shared the belief that writing is a powerful tool for communication. We saw it as a process involving thinking, feeling, reading, and writing. When I compare notes from our first attempts to write down our beliefs with later ones, I am struck by the change in tone. In our final workshop notes Evie wrote, "We strongly believe writing empowers our students — hearing and deaf. Perhaps this is the most important life skill we can help our children develop — the ability to see and make choices and to exercise some control over their own lives." Our work together had not altered our initial assumptions but had made them clearer, stronger and more explicit.

Besides this shared understanding and commitment, we also set our own agenda and retained control over our program. This sense of autonomy gave us a feeling of empowerment. As our confidence grew, we became more comfortable about sharing our ideas with others. We had ownership of the good ideas as well as the mistakes in our program. Just as Calkins (1986) talks about student experts in the classroom, we had become the school experts about our program. The feeling of satisfaction created is just as strong for the adult as for the child.

It is also important to mention here that, throughout our inquiry, we had the support of our administration and were given the resources necessary to conduct our program. We were not given deadlines or schedules to meet and this allowed us to carry out our action research over time as part of an ongoing process. Both Jaggar (in *Teachers and Research,* 1989) and Tharp and Gallimore (1988) regard these as necessary to the organization of a school if an atmosphere conducive to teacher research is to be created.

All of the issues I have discussed in the preceding paragraphs were important to our action research, but I have not yet touched on the aspect of our work that was most important to me — our partnership. Of all the areas I had considered, this one seemed to be the most critical. I wanted to understand how I had grown so much as a teacher through my association with Evie. To be better able to work in a new situation, I needed to reflect on the past.

When I consider my collaboration with Evie, one feature stands out above the rest — our conversations. Evie herself noted, "We have come to our beliefs through observation, thinking and countless discussions over cups of cafe au lait." I have been trying to analyze the tone of these conversations. What was it about this talk that moved it beyond the realm of spontaneous chat?

Our partnership was forged 'through dialogue, through the questioning and sharing of ideas and knowledge that happen in conversation' (Tharp and Gallimore, 1988, p.23). As well as being my partner, Evie had been my teacher during our discussions. I don't know if she was conscious of doing so, but she was guiding me in my learning about the writing process. Perhaps our discussions were what Tharp and Gallimore call 'instructional conversations.' They explain that 'instructional conversation is pointed toward a learning objective by the teacher's intention; and even the most sophisticated learners may lose consciousness of the guiding goal as they become absorbed in joint activity with the mentor' (p.25).

I feel the notion of instructional conversation partially explains the tone of the dialogue Evie and I had. However, in some ways it strikes me as being somewhat simplistic. Our conversations had had a greater feeling of give and take. Under the umbrella of our shared beliefs about writing, we each had much to offer during our talks. Depending on the topic, we alternated the roles of teacher and learner. In an atmosphere of mutual respect we learned from each other.

The term 'instructional conversation,' as defined by Tharp and Gallimore, seems to suggest a leader-follower relationship during the conversation. I find it somewhat troublesome to think that only one participant is directing the talk. I would agree this type of conversation frequently occurs in the classroom and is necessary, but I would also argue that it may not always be the most productive. When I consider my talks with Evie, I see them in terms of two people making sense together. Initially, our knowledge was unequally distributed and it was up to the less knowledgeable partner (usually me!) to extend and modify her knowledge in order to come to a shared understanding. Chang and Wells (1988) make this point and continue by saying it is not so much the relative familiarity of the information involved but the amount of constructive mental effort put into evaluating and utilizing existing knowledge that allows one to make sense of the other participant's contribution to the dialogue and to increase one's own knowledge. I feel this better describes the tone of the early conversations that Evie and I had.

As we created new knowledge together, our dialogue became even more comfortable and ideas flowed freely. Tharp and Gallimore state 'all intellectual growth relies heavily on conversation as a form of assisted performance in the zone of proximal development' (op cit p.25). Certainly my growth as a teacher in my zone of proximal development came about largely because of my conversations with Evie.

Of the many thoughts I have had about my years of partnership with Evie, the one that remains foremost in my mind is the importance of 'talk.' It was the crucial element from start to finish. It helped us come to a joint understanding about our work in the classroom. It fostered our mutual trust and respect for each other as teachers. And finally it formed the foundation for a lasting friendship.

When I continue our action research with a new partner, I hope to be able to use this powerful tool to recreate the warm, interpersonal and collaborative atmosphere that Evie and I shared in our teaching and learning.

This would be a most fitting tribute to my teacher, partner and friend.

8

Who Teaches the Teachers?:
Community, Collaboration and Conversation in the Learning Process

Maria Kowal

Starting Over

The first time a teacher teaches a new grade or a new course can be a time of excitement, challenge and learning. But it can also be a time of anxiety. You leave behind the security of familiar materials and confidence gained through foreseeable teacher-student encounters for the challenge of the new. You may have strong beliefs and principles to guide your personal approach to teaching and learning, but putting them into practice is like a singer performing a new song in front of an audience far from home: the activity is familiar, but the content is new and the reception unknown. The experienced teacher becomes the first-year teacher all over again.

Such were my feelings when I was seconded to the Faculty of Education, with teaching responsibilities in the primary/junior math program. I was successful in my own teaching, but I was uncertain of how to approach the task of helping novices — pre-service teacher education students on their way to becoming competent teachers — when I too felt like a novice.

I saw many of my own beliefs and practices about teaching and learning reiterated in the Faculty of Education's program statement for this option, but it was I who was responsible for creating the conditions for learning within my own teaching situation. What follows is an account of an experienced, yet 'novice' teacher, learning with, from, and in a similar way to, the students she was teaching. It is an account of the benefits of inquiry-oriented approaches to thinking about the art of teaching and of the unanticipated outcomes, which can be more striking than the original aims of the inquiry. It is an account of an action research project conducted by a first-year teacher educator in the pre-service classroom. I believe it illustrates how action research can be an important tool to "enable teachers to acquire the competencies and resources to be systematic and intentional learners in and about (our) own professional situations and the confidence and disposition to use them" (Wells, 1992, p. 170).

My experiences as an action researcher, and the data I collected throughout the year, raised many interesting issues. This chapter focuses on three issues which I believe contributed to the richness of our learning environment. The first is the various levels of teaching and learning inherent in the situation: the children, the pre-service teachers, myself — their instructor, and my peers — graduate students of education, who were also taking the action research course in which I was enroled. These levels of learning not only contained many parallel experiences for the 'teachers' and the 'learners'; they also proved to be mutually enriching.

The second issue is the importance of reflection and action research as means of promoting intentional learning in the attempt to become a more effective practitioner. The third, which is central to both of the previously mentioned issues, is the importance of community, collaboration and conversation in all learning experiences. These issues are discussed in the context of one particular part of the pre-service teachers' math program. It involved setting up opportunities for the student teachers to work with small groups of children on mathematical activities and to observe each other in the process.

New Approaches to Teacher Education

The program in which I was involved was a collaborative teacher education venture between a Board of Education and the Faculty of Education in a local university. Interaction was a key component of its structure and of its teaching philosophy (Sydor and Hunt, 1991). The program itself was based in an elementary school. Student teachers spent two days a week in classrooms observing and helping the classroom teacher, in order to gain familiarity and experience in working with children before they went on to complete their practice teaching. For two days a week, students were in faculty classes, which were taught by university instructors, seconded teachers such as myself, and other school board members with a particular area of expertise. One day a week, students' classes were held at the university.

Part of the richness of the program was that it brought together teachers, student teachers and faculty of education staff, all learning about teaching and all interacting to varying degrees with school children (Sydor and Hunt, 1991). Three strategies were identified as being essential to the program: reflective conversation, inquiry, and theory grounded in practice.

In my teaching I was looking for a way of encouraging the students to reflect upon their performance as prospective elementary school math teachers and of making use of the increased exposure to working with children that was provided by their teacher education program. These classes were, after all, being held in an elementary school and I was a practising teacher. What advantages could the setting yield for the student teachers' learning?

Action research was one vehicle used within the program to promote reflection and inquiry. As part of my own professional graduate studies, I decided to adopt this approach as a means of gaining a better understanding of the program's objectives and of reflecting on my teaching, in an attempt to realise some of my own goals and objectives for the course.

Developing a Framework

Classroom interaction became an important feature of my action research project. Many educators today would agree that knowledge is not something that can be passed on from the teacher to her students in a steady stream of information, but that knowledge is constructed and reconstructed systematically by individuals who are continually assimilating new information and revising previously acquired information in the light of it. There is an important social dimension to this process. As Vygotsky (1978) has shown, an individual's learning takes place largely through interaction with other people. Wells, Chang and Maher (1990) see conversation as a key factor in the learning process, as it provides "a forum in which individuals calibrate their representations of events and states of affairs against those of other people, and realign and extend their existing mental modes to assimilate or accommodate to new or alternative information" (p.97).

A metaphor central to my regular classroom teaching was that of a community of learners, similar to Carl Bereiter's 'community of scholars.' He suggests that an important instructional method for promoting learning as a constructive process in the classroom is to create a community of scholars, "turning the classroom into a social setting for mutual support of knowledge construction, a setting that could eventually be internalized by the individual students" (Bereiter, 1985, p.221).

This is also an important consideration in the professional education of adults, for they bring with them to the classroom their own life experience. In the case of student teachers, many have already had considerable relevant experience as teacher aides or assistants and as parents, and possess important knowledge that can contribute to others' professional development. It is important that this be recognized by those responsible for teacher education (Hollis and Houston, 1990; Sydor and Hunt, 1991).

Many teachers, myself included, see ourselves as facilitators of our students' learning, who work within their "zones of proximal development" (Vygotsky, 1978, p. 86) to help them become independent learners. With this as a guiding principle, our task is a complex one, for it demands that we adopt various roles appropriate to different learning situations. At any time we may be required to adopt the role of listener, motivator, expert, comedian or any one of the countless others which make up the teacher's repertoire. With experience, we increase and refine our repertoire and are better able to respond to the needs and interests of our students. Similarly, the pre-service education of teachers can and should provide ample opportunity for student teachers to work with and observe children learning, so that the student teachers can experience for themselves what it means to be a facilitator of a child's learning. They also need to be provided with an opportunity to reflect on their performance in this role.

Reflecting on our practice is seen by many as an important means of bringing about improvements in our teaching. Schulman (1987) defines reflection as:

> What a teacher does when he or she looks back at the teaching and learning that has occurred, and reconstructs, then reenacts, and/or recaptures the events, the emotions, and the accomplishments.... Reflection is not merely a disposition ... or a set of strategies, but also the use of particular kinds of analytic knowledge brought to bear on one's work. (1987, p.19).

Good teachers are able to reflect-in-action (Schön, 1988), as they respond to the needs of the situation. However, for reflection to transform practice, it needs to be conducted from a perspective of reconstructing experience. Such reflection may require us to analyze ourselves as practitioners, to uncover some of our underlying assumptions about teaching, and to reconsider our practice in the light of these assumptions (Grimmett, Erikson, MacKinnon, Riecken, 1990). In this process, the prospective, reflective practitioner can be helped by the educational setting and by having appropriate tools and vehicles with which to work (Zeichner and Liston, 1987).

I was looking for a framework which would allow the student teachers and myself to draw on our practical knowledge, whilst simultaneously causing us to reflect, through discussion, on our teaching performance as we learned about improving our practice. As I struggled to articulate this objective to my classmates in the action research course, I was introduced to the writing of Eleanor Duckworth and Tom Brissenden. Reading the work of these writers enabled me to develop a project for part of the math program which had the potential to help me achieve my objective.

Eleanor Duckworth's (1987) collection of essays deals directly with issues concerning teacher education, and with children and teachers learning from one another. Among the topics she discusses are the practical implications of implementing Piaget's theories of learning, how to discuss controversial issues in the classroom, and how she encourages teachers to become more reflective about the processes involved in teaching and learning. At one point, she describes a four-stage model for teacher education which I was able to adapt for use in the program's math course. In her model, teachers learn something new, watch her teach it, teach it themselves in a non-threatening situation, and then go into schools and teach it themselves.

This apprenticeship model interested me because our students' own program involved them in learning by watching experienced teachers at work, and its school-based site made it relatively easy for us to invite children into some of our math sessions. There was also the possibility that some of the student teachers would take what they had taught in an experimental situation and try it out in their math class in subsequent practice teaching sessions.

Tom Brissenden's work (1988) pays close attention to the role of talk in children's understanding of mathematics. He describes the math teacher's role in facilitating her students' learning in four stages. First, she plans effective mathematical situations, which use well-planned materials to generate and support mathematical activities by groups of learners, including talk and discussion (1988, p. 34). Then, when the children have been introduced to the activities, she becomes an acute observer and a good listener and uses this information to intervene in ways that keep the children thinking, either in a mathematical role, for example asking challenging questions or injecting mathematical language, or in a procedural role, for example finding out about students' progress, drawing out students' ideas, encouraging and supporting. She then systematically organizes group work to be completed both with and without the teacher present.

Preparing for the Learning Experiment

At an appropriate stage in their course work, just after the completion of the first of three practice teaching sessions, I introduced the student teachers to problem-solving activities which met Brissenden's criteria for creating effective mathematical situations. This was to prepare the student teachers for a future session where they would be required to assume the role of teacher as described by Brissenden. In a controlled setting, working with small groups of children, the student teachers would be required to introduce a math activity to the children and to act as a facilitator of the children's learning, whilst being observed by a peer who would be taking notes on the activity.

The student teachers worked cooperatively in small groups for two sessions to complete the activities, and we also discussed, in small and large groups, the implementation of such activities. Throughout these sessions, I was careful to model the type of teaching I would be asking the students to adopt in their next class. We discussed together some of the techniques used, and this brought out into the open many of the features contained in Brissenden's model, for instance, how to ask questions that would help the children to focus on the mathematical principles underlying the activity and how to encourage children to use mathematical terminology in talking about the activity. Our discussions also required the students to draw on information from their previous classes and on observations from their classroom placements.

Next, using the suggestion from Duckworth that teachers should be able to try out new ideas in low-risk situations, we arranged for children from the school to visit one of our classes and to participate in some of our math activities. In preparation for this, the student teachers worked in groups of two or three to select two different activities that they could try out with the children in our 'laboratory classroom.' The student teachers were responsible for selecting the activities, which could be from any source but should aim to meet the criteria of creating an 'effective math situation.' During the class, one student would work with the children and the other would take notes on the type of questions, open or closed, asked by the student teacher, and note the quality of talk that was produced by the children.

Working together, we drew up a list of what to look for in the children's responses. This included the types of questions the children were prompted to ask, the degree of cooperation the activities gave rise to, and any hypothesizing that the children engaged in. The student teachers would assume the role of teacher as facilitator of the children's learning. Upon completion of the activities, students were asked to discuss their notes with each other, in particular the way in which they thought the activities had gone. They would concentrate on two areas: How effective were your activities? How well did you fulfil the role of the teacher as facilitator? Two of the groups, chosen at random, were video-taped, with the intention that their work would be discussed by the whole class at a later date.

I was hoping that the student teachers would be encouraged to listen to themselves as they talked with the children and that this would lead them to reflect on the ways they interacted with them. Were they encouraging the children to be curious about the math activities, to take risks, to listen to their peers, and to learn from them as well as contributing to the discussion? I also wanted to see how well the student teachers had understood the notions of effective mathematical situations and of the teacher as facilitator.

An important point that should be raised here is that the learning experiment was a deliberate attempt to encourage the students to take the knowledge gained from their course work and from their apprenticeship in regular classrooms and to create the conditions that would allow them to apply this knowledge to a practical situation in which they were given ownership over the choice and implementation of the activities. Unless learners are given such opportunities, "there is a danger that the theory of learning as 'assisted performance' will be used to further bolster the traditional practices of transmission-based instruction, rather than providing the basis for a radical and empowering alternative" (Wells, 1992, pp.31-32).

Until this point in their course work, I had been assisting the student teachers in their learning and had, to a large extent, been in control of the course work. At various stages, groups of students had agreed to be audio-taped as they were discussing and completing some of the problem-solving activities. In listening to the tapes, I was able to listen to myself in my interactions with the students and to reflect on *my* performance as a teacher-facilitator. I was also able to increase my understanding of what the student teachers were learning from these sessions and what direction to take in planning for subsequent sessions. I was learning from their learning.

As the students began to introduce themselves to the children with whom they would be working, I was excited to see which activities they had selected and how they would interact with their students. From this point on, the direction of my action research project would be determined by the student teachers. As Judith Newman says, "Becoming a learner-directed teacher involves being receptive to the unexpected ... offering students an invitation to explore in some specific direction and then following closely behind" (1989, p.9).

At the end of the session, we discussed what the students had noticed about the interactions. I was looking for general feedback regarding the usefulness of the activity and what had gone on during the session. The following comments are taken from the subsequent whole group discussion.

1 Maria: How about the talk that went on between the students?

Was there any dialogue that went on between them? And when they did, did they talk to each other?

Was there anything you noticed from it? A reason for it?

2 Diane: I remember the students we had, even though they were playing against each other, they would still help each other out. They — like, sometimes the object was to win, but they still helped each other out. So there wasn't really a lot of competition there. They kept dropping hints and it was quite interesting to see that.

3 Eric: We were prompting them a little bit too in terms of trying to get the focus off who's going to win and put it on more to the strategy to win.

We were doing a game like the toothpick game (a game we had studied in class) but with a calculator... adding ones and twos to come up with the number seven.

And once we got them to focus more toward what they were doing as a group it was really good.

They were helping each other out and trying things.

4 Diane: We had two girls who — the one was very verbal and the other one was quite quiet. And the one would take over for the other one and help her all the time. It was difficult because... um... like... we were doing our activi-

ties, we were trying to get the balance and you
know sure help her out but let her have a
chance to try for herself. And it was interesting to see how the one sort of took over for her.

5 Eric: We had that same thing in our group.
There were three and one girl was definitely
the strongest and caught on to the concept.
And at one point she was trying to show the
other girl — this is in tangrams — how to do
it.
And the slower girl said: "Don't tell me I don't
wanna know I wanna do this myself." It was
really neat.

6 Fatima: Yeah, they were very persistent our bunch.
They did not give up. They did NOT ask us
"How do you do this?" or "Tell me the answer."
They wanted to work it out for themselves.

As I listened to their comments, I was pleased at the enthusiasm
with which the students talked about the session. It had obviously
been a worthwhile experience for them. They were being encouraged to look at how children collaborate with one another in a
group situation, to see advantages and possible disadvantages of
different grouping decisions. On the other hand, I was a little
disconcerted by what I thought at the time to be the rather
general nature of their observations. In retrospect, however, I realised that this was the first time that the students had engaged
in this type of activity and it was still quite early in the year. I also
discovered from subsequent remarks that many of the students
had had little time to observe children working in small groups
during their classroom observations. I shared their enthusiasm
and maintained the role of listener. It was in a later session when
we had the opportunity of viewing some of the video footage that
there was an opportunity to adopt a more critical-analytical
approach to our discussion.

    Further feedback from this discussion raised two interesting
points for me as the instructor. Even though the students were
able to observe and help out in classrooms two days a week as part
of their program, many appreciated the opportunity to work in a
small group, away from the eyes of their associate teacher. This
was so, even though the classroom observation period was not
evaluated by the associate teacher. Secondly, the student teachers did appreciate being given certain things to look out for in
their observations, no matter how strictly they did or did not
record occurrences of them in their notes. The students' com-

ments suggested that the list we had made gave them an idea of things they could be self-monitoring for in their own teaching in the future. From the student teachers' point of view, this had been an important learning opportunity and one which many felt it would be appropriate to repeat in subsequent years.

"So How Are You Finding the Activities?"

During the session, I tried to visit as many of the groups as possible to get an idea of how the activities were progressing. I came to one of the groups being video-taped just as the children had left for recess. The activity the students had chosen was called The Paper Cup Game. It was designed to provide practice in addition-facts for students in the primary grades. It had been set up in the following way. Each player had their own board and set of dice. The brightly colored board had twelve cups, numbered from one to twelve. Each child had twelve kidney beans, which she was to use to fill the cups. A cup was full once a bean had been placed in it. Students took turns at rolling the dice and, on each turn, were allowed to place a kidney bean in either the cup of the number rolled or in any two empty cups whose numbers, when added together, totalled the number rolled. The object of the game was to be the first player with a bean in every cup.

Paper Cup Game

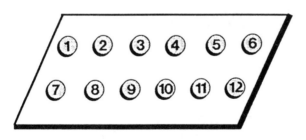

Player rolls

Possible moves:

1 bean in (10)

1 bean in (9) and 1 in (1)

1 bean in (8) and 1 in (2)

What follows is an extract from our discussion.

1 Maria: How are you finding the whole activity here with the children?

2 Judith: It's great.

3 Maria: (excitedly) Is it really?

4 Judith: Yeah, 'cause you can <really notice things> Like I picked up so many things from you (addressing Taras)... the way you were asking the questions then you summarized with them and you were saying, "Well what strategies did you use?" and they said, "Yeah, we wanna try again and use those strategies again" ... and it was great.

5 Maria: Oh good, uh-huh.

6 Taras: **

7 Maria: So like, how maybe to win the game? Is that what you were looking...trying... <to do> like we did when we did that um...

8 Taras: The balloons (reference to a strategy I had used in a previous activity with the students)

9 Maria: Yeah the balloon race.
              Oh good, oh good, that's lovely!

10 Diane: They did seem to enjoy that and I think it was right at their level.

11 Taras: Do you think it was? I thought it was too easy for them.

12 Diane: Well... um... I'm not so sure. Like... er... this girl was still counting with her hands at the beginning she was very hesitant.

13 Taras: That's right, you're...

14 Diane: Especially at the beginning she was very, um, hesitant.

15 Maria: How did she carry on? How did it go later?

16 Diane: It's like she was more confident.

17 Maria: (encouragingly) Was she?

18 Taras: But this kid Bonnie she was right up <there> - She'd mess up with whole things, like adding <skills> like <she'd say> six no seven no eight.

But I do that too .
But she had she had an idea that the idea is
to try and fill the <high> ones first and then
you have the little ones (low numbers) you can
use at any time.

19 Maria: Oh and you got on to- OK, I wrote that down
in my notes. Did you actually ask if there are
more numbers that come up more regularly
and why that is?

20 Taras: I didn't actually come up with that.
I think that's the basis for it, I guess.

21 Maria: It's probability.

As I sat down with the student teachers, I wanted to try and
gauge what they had learned from the session so far. I was careful
to be encouraging without at first trying to direct the conversation
in any way. I wanted to see what the student teachers would
choose to discuss. Very little discussion of the activity had taken
place before my arrival so these were some of their first reflections
on the activity.

Judith's comments suggested that she had learned a lot about
how to encourage students to think about developing strategies
for winning the game from observing Taras. In an earlier session,
we had talked about looking at winning strategies as a means of
encouraging students to think about the mathematical principles
behind some games, and I wanted to reinforce this point (turn 9)
in order to underline how skills learned in one situation can
readily be applied to new situations.

A general concern of many of the student teachers, and one
which is often a problem for newly qualified teachers, was
whether or not the activities they had chosen would be pitched at
the right level for the children participating in them. It seems
from this extract that, although the basic math skills required
may have been mastered by the children already, Taras was able
to pitch the activity within the children's zone of proximal
development by concentrating on developing winning strategies.
In doing this, he was presumably drawing out the students'
thinking about the different combinations of numbers that could
be used to obtain the number required by the roll of the dice. This
short extract suggests that, as the game progressed, Taras was
required to reflect-in-action according to his students' needs and
that, in doing so, he provided not only an occasion for his students
to be challenged in their thinking but also an important learning
opportunity for one of his peers.

As I listened to the student teachers talking, I too was learning from them, and the value of the session was becoming apparent to me. At turn 19 I decided to see if the student teachers themselves had thought about the role that probability was playing in the roll of the dice and the outcome of the game. I was not sure if they had recognized one of the mathematical principles at work. I judged this moment to be the right time for me to start drawing out the thinking of my own students, as it appeared that Taras had done with his.

At the end of the session, I took the videotapes home to view in order to decide which parts to play to the student teachers at a later date. The final step in the action research would be to watch clips from the videotapes and to use them as texts for further reflection on the learning/teaching process.

The Paper Cup Game

My action research until now had provided me with many moments of excitement as I tried out new ideas and watched them at work in my classes. But I had not yet been surprised by any of the results. However, the surprise came as I sat down to watch the videotapes, and it was quite a shock. It was caused by the board game, discussed above.

We join the game in progress after Taras has very capably explained the rules to the students.

14 Taras:	Now, so Alex's off and running.	
15 Bonnie:	She can roll the dice.	
	(Alex, the other student, is unsure of how to begin.)	
16 Taras:	Yeah, (laughing reassuringly) eight again.	
	(Pause of approximately 8 seconds while beans are placed by Alex in the cups. She is clearly hesitant about where to put them. This is her first turn. She puts two beans in cup 4.)	
17 Taras:	Now you've put two in 4?	
	(Alex looks as if she thinks she has done something wrong.)	
18 Taras:	No, that's fine but the only thing is we only have twelve beans... so how many are you gonna put in there?	
19 Bonnie:	<Just one>	
20 Taras:	Just one. That cup's filled when you get a bean in the cup. That cup's full.	

So that's fine, or do you want to change your idea?
(Pause 4 seconds. Alex takes her turn again, more confidently this time.)

21 Taras: OK, what did you put down?

22 Alex: Eight — one and seven.

23 Taras: One and seven

(Alex looks more confident)

24 Bonnie: (rolling the dice) Eight.

25 Taras: Eight?
Loaded dice? ... (children look puzzled) You're always rolling eights.

(5 seconds pause while Bonnie places her beans.)

26 Taras: Where did you put it in?

27 Alex: 5 and 3.

28 Taras: 5 and 3...
You have to check, Alex, to make sure her answers are right. OK? (Alex had been looking about the room while Bonnie was taking her turn. There is clearly no reason for her to be paying attention while the other player is taking a turn.) Go ahead, Alex. Your turn.

(Alex rolls the dice. 10 second pause. Alex is studying the game board and puts a bean in cup 1 and another in cup 2 and then looks across at her partner.)

29 Alex: It's 1 and 2 (looking at Taras for reassurance.)

30 Taras: (Turning to Bonnie and trying to distance himself from the activity) As long as it's all right with Bonnie.

(However Bonnie has already rolled the dice for her turn and is clearly not interested in seeing what move Alex is going to make.)

31 Bonnie: Can I do the same like this like this? (She has rolled two and three and wants to know if she can use them to fill these cups.)

32 Taras: Sure, yeah.

(Play continues in silence until Alex finds

that she is unable to take her turn.)

33 Taras: Is there a problem, Alex?

(Alex nods and smiles and appears to be glad of the help.)

34 Alex: <I can't go>

35 Taras: No. Well, what happened?

36 Alex: I've got * * *

37 Taras: And ... how do you know you can't do anything?

(Alex counts on her fingers, trying out different addends for the numbers she still has left to fill.)

38 Alex: * * *
There's 3 and 5 they make 8 and... (thinking of alternate addends.)

39   Taras: Is it just 3 and 5 you need? Anything else?
So you're just going through (perhaps trying to discover whether Alex has a method for checking all of the possible addends)
How did you pick number 3 -   * * *
Why didn't you pick 7 for instance?

40 Alex: Because it's already filled up?

41 Taras: Because it's already filled up.
So you've checked all the cups (looking at the game board). So you'll just have to wait. Now it's Bonnie's turn. You see, at some time Bonnie you might get stuck too. This is where it gets tougher.

In our math classes we had talked frequently about the importance of creating a cooperative atmosphere in our classes. This might be a way to increase student interest in math, to help some students overcome feelings of math anxiety, and to stimulate all students' learning through discussion of the activities in use. As I watched, I saw quite clearly how the wrong type of activity could undermine even the best teacher's efforts to create such an environment. Here was proof of the importance of the first stage in Brissenden's model: the selection of 'effective math situations.'

As the preceding data show, the game did very little to stimulate student collaboration, to contribute to a sense of community, to encourage conversation — to say nothing of promoting creative thinking, hypothesizing, or boosting student confidence. At Alex's first turn, Taras has to point out that 4 and 4 is not a good move to make because there are only twelve beans and it is not possible to put more than one bean in the same cup.

Both students are playing independently and, without Taras' intervention (turn 14), have no incentive to watch and thereby to learn from each other's moves. All of the interaction takes place between the teacher and the students. There is no reason for the students to talk to each other about what moves they could make, or to hypothesize about winning strategies. The element of competition makes sure of this. Taras, who appears to read the situation well, does his best to distance himself from the game (30) but is obliged to continue in the role of "expert" to help the game along.

A little later, as the students have gained considerably in confidence and understand better the rules of the game, Taras begins to turn the students' thoughts towards winning strategies. Both students have high numbers left to fill and have been experiencing difficulty in completing their turns.

57 Taras:	What numbers do you need Alex? Do you know?
58 Alex:	... um...12 ... 9... 8 and 5 (looking carefully at her board)
59 Taras:	12, 9, 8, 5? (to Bonnie) OK, what numbers do you need?
60 Bonnie:	Well all the low ones usually go.
61 Taras:	All the low ones usually go?
62 Bonnie:	Yeah, right.
63 Taras:	(to both students) If you were to do this again what would you fill up first? Do you know? Do you have any idea what you might fill up first?
64 Alex:	Maybe I'd probably fill the high ones first and leave the high ones and the... and then have the low ones and just in case you get eight and this (pointing to 8) is filled up... um... well... (implying the smaller addends like 3 and 5 could then be used to fill the cups of a lower value)
65 Taras:	What about the 1 Alex?... Would you leave the 1 till the end? (Alex nods her head looking at Taras)

66 Taras: You'd leave the 1 to the end?
             So you're using two dice? Is that a good one
             (i.e., strategy), 'cause YOU (addressing Bon-
             nie) were saying keep the low ones — which is
             a good idea.
             But what about the 1? Would that count in
             with one of the one's you want to leave to the
             end?

             (Bonnie shakes her head.)

67 Alex: Well, maybe not.

68 Taras: Maybe not.

69 Alex: 'Cause like, if I were to get an eight and this
             was filled up (pointing to 8) and this one was
             filled up (unclear to which cup she is pointing)
             I wouldn't be able to do nothing — then I'd be
             able to <put> it in that one (pointing to cup 1)

70 Taras: Oh, right, right (hesitatingly because he has
             not quite understood the logic of Alex's expla-
             nation). Do you wanna try it again and start
             fresh and see if we can get it all filled up?

             (Both students nod)

Utterance 60 suggests that Bonnie is already analyzing the situation and formulating some hypotheses about how the game
works. Taras seems to realize this (61) and turns the students'
thoughts towards useful strategies for playing the game. Alex
does not seem to have started to think about strategies and is
perhaps following Bonnie's lead of leaving low numbers to the end
when she replies affirmatively to Taras' question (65). She has not
realized that leaving herself with just the number one will make
it impossible for her to complete the game, two being the smallest
number she can roll. Taras, sensing this perhaps (72), decides it
will be best to let the students experiment instead with their idea
of filling the high numbers first.

As the game progresses the going once again becomes more
difficult.

85 Taras: What do you think Alex? Can you go?

             (Alex rolls the dice)

86 Alex: Ten (she places a bean in 10).

             (Bonnie rolls the dice and is unable to take her
             turn. Alex rolls the dice. 25 second pause
             while she thinks then puts three beans in
             three different cups.)

87 Taras:	Can I ask you what you just did?
88 Alex:	2 and 3 makes 5 and 4 makes 9.
89 Taras:	Um — that's pretty good thinking, except we can only use two at a time. <it's> the most we can use. But I'll give you marks for that. That's pretty good thinking, Alex, but you have to... unfortunately you can't use that, you can only use 1 or 2 beans at a time.

(Bonnie rolls the dice) -

OK, Alex? So you have to take these ones out. That's pretty good thinking, Alex.

(7 second pause. Bonnie is not listening but continuing with her turn.)

(to Alex) OK, so you have to take those three out because we're only using one or two at a time. OK, is there any other way you could make 9?

(Alex shakes her head)

No? OK, try again.

Alex, who is now more familiar with how the game works, has thought of a creative solution to the problem of cup five already being full, and fills cups two and three instead. Unfortunately the rules of the game do not allow this, and her creative solution to the problem is rejected. The restrictions caused by the rules of the game are something the student teachers might want to think about changing if they were to use the game in the future.

Student Teacher Reactions to the Session

Once the children had left, the student teachers sat down in their groups to discuss the effectiveness of the activities and how they might adapt them in the light of their experience. At this stage, the student teachers had not had the opportunity to watch the video and were working from memory and the notes that they had taken during this and the second activity. In contrast to the children, the student teachers collaborated well in reflecting on their experiences and observations.

| 1 Judith: | Bonnie was so overbearing and so I was trying to balance them out. I found it difficult to... direct questions at Alex without putting her on the spot. |

2 Taras: How did you get around that?

3 Judith: I don't think I did.

4 Taras: One thing that I could think of is to... er... like she wouldn't work well with a lot of group work.

             (General announcement is made to the class)

5 Diane: Does anyone else have anything for Judith?

6 Taras: What I was going to say was that I think that shows a good example of why you can't always do group work.

7 Diane: <Yeah, you know what> sometimes you have to know *who to pair with*.

8 Taras: *That's it* and also pair her with another weak person another time so that it brings out her leadership qualities. You grab that weaker person and aim for — at some point that she * * aim for one activity which is one of her strengths so that she feels good. That way — so that at least in turn someone's gonna feel good someday.

9 Diane: (To Taras) Actually I thought yours was a good <activity> for working independently too. You could set that up on your own time.

             (Taras goes on to talk about how he might take the idea of probability and try to develop it with the class.)

10 Diane: That does sound kinda neat. Yours (to Taras) was also, you know ... when I was watching the kids I thought it could have been more difficult if they'd subtracted... if they could have either added or subtracted.

11 Taras: That's what I was saying to Maria too is that — that's before she suggested probability — my suggestion was to get them adding or subtracting.

12 Diane: Yeah then they would have had to think out which would be best in this situation.

13 Taras: Like I thought that Alex — when she dropped three beans in — that was great.

14 Judith: Yeah, oh. She was really thinking.

. This peer group discussion provides a good illustration of the type of collaborative talk referred to by Chang and Wells (1988), which they consider to have "the potential for promoting learning that exceeds that of almost any other type of talk" (p.97). The student teachers have identified for themselves a problem which arises frequently in the classroom: how to group students so that the learning situation is beneficial to all those involved in it. In the discussion, Diane and Taras assume the role of "experts" and, together, the group starts to come up with strategies that could be used in future situations to help students who may be reluctant participants in group work. They then look at ways of making the activity more challenging for their students.

It was striking to me that none of the student teachers commented on the lack of communication between the two children in the first activity, given the emphasis we had placed on 'talk' in our previous classes. Secondly, the student teachers discussed the question of the appropriateness of the task in terms of the level of difficulty, but its inappropriateness in promoting discussion was not questioned.

At this stage, where the students were setting their own agenda, this was not unduly important. For me, in retrospect, however, the tape raised several issues. I had learned a lot about the importance of talk in learning, but had I communicated this clearly to my students? Was I struck by the absence of conversation between the two students because I had had the benefit of looking at a video of this episode and of comparing it with a strongly contrasting one in which the children were working together to complete their activities. Perhaps the student teachers were aware of the lack of communication but had chosen, instead, to concentrate on issues that were of more relevance to them in their discussion.

Using Video as a Reflective Text

Whatever the reason for these differences, having a video text to look at closely had provided me with an opportunity to observe the interactions in a different way from the students, who were relying on memory and rough notes. I was able to use the video recording as a "reflective text" (Wells, 1990a) to increase my understanding of the role that learning materials play in the learning process. It is easy to say that non-competitive activities promote collaboration between students and that, as a result, more learning accrues from the interactions that take place. But we still make competitive games for our math centres and for our children to work on in unsupervised groups because we know that they 'like to play.' However, it would seem from this video that there is a big difference between playing and learning. The video contained a powerful message to all of us to be careful in choosing activities for children to work on unsupervised, under the assumption that all resulting interaction is quality interaction. It is easy to overlook the important role played by learning materials, silent participants in classroom interactions, in determining the quality of the interaction that takes place.

It was this discovery that I chose to share with the class. I made a conscious decision not to follow through on the points that the students had identified in their discussions. This was not because I did not consider the students' issues worth discussing further, but because the videos could show us two quite different learning situations and give the student teachers a chance to be aware of what was going on in other activities in which they had not personally been involved. This was an opportunity that a classroom teacher would not often be given. I hoped, too, that it would provide the student teachers with something new to think about, as it had done for me.

I showed excerpts from two activities, a cooperative one involving ratios, and the Paper Cup game. In the first activity, the children were all given the same set of problems to solve as a group. These problems required them to guess and to refine their answers as they worked. It was obvious the children were enjoying the activities. Although one child had a tendency to dominate the discussion at first, all the children participated enthusiastically and were not afraid to offer suggestions or to improve on a peer's previous comments. Once satisfied that they had solved a problem, they presented the answer to the student teacher and successfully explained their reasoning.

The contrast between this activity and the Paper Cup game was striking, and the student teachers were quick to pick up on what I had noticed. They were also quick to offer possible solutions to the problem, unprompted by me.

2 Eric: Well, the first one there was definitely a group activity. There were lots of comments coming from all the kids working together. Just in contrast to the second one which was more of an individual scene as smoke came out of the kid's ears as she was trying to figure it out.
I suppose they learned more * * * than individual effort.

3 Fatima: Yeah, there was more discussion in the first

one. They really discussed what they were doing. Of course we stimulated that because we asked them why they did it the way they did.

4 Maria: OK, so the teacher had a role to play as well. Diane? Can you shout really loudly? (she is a long way from the microphone)

5 Diane: I was thinking the one Taras did. Because of the element of competition perhaps they didn't want to talk too much in case they gave the <secret> away. And actually I was involved in that one and uh... sometimes I think they wanted to keep it to themselves, so that if the next person rolled that number then they... <hadn't helped the opponent>.

6 Maria: It stopped the talk didn't it?

7 Diane: Yeah.

8 Maria: And I've used games in my math program as well and I never really thought of any sort of effect that <competition> might have. And I guess I read that, in cooperative learning, children share and they work together. But this really did strike home to me — one of those things where you experience it for yourself of, wow, look at the difference between the two situations . Although I think that Taras' role as the teacher there <was important> — you were helping the students and trying to show them — to give them strategies for using within the game. But they really did sort of just isolate within themselves rather than discuss it.

9 Bonnie: If he could have had one board it would have made the difference.

10 Maria: Yeah, that's a neat idea. Is there any way you could take that game and make it into a cooperative game?

11 Carol: You could make it a timed...

12 Diane: Two teams.

13 Maria: A timer?

14 Carol: Yeah, limit the time to see if they could do it under the clock or beat their last time and to work cooperatively over one set of cups.

| 15 Maria: | OK, so how many boards do you have then? |
| 16 Carol: | One set of boards for two kids. |

I was pleased at the way the student teachers identified the problem and then proceeded to find ways of overcoming it. Such an approach forms the basis of all effective reflection.

The Benefits of Conducting Action Research in a Community of Learners

By undertaking a systematic inquiry into how knowledge can be constructed in a community of learners, of which the above data represents only a small part, I have greatly increased my understanding of the collaborative learning process. My readings and observations encouraged me to look in more depth at the quality of the interactions that were taking place in our classes, and to take a closer look at my role within them. As a teacher-researcher, I was also a learner. At each stage in the research I was able to reflect on my actions and to work on changing my practice accordingly. However, it was in reconstructing the research in writing that, through inner speech, I finally came to understand much of the theory and its application to my research. It is this final stage of reflection that will lead to changes in my future teaching.

As I review the project in retrospect, I can see flaws in the process that I was not able to see at the time of conducting the research because I was so involved in the events taking place. I have also experienced for myself the importance of the types of interaction that occur in the collaborative classroom. My student teachers experienced it too. This year I was not able to make as explicit to them as I would have liked, the processes that we were engaged in in our community of learners, although I do not know if this would have been more beneficial for them as learners. In future years I will make more specific references to the frameworks I am using. I will also not assume that being exposed to good mathematical materials is enough. I will invite the students to talk about what makes them good for group-work and encourage them to adopt a more critical eye when choosing from published materials.

From their comments, the student teachers appeared to have learned a lot from being introduced to activities that they had not experienced as elementary school students in math classes and from observing themselves and children working on them. As individuals within a community of learners, we were all given the chance to learn about and to reflect on our teaching practice.

This piece of action research brought together three different groups of learners; first, students in a graduate class in education and their professor, who were all conducting and learning about action research; second, the student teachers and myself, their instructor; third, the student teachers and the children with whom they were working. In each group of learners there was a dialectical relationship between the 'teacher' and the 'learner'; both were learning from each other. This multi-level interaction is one which, as Nona Lyons (1990) has pointed out, deserves greater attention from researchers and teachers. It is central to the learning process. These three groups were not working in isolation. The action research project provided a thread which linked all three groups and established an interdependence between them.

In addition to these vertical levels of learning between teachers and learners was the horizontal aspect of the learning which occurred in peer interactions. It is possible to say that, in this respect, the knowledge we constructed was communicated beyond our immediate community of learners to the peers with whom we were in contact outside of the action research.

One of the reasons our learning experiment was a success was that the student teachers and myself were open-minded and curious about what was happening. As Wells (1990b) has pointed out, these are essential elements for teaching and learning in a collaborative environment.

I have learned from my action research that collaborative interactions can produce learning which possesses both depth and breadth, in that it extends to one's peers and also to one's students and teachers. Everyone can benefit within a community of learners, and knowledge that is relevant to the needs of the participants is created like the product in a chemical reaction.

So Who Teaches the Teachers?

Perhaps the best answer to this question is that it is the teachers themselves, aided by all those with whom they come into contact. How we respond to the influences around us is very important. Will our minds be open to new ideas? Will we be able to recognise a problem and be able to respond to it appropriately? How will we react if some of our peers or superiors make suggestions which may appear to be unsuitable in the light of our own understanding of the classroom in which we are operating? How refined an eye do we have for dealing with the situations that arise in our classrooms? What motivation do we have to refine our understanding or conoisseurship of classroom interactions? The way in which we resolve — or, as Maggie Lampert (1985) says, "manage" — our classroom problems will depend on the image that we have of ourselves as teachers.

After having experienced the powerful potential of talk in my math course this year, I shall probably decide to work on refining my in-class experiment for the forthcoming year. The approach I used is not without problems, however. It requires time if it is to be successfully completed, more than I was able to devote to it this year. Other elements of the program will need to be adjusted; perhaps some of the content covered will need to be omitted, or just covered in a different way.

From my own experiences as a teacher of math, I know that it is easier to learn to adapt a good comprehension of the learning process to new concepts in the math curriculum than to have to think of suitable strategies each time one encounters a new concept. However, I do not claim that, in making a decision to concentrate on the learning process, there are not other problems in the program that still have to be resolved. If I have come to see myself in Lampert's terms as a dilemma manager (1985, p.190), then what I have decided to concentrate on is helping my students to provide conditions in their classrooms which will help their students to learn and to develop a positive attitude towards mathematics. In so doing, I may well find new ways of dealing with some of the other problems that I have not yet resolved.

The students' reactions to the learning experiment were all very positive, so it seems fitting to close the chapter with their words. The following comments are taken from one of the final term papers, written about directed play in the primary mathematics program:

> Our understanding of the importance of play was strengthened through our own learning experiences, and also through our observations in the classroom. The approach to math we as student teachers have been exposed to by our instructors has left us with a different and much more exciting view of mathematics and its importance.

9

So You Think it's the Children You're Observing

Leona Bernard and Christina Konjevic

Traditionally, teachers have looked outside their classrooms for answers to questions about their teaching and their students' learning, seeking other, more knowledgeable, voices to address their classroom concerns. Teachers have been relatively silent in this approach to professional development. We (Christina and Leona) were no exceptions. In this sense, our relationship started in the hierarchical mould, with Leona, in a consultative capacity, providing advice and assistance to Christina, the teacher, who was seeking support for modifications in her classroom program. However, when we started to address Christina's problem as teacher-researchers we found that these traditional assumptions and expectations were challenged and changed.

In the foreword to *Jevon Doesn't Sit at the Back Anymore*, Connie White's (1989) account of her teacher inquiry, Jerome Harste discusses voice, conversation and community as essential components of the process of teacher-research. It was our involvement in teacher-research that helped us to develop our voices, to engage in new conversations and to become members of the teacher-researcher community. What follows is an account of our teacher inquiries and our partnership. Following some background information, we share our inquiries; through them we found our voices, while discovering the powerful impact we had in influencing another's learning. We share some of the conversations we had together, showing how they took our questions beyond our initial inquiries to ones that challenged our pedagogical principles and everyday practices. We also describe how we joined the community of learners. Not only were we observing the children — we were observing ourselves and our learning. Finally, we offer some reflections on our current roles in collaborating with other teacher-researchers.

Background

As a resource teacher for primary teachers who provide instruction for English as a Second Language (ESL) children directly within their regular classrooms, I (Leona) wanted to learn more about how I could assist teachers in making meaningful discoveries regarding the language and cognitive development of these children. By taking a course in action research, I thought I could become versed in the subject and therefore able to subsequently transmit my newly acquired expert knowledge to teachers. After all, isn't that what consultants or curriculum experts are supposed to do?

From the very first class, however, my assumptions were challenged and questioned. The principles underlying the course in action research were based on the premise that teachers learn as all human beings learn; therefore, a didactic approach by the teacher, which assumes a passive receptive role on the part of the learner, is contrary to the natural learning process. In an attempt to explore this approach to learning, all participants were expected to engage in a practical investigation in a classroom. Because of my consultative position I did not have my own classroom in which to conduct an inquiry. As a result, I decided to collaborate with a teacher-researcher while I investigated the role I played in providing assistance to that teacher-researcher. Having set my task, I began to search for a potential collaborator. The ideal partner would have to be inquisitive and professional, intrigued by challenge, and willing to sacrifice some personal time. I was also anticipating that the experience would be a successful and rewarding one for both of us; for my part, one of my objectives was to complete the course requirements with a good grade.

Christina, a Junior Kindergarten teacher with a large number of ESL children in her class, seemed to be just the person I was looking for. I had met her a year earlier while I was a Primary ESL Resource Teacher. She was always asking questions about the ESL four- year-olds in her class and her conscientiousness in meeting their needs had led to many discussions on program-modification. While I was visiting her school one autumn day, soon after I started my course, Christina approached me in the corridor with a concern about the ESL children's inattentiveness during large group reading time. That question turned into an invitation and the beginning of a valued partnership.

Our Inquiries

As we began to work together, each of us had our own specific topic of inquiry. These can be briefly stated as follows.

Christina's Inquiry

I was concerned that my ESL children were not attentive during large group storytime. My goal was to develop strategies to elicit appropriate behavior from these children when I was reading to the whole class. I chose to begin the classroom research by trying to discover possible reasons for my ESL children not being interested in the book while they were in the large group. To find out if language was a factor, I observed and videotaped the group while a story was being read in the ESL children's native language. I quickly realized that language was not the dominant factor in accounting for the children's inattentiveness. I observed something rather unexpected: the English-speaking children were visibly trying to make sense of the story, despite the barrier of a foreign language. They drew closer to the book and storyteller and their eyes were fixed on the book. The ESL children, however, were still not as interested as their English-speaking peers.

It became apparent to me that these ESL children were at a different stage in their literacy development than the children who were engaged with the story and would, therefore, benefit from more individual interaction with books. I audiotaped and transcribed myself reading to the ESL children in small groups and discovered many things about myself as a teacher. I found I was using teaching strategies that had the effect of inhibiting the children's learning, rather than enhancing it. I asked questions that limited responses, I gave little opportunity for the children to talk or physically demonstrate understanding, and I held the book at all times. This is when my inquiry shifted from trying to change the children's behavior to changing my own.

I began to question my beliefs about literacy development in young children. If I believed children's experiences with print should be naturalistic, why was I controlling their interaction while sharing a story? I could not answer this question satisfactorily. I was so frustrated, because I could not articulate why I was doing what I was doing. There was a mismatch between what I said I believed and what I was doing in the classroom. Since I still held the beliefs, my practices had to change. I continued reading in small groups but I talked far less. I changed my questioning technique to allow for lengthier responses and I provided opportunities for the children to handle the books. I began to question the purpose of large and small group and individual reading activities. This led to the creation of "Booktime." Now, every child selects a book from the baskets available and reads alone or with a neighbor. I still read books to the large group, but these books are put into the baskets for individual children to peruse during "Booktime." I also use large group time as an opportunity to discuss appropriate book management (i.e., treating books with care) and to introduce new books and other print material (i.e., cookbooks, maps and magazines). I have designed small group storytime primarily for children to respond to the story by linking their own experiences to those in the story and to make connections between their worlds and the world of print.

What began as an inquiry into ways of increasing ESL children's attentiveness in large group storytime resulted in the enhancement of literacy experiences for all children in my class.

Leona's Inquiry

My inquiry was to find out what my role was — and what it might become — in providing support to Christina while she pursued her classroom inquiry. As a start, I wanted to uncover the characteristics and qualities I displayed when supporting a teacher-researcher. Since my focus was on our interactions, I decided to collect data by audiotaping all of our meetings.

As I looked carefully at my contributions to the second conversation that I had transcribed, I discovered that I was imposing my hidden agenda onto Christina's research. In a two page transcript, I tried — five times — to get Christina to do the research "my way." My intentions were disguised as follows:

"What do you think would be better? To read the story with them in the small group first?" I CERTAINLY BELIEVED SO!

"What would be better, use the story like — sort of preservice?" AGAIN, I KNEW WHICH WOULD BE BETTER!

"And then, when the book is there in the large group, they'll know what it is about." HERE I AM RATIONALIZING THE "PRE-SERVICE" READING OF THE BOOK!

"Or the third alternative is doing all three. Pre-service, story and, then, follow-up. So they're hearing it three times and are even more familiar with the book." THIS IS MY ATTEMPT AT COMPROMISING!

"So — you want to read the story again with a small group of the ESL children after you've read the story in large group? Then they can have a positive experience because they know about the story. You can also do it the other way — read the story in the small group before introducing it in the large group." I JUST HAD TO TRY TO GET MY INTENTION ACROSS ONE LAST TIME!

The realization that I was interfering with, rather than supporting, Christina's research was a turning point for me. I had expounded on my belief in supporting the ownership of another's learning on numerous occasions, yet the undisputed evidence from the tape showed my behavior to be quite contrary. In fact, I was trying to control not only Christina's research, but also her own learning. This revelation led to changes in future meetings. I spoke far less, listened more attentively, and limited my comments to those points that were most relevant. More importantly, I openly stated my agendas and confronted them with Christina, thereby eliminating my previous subversive behavior.

What began as an investigation into what I was doing to support a teacher-researcher turned into an exploration of what I should be doing to enhance the learning of another individual. In this way, I, too, was a learner.

Conversation

Although the discoveries we made through our inquiries were important for our subsequent practices, what we want to explore fully in this chapter is what we discovered in the process. Our contribution is thus more about what we learned about learning from the experience of working together than it is about the specific results of our inquiries. In the following sections we attempt to show how conversation and community were instrumental in our investigation, both of what we were learning and also of how we were learning.

Our conversations were especially valuable for three reasons. They assisted us in becoming familiar with, and increasing our competence in, the concrete aspects of the inquiry process. The conversations also contributed to the further development of our relationship, both personally and professionally. Most importantly, our conversations guided us beyond learning solely through the inquiry to reflecting upon what we were learning. Although these topics can be identified separately, they were interwoven and interconnected throughout our conversations. As we were increasing our understanding of the inquiry process, we were also enriching our relationship; we were also coming to a fuller realization of the fact that reflection is an integral part of the learning process. In this section we attempt to relate the evolutionary development that occurred during the course of our conversations.

In the beginning, we were focused on the organization and management of our inquiries. To meet these goals, we established regularly scheduled meetings, primarily for practical purposes: to report information, set goals and identify tasks to be completed for the next meeting. Initially, our conversations addressed these topics.

The first session was one in which we established the concern or problem we wanted to pursue and planned our means of data collection. Leona had come to the meeting having defined her question regarding her role in assisting a teacher-researcher and had selected audiotaping as a form of data collection for her inquiry. Therefore, the objective in this meeting was for Christina to do likewise. Because she had so many questions, we tried to focus on her primary issue: "How can I engage the ESL children in the story being read in large group storytime?" She considered two hypotheses: the children's lack of interest might be related to cultural/linguistic factors and/or to their inexperience with large group activities. After deciding to have someone read a book to the children in their home language, we had a lengthy conversation about the best way to collect observational data. Not having had previous experience of formally collecting data for analysis, Christina needed some explanation and a description of the mechanics involved. Once she had understood the various possibilities, she selected videotaping as her vehicle for observation. We stuck to our plan in the first meeting, at least.

As we gained some experience in formulating a hypothesis and collecting and analyzing data to test it, the focus of our meetings began to shift towards discussing aspects of the process. We were not just reporting on our observations, we were trying to interpret them. For example, witnessing the English speaking children trying to make sense of a story in a foreign language resulted in a hypothesis Christina had not considered: the children's experience with literacy, or lack of it, might be a factor in their inattentiveness in large group storytime. We were beginning to see the value our meetings were having in the process, as is articulated by Christina: "I realize what's happening more when I talk about it than when it's happening because when you go back to the fact you realize all those other things are coming at you." Our meetings provided us with the opportunity to identify and discuss a particular event in depth, without the countless distractions taking place at the time of the occurrence. We still set goals and tasks to be completed for our next meeting, but our discourse began to move a little beyond the concrete.

As our familiarity and expertise in the inquiry process grew, our meetings started taking on a rather loose, but flexible, format. Christina would report on her latest observations, interpretations and courses of action, while Leona would report on the latest information she had gained from her course in action research. One day, we were discussing the cyclic pattern of action research and relating it to our personal inquiries (Figure 1). Christina offered this analogy: "In a way it is like a molecular chain because from that action develops a new one. This is what's happening to me. I do these things and I've got a new question and from there another one." We were attempting to make sense of our inquiries through the utilization of a more abstract, symbolic representation.

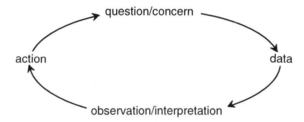

Figure 1 / The cycle of action research

The inquiry process not only provided evidence of the learning behaviors of the children but also of our teaching behaviors. This was a rather humbling experience. Judith Newman states: "... the incidents which help us change as teachers aren't big events — they're small, everyday, ongoing occurrences" (1987, p.728). Indeed, when we both transcribed our audiotapes, it was the small, everyday behaviors we displayed that irritated us to such an extent that we were determined to change them. These revelations were turning points in both of our inquiries. Christina found she was not allowing enough time for the children to respond to the book and Leona found she was interfering with Christina's research. We discovered the true meaning of the saying: "actions speak louder than words" and found a cathartic comfort in sharing our embarrassing discoveries with someone we knew would understand.

Not only did our conversations contribute immensely to our understanding of the inquiry process, but they were also instrumental in the enhancement of our relationship. We soon found that we had to be willing to accept a certain degree of vulnerability to engage in teacher-research, since many of the things we were learning and revealing about ourselves were embarrassing. Leona confessed her discovery that she had hidden agendas and outlined the changes she planned to implement in future meetings. Christina's transcription of an audiotaped session, in which she read books to the ESL children in small groups, was another source of revelation:

> What I felt when I did that is that I talk way too much. It was very "yes/no." It wasn't too open-ended. A lot of broken English, which I have quickly, finally, recovered from and am very conscious of. I still talk "ESL" but not like I did before. If I do, I always catch myself and repeat it in appropriate English language. I listened to the second one but I didn't transcribe it, but I noticed. I noticed that I talked much less. When I did talk it was just story words instead of my words seeking out knowledge from them. I think they (the children) talked a lot more because I talked a lot less.

Although these could have been relatively awkward experiences, having non-judgmental and open partners made it easy for us to share our discoveries.

We had developed an excellent rapport and relationship; however, there was still some amicable tension. Although Christina was making significant changes in her program to accommodate the emergent literacy needs of her ESL students, much of the evidence she collected did not support her belief in the effectiveness of large group storytime for these children. Yet she continued this aspect of her program. Leona tried various ways to heighten Christina's awareness of this incongruence through conversations in which she consciously tried to incorporate curriculum expertise with her knowledge of the learning process. Leona subsequently confessed her frustration to Christina in this way: "It was very difficult for me because I just wanted to tell you to drop the large group reading as an emergent literacy experience for these children. However, I knew I had to find an avenue for you to come to this realization for yourself if it was to be meaningful for you." Finally, after three sessions, Christina came to the realization on her own.

The conversations that encouraged this shift began with Christina's recognition of the incongruence. "These kids love the book in the small group....It's like having an old blanket you don't want to let go of. I feel the same way about the large group reading. I don't know why. Why? Why, when I see this, do I want to hold onto large group?" Obviously, recognition of the fact that the children benefited from the small group reading time did not prompt immediate change in the classroom practice. Christina had not yet taken ownership of the problem; however, recognition of it was the first step.

Christina could not satisfactorily answer her own question as to why she was maintaining large group reading, despite several prompts on Leona's part. In addition to hanging on to the "old blanket," Christina provided the following rationalization: "Maybe there's a norm within grade levels and teaching that you do small group things, you do individual things and you do large group things." That still did not answer the question as to why she was using large group reading as a method for literacy development, particularly when further evidence from the classroom pointed in the opposite direction. The following transcription is an excellent example.

Leona:	They (the ESL children) may not even be giving explanations. They may be pointing at things they know in the book.
Christina:	Or they relate to their home. Like Mahan did that again, "My Mommy have that house. My house," and it went on and on, relating it totally to her own experience. I just found that very fascinating. She does that. Nobody else does that.
Leona:	Can you do that in a large group?
Christina:	No. You sit there and you have to shut up and don't talk.

In the course in which Leona was enroled, there had been a discussion of two aspects of learning: the concrete, data-derived learning from one's inquiry, and the less tangible learning that results from reflecting upon the data as it applies to oneself as a learner. This was an opportune time to assist Christina in reflecting upon why she conducted large group reading, how she learned as a learner, and how that applied to her inquiry. Up until this time, Christina had been focused on the first aspect of learning described above; however, Leona's intention was to assist her in making the shift to the next aspect. Christina was encouraged to consider how she learned as a learner. To assist her in this task, Christina listened to the taped conversation of the previous meeting. (Up until this time Leona had been the only one to use the tapes as data).

When we next met, Christina reported with excitement the numerous observations she had made while listening to the tape.

The conversation that followed was no longer about the data from the classroom seen from the point of view of her inquiry about the children, but about what she was learning in the process of her inquiry. We share our conversation on the topic:

Christina: As you go through you realize why all the things you did—why did you need to do those things? Why didn't I do something else? That's equally as important as the actual end data.

Leona: I would argue more important.

Christina: It's true, yeah. The end is important because it puts everything together. How can I say?

Leona: You mean, the initial question you had?

Christina: Yes, by coming to some kind of answer, and I wouldn't even say it's an answer so far as the research, I can say this is why...

Leona: But I see a difference. Maybe it's the generic aspect of teacher-research. The initial focus was on something for the students. The whole focus has now become something internal.

Christina: Oh, yes, and it makes you think about teaching. (reading from notes) 'I'm looking at what I am doing as it is affecting the child as learner. Need to look at how I learn.'

Indeed, the focus shifted from the children and the classroom practices to Christina and the pedagogical principles underlying her practices. She had recognized the incongruence between pedagogy and practice in previous sessions but had not been aware of their interconnectedness. Nor had she been committed to making any changes. Now Christina had taken ownership of the problem, as she expressed in her own words:

I understand the inquiry process but why do I do what I do? I couldn't answer my own question. I thought, parents don't challenge us in school and I think that almost we don't have to defend why we do what we do. I realize, when you asked that of me, I didn't hear Leona saying that, I just heard a parent, or a principal or a colleague, but not Leona, who's helping me with my research. It was funny. It was like a different voice in my head.

It was a different voice. It was Christina's voice, which she had just newly discovered.

When Christina formulated her understanding for herself, it

was a day of celebration. It was also a turning-point in our relationship. We were now genuine partners. We were on the same wavelength. We shared a similar experience that took us beyond the cyclic pattern inherent in teacher-research to one in which we were confronting ourselves. Our collaboration changed, in that we were mutually providing each other with input and support, instead of most of that responsibility falling on Leona's 'expert' shoulders.

"Knowledge is not something 'gotten,' but something socially created through conversation," says Harste (in White, 1989, p.ii). Although we believe this to be true, talk was not enough for us to arrive at the revelation that our pedagogies were incongruent with our practices. The conversations were indeed helpful for us to sort out our thoughts publicly but it was only when we listened to the tapes of the sessions that significant discoveries were made. That is how Leona became aware of her 'hidden agendas.' Christina describes her experience while listening to one of the taped conversations in this way:

> When I first listened to the tape I wasn't thinking about the research, like what your question was of me — 'Why do you do large group reading?' I was just listening to the tape and it was funny. It came about three or four times. I kept asking myself. And I realized at the end, 'Oh, Leona's asking me to —'. But I was asking myself as I was starting to realize. There was the next stage. Even though you helped me go toward, I think that, even if you hadn't said that, I would have come to it. After listening to the tape and realizing that I had to look at why I'm doing what I'm doing.

Listening to the tapes and transcribing them was a reflective act. Through reflection we were not just exploring our inquiry questions, we were also exploring ourselves. We were asking: How are our actions and practices affecting the learning of others? Are they a help or an obstacle in attaining the ultimate learning experience we are trying to provide our learners?

We believe that it was listening to and/or transcribing the tapes as reflection that played a major part in shifting our relationship from that of expert-novice to one of true partnership. Leona's questions were no longer focused on assisting Christina to become aware of the discrepancy between data outcome and her practice. We were sharing our experiences and thoughts. We were each genuinely interested in the other and our questions reflected that.

The type of questioning Leona employed and the interaction in which she was engaged with Christina, while trying to guide her toward her own revelation, was in some ways similar to the 'hidden agenda' strategy. However, there was a major difference. In attempting to lead Christina to self-discovery, Leona did not want Christina to take on 'Leona's' understanding. Leona knew that the learning could only be meaningful if it was Christina's understanding. It was frustrating because it would have been more expedient if Christina had been given alternatives to large group reading as a means for developing emergent literacy. Leona had this concrete knowledge but she also had knowledge about the learning process and a firm belief in John Dewey's philosophy that education is experience. Leona was challenged into putting her beliefs into practice. Christina summed up Leona's role in this way:

> It had come from me and that's really the key to you helping me. From reading the articles and things like that it's like you start off talking a lot, which I think is important. And one of the articles mentions its importance. Because you need to help me to seek direction — like, what am I doing? You need to help me focus. As I became more focused you became less, uh, you didn't need to help me do it any more, because I was already doing it. All you would do, at the same time, if I said something you would just say, "Well, then, why are you doing that?" — questioning and reclarifying, etc.

Community of Learners

As a result of our collaboration together, we feel that we are now members of the community of teacher-researchers but, more importantly, members of the community of learners. (Perhaps there is no need to make a distinction between the two terms.) Our relationship is no longer defined by the roles and titles we hold but by mutual respect for each other as colleagues and learners.

Our most difficult and humbling experience was when we realized that, to become effective partners in learning in and out of the classroom, we had to relinquish control. Leona wanted to tell Christina what changes to make in her program and Christina wanted to regulate storytime. Relinquishing control in these areas and others became considerably easier when we felt empowered as teachers; when we, personally, felt we had developed our own inner voices and had gained some influence over our own learning. It was teacher-research that provided us the tools to engage in this type of learning.

We learned that, if we truly valued and respected people's ownership of their learning, we had to change our learning environments and atmospheres. We found there were common strategies that emerged as a result of our conscientious efforts to relinquish control over another's learning. In practice, the following features do not occur in isolation from each other, but for convenience of presentation we have separated them.

1. We were providing more **time for talk**, thus allowing the learners to sort out their thoughts aloud. That placed us in a relatively new position of being genuinely attentive listeners.

Christina: Throughout my inquiry I realized the more owner-ship for books I gave the children (i.e., time to look and hold books in *their* hands) the more talk occurred. It was a 'tool' that they seemed to feel in control of and could use to make connections with their own personal experiences. 'Booktime,' as I have termed it, evolved from these observations. It is a group activity in which the children choose their own books and are given the opportunity to look at the pictures, make their own story, or read and share with their peers. I also interact with the children at this time but I am much more of an active listener.

Leona: Talking assisted in the process of internalizing Christina's inquiry into a personal, meaningful experience. In one of our meetings she expressed the need to talk and to have a listening companion, "Here I am talking to myself. I am. I'm not talking to you. I'm telling what I did and you're here!" My role as the teacher-researcher companion was to be there; to listen atten-tively. Interruptions were best limited unless absolutely suppor-tive to Christina. During the interaction I responded with nods, uh-huhs and yeses, while taking notes which were shared at the end of Christina's time to talk. It was then that I made comments and a summary of what I thought she was saying; the result of my listening between the lines.

2. We provided relevant and immediate **feedback** at crucial moments while the learner was talking.

Christina: Interaction with the children, since I have devel-oped 'Booktime,' is very different. It has changed dramatically from teacher-directed to child-initiated. The children have a keen interest in books and will go to the basket of books during activity time. This allows many opportunities for me to sit with a smaller number of children. This situation brings forth much more dialogue, questions and observations from the children. Also, they provide me with, not only a forum for personal observations about the child but, an indicator of their interests, assisting me in selecting a variety of books.

Leona: The feedback I offered Christina was no longer prescriptive advice. It took the form of questions, clarifications, observations, rephrasing and summarizing. Here are a few samples:

Christina: Why is it that logical things aren't clear; like, why wouldn't I see it? (the relevance of small group reading sessions)

Leona: It's not logical.

Christina: Do I need to see everything? Sometimes I wonder.

Leona: Why do you think you have to go through this process?

Christina: Because I'm learning.

Leona: What are you learning?

Christina: I'm learning by doing.... I have to become more confident in me!

Leona: You mean you're swayed by what others do. You have to decide things for yourself and until you build that certain kind of confidence you can't speak confidently to anybody else.

Christina: No, you're right.

Leona: So, if somebody said to you, "Oh, I see you don't do large group reading anymore," now you can tell them.

Christina: You're right. I see what you mean. That's much better. That's why I wish everything I did I could articulate exactly. Like, why do I do it that way and not that other way?

Leona: You haven't done the reflection and coming to terms for yourself. You said teachers ask questions but don't go beyond to pedagogy, but you're not either.

3. We provided **modelling**, as opposed to transmitting information, as a means of empowering learners to take responsibility for their own learning.

Christina: Leona's use of audiotapes was also a tool that I used to monitor not only my language but the children's language as well. Also, watching and listening to her as she interacted with the children I noticed that she modelled such things as 'pausing' after she asked a question, allowing interruptions during the story and making connections to their own experiences.

Since language is so crucial to all learning, story and books provide an excellent resource not only for the English-speaking children but also for those just learning the English language. Not only am I a language model but I also model storytelling, book management (how to hold and care for a book) and a variety of book skills (i.e., recognizing the front from back and the like).

Leona: Being a mother of a two year old son who is beginning to speak, I am hearing so many of my phrases coming out of his mouth. Similarly I have witnessed Christina incorporating some of my interactional patterns into her own inquiry. In the above transcript segments she was asking "why" of herself, not because she was instructed to do so, but, rather, because she has developed this skill through example.

Another way that I acted as a model was by sharing what I had been doing and thinking about in relation to my inquiry during the intervals between our meetings. Since I was using the audiotapes as my means of data collection I focused my discussion on the transcripts and relevant observations I had made. Christina began to listen to the recordings of the sessions and reflected upon them in terms of her own learning. Additionally, she provided me with feedback as to her perception of my role in assisting her: "You'd often repeat what I said. When you did it, it was like you wanted me to clarify something, but you made it seem like you wanted it clarified, but, in turn, I was clarifying. That was important because that was another thing I learned about learning."

4. We **provided resources** appropriate to the task and at the learners' level to supplement and broaden their learning.

Christina: I made decisions about the kinds of books that I put into the 'Booktime' basket. Initially, I began with only board books since I wanted to observe how much experience the children had with them. Gradually, I added picture books, predictable, lift-flap books and theme books, as they became more experienced with handling books, and I modelled good book management skills. We now have books and magazines throughout our classroom (i.e., recipe books, catalogues, telephone books), as well as non-fiction books about insects at our nature table.

Leona: Last year I gave Christina an article to which she referred many times during our action research collaboration. It was obviously extremely relevant to her and to the research she was conducting. To assist her in her inquiry I sought out materials on the topic of classroom research but failed to consider articles related to the topic of her inquiry until she requested them of me. My role was not only to find the articles but to take into consideration the timing of the giving of them to Christina. I did not want to overwhelm her by giving the resources all at once; rather, I was conscious of selecting and providing the materials when they would have the greatest impact on various stages of her inquiry. As a tool for learning, resources are essential, but it was evident that they should not be doled out indiscriminately.

5. We provided **opportunities for ongoing evaluation**. This is an essential aspect of any purposeful activity and teacher-research is no exception.

Christina: Having ownership over one's own learning (teacher or child) is just one part of evaluation. Once I was able to take on the responsibility for initiating new actions to bring about change, I could reflect upon and evaluate what I was or was not doing. For example, once I allowed for a variety of natural opportunities for children to interact with books, I noticed that the more exposure they had to books, the greater was their interest in them.

Leona: There were two interrelated components to Christina's and my ongoing assessment:the inquiries and the reflections. In evaluating our respective inquiries we were continually asking, "Am I making progress toward my goal?" This process assisted us in making adjustments to our initial inquiry question, methods of data collection and subsequent actions. Evaluation also moved us from the external inquiries to metacognitive reflections on learning itself, and the conditions which support it.

6. Our **learning environments** became different places from when we commenced our partnership in teacher-research — much improved, we think. We shifted from doing something 'to' the learner to doing something 'with' the learner. As members of the community of learners, we have gained a renewed respect for the value of observing children and, indeed, all learners because we know such observations provide a window into our own learning.

Reflection

It has been three years since we launched into our collaborative teacher-research project. Many things have changed in the interim but not the powerful impact the experience has had on our lives. Surprisingly, the partnership endures despite the great distance that has separated us since Leona's move from Toronto to Houston, Texas. We still converse across the miles and anxiously await the cassette tape, with the latest instalment, in the mailbox.

We have taken our relationship for granted. Absence has been our teacher with the uniqueness of our partnership coming into focus of late. When engaging in new partnerships we have been frustrated and disappointed because they have not even come close to the collaboration we experienced together. We should have entered those partnerships without preconceived expectations and assumptions, but we did not. We anticipated that the experiences would be very similar to our own. "Uncovering these assumptions" (Newman, 1987) has been a learning experience in itself and has prompted us to consider the unique elements that led to our professional growth and lasting friendship.

Some teachers with whom we were interacting were separate from, not a part of, their research. They engaged in the formalized, systematic, cyclic approach of an inquiry method: they articulated a concern or issue, collected and interpreted the data, set hypotheses and tested them. Oftentimes, the mismatch between practice and expressed pedagogical beliefs was not recognized. Subsequently, aspects of their program have changed but the teachers have not.

Bissex (1986) and Harste (1989) see the teacher-researcher as a learner; Atwell (1989), the thoughtful practitioner; Schon (1983), the reflective practitioner; and Goswami and Stillman (1987), the transformed teacher. Whatever the title or description, all concur that an analysis of the teacher's own role in teacher-research does not only occur through formal evaluation of one's actions but also through reflection upon them. This was what we experienced in our collaboration.

Prior to writing this chapter, we shared what we had learned through our inquiries — as they relate to educational practices — in such presentational formats as conferences, workshops and seminars. However, focusing on the significance and evolution of our relationship through writing about it here has helped us in our consideration of the role of a partner in assisting another teacher-researcher. Previously, we had lacked the recognition and understanding of the process we had been through to become equal partners. And so, in working with new partners, we expected to be at the same stage of awareness, at the outset, as we are in together after years of collaboration. This was a completely unrealistic expectation.

At a very early stage in our collaboration, Leona phrased her inquiry question using a metaphor: What is the role of the CATA-LYST in providing support to a teacher-researcher? Later, she decided to look up this word in a dictionary. *The New Webster Encyclopedic Dictionary* defines catalyst as "an agent that induces a modification in the speed of a chemical reaction, but is not itself chemically changed." However, as she discovered, the term "catalyst" was an inaccurate term to describe Leona's role in supporting Christina's research. Her collaboration with Christina did not leave her unchanged; quite the contrary, the role she played was dynamic in its evolution.

The catalyst speeds up change in a chemical reaction but does not itself change. However, in a human situation, change in a person has to come from within. A catalyst can speed up this process but, once the change is proceeding effectively, the catalyst becomes obsolete. Christina certainly did change from within, but in order to do so, she benefitted from Leona's help. Although Leona was aware of where she wanted to guide Christina in her research, Leona's transaction was in an open manner so that she, too, was changed. Therefore, to be of most value the person who attempts to support a teacher-researcher must be open to change — must be willing to learn from the collaborative relationship.

In addition to developing our voices, we have confronted ourselves and, in the process, feel we have taken ownership over our own learning. Now, however, we are faced with a new challenge as we engage in new partnerships. Valuing and respecting the ownership of another's learning does not only apply to students in the classroom but to all learners — teachers included.

We have moved into another meaningful stage of learning as a result of our collaboration. Unfortunately, moving to different levels of learning can sometimes breed arrogance and superiority. An anecdote illustrates the point well.

Leona: Andreas, my son, is a consistent teacher and he humbles me greatly. One morning, when preparing to go to his daycare, he wanted to take some picture books with him. Aware of his possessive nature I coached him into sharing the books with the other children. He agreed to share with everyone except one individual. When asked why, he responded, "S_____ only reads the pictures and not the words." Andreas had made the connection that it was the print in books that told the story and S_____ was still at the stage where the pictures told the story. He considered himself superior!

Andreas is an excellent teacher! He had graduated from one stage of literacy development into another and found little satisfaction in sharing his book with someone who was not at the same stage as he was. Parallels exist between Andreas' behavior and ours. We only wanted to interact with teacher-researchers who were in the same state of awareness of the learning process as we were, totally forgetting that we had had to go through the process to arrive at that awareness. In our new partnerships we have been far too focused on our own needs, not the collective needs of the teachers with whom we have been interacting. We need to recognize that our roles have changed. Both of us are now in positions of providing support to other teacher-researchers. But no longer as catalysts. Writing this chapter has helped us to see that our role can be much more creative.

10

Promoting Growth Through Dialogue Journals

Catherine Nicolaou Keating

I remember just how thrilled I was the first time I got a reply from Bill, my dialogue journal partner. It was not only exciting, but also reassuring to receive positive feedback in the first response. Just getting a reply was a monumental experience. Bill wrote the following words of encouragement: "I'm looking forward to dialoguing with you because I want to learn more about the power of the process and about where it can lead me." These words made me feel validated by Bill, who is one of my superiors, and opened the door of reciprocal learning. I was inspired to continue with the writing and sharing of the journal in order to hear more about what Bill thought about my ideas.

At about the same time, I also started sharing dialogue journals with some of the teachers at the school where I was vice-principal. I wondered if they experienced a similar reaction to getting a response to their journals from me. Talking about the experience later, Linda recalled how she felt at the time about starting the dialogue journal.

> [I thought] it would be a new experience for me. I've never done it before. I enjoyed it. I get excited about finding out what the administrator's responses to what I say will be. I like writing my thoughts down on paper, because it makes me think. I realize things that I didn't realize before or I'd organize my thoughts better. And get a chance to find out what other people think.

In the Board for which I work, we have recently instituted a new form of supervision. Entitled 'Supervision for Growth,' this scheme represents a radical change from the traditional evaluative mode of supervision towards a growth-oriented model, the aim of which is to encourage and support teachers as competent educators who accept responsibility for their own professional development (York Region Board of Education, 1991, p.10). A key feature of this approach is that teachers identify their own areas for growth and development, based on personal, professional knowledge, and then develop and implement activities for achieving the goals that they themselves have set. Since it is the responsibility of principals and vice-principals to assist them in this process, 'Supervision for Growth' offers a new opportunity for teachers and administrators to work in a collaborative partnership.

In the traditional mode of supervision, as Yonemura (1982,) says, "experienced teachers as sources of knowledge about practice, are rarely utilized in imaginative and productive ways" (p.239). However, this need not be the case, as I hope to show in describing the project in which I was engaged. This involved me, in my role as an administrator, in supporting the professional development of three of my colleagues through the discussion of issues that the teachers chose to raise through the medium of dialogue journals. In response to Yonemura, I would like to present this action research project as an imaginative and productive way of treating teachers as sources of knowledge which they themselves can build on to further their growth and development.

The idea of using a journal to communicate with a teacher was an intriguing one to me. I had first learned about the use of a dialogue journal between administrator and practitioner in an article called 'A Superintendent and a Principal Write to Each Other' (Beatty and Diakiw, 1991). In reading this article, I discovered that the idea of promoting and supporting teacher growth and development from within the school milieu was possible through the sharing of such a journal. The article described some of the risks involved and some of the developments each partner benefited from by taking part in the activity. It seemed like a good way to work collaboratively with Carol, Linda and Jane in relation to their growth plans. It also promised to be a valuable experience for me in allowing me to learn more about my role in supporting their development.

Dialogue journals can take many forms, as is clear from the other chapters in this book. In my case, a dialogue journal is a diary, log or journal in which one is encouraged to write about feelings, questions, concerns or important issues to explore. The journal is then shared with an administrator, who responds in writing as coach or mentor. The dialogue journal strategy is presented by two Boards as part of their Supervision for Growth (North York Board of Education,1991, York Region Board of Education,1991).

In line with Board policy, I first saw my use of a dialogue journal with teachers as a way for me to mentor and support them. In the same spirit, I established a relationship with Bill in order to experience the benefits of being mentored through the dialogue journal process. I convinced Bill that sharing a dialogue journal would be a worthwhile activity for both of us and he agreed to give it a try. To start the exchange, I sent him some articles about the dialogue journal process. In his reply, he included the following comment.

> Thanks for the articles, I found them interesting and relevant to the writing I've been doing. I'd be interested in seeing other such articles you come across. I'm looking forward to dialoguing with you because I want to learn more about the power of the process and about where it leads me.

This statement was an indication that the learning was going to be reciprocal. I wondered if the same reciprocity would develop in the dialogue journal sharing between me and the teachers.

Negotiating Expectations

Each of the teachers I worked with, referred to here as Linda, Jane and Carol, agreed to write and share a dialogue journal with me as part of the process of developing their growth plans according to the Board's Supervision for Growth (York Region 1991) framework. The idea of sharing a dialogue journal was an added benefit for me.

I had already met with the teachers, both formally and informally, during the first term of the school year. Following Board policy, each of them was required to develop a personal growth plan and so my purpose, at that point, was to discover their ideas about what to focus on so that I could help them to write their action plans. In these discussions, I was acting in my role as administrator and coach, as Schön (1975) describes it, "... of helping the student (in this case the teacher-as-learner) formulate the qualities she wants to achieve, and then, by demonstration or description, explore different ways of producing them" (p.296).

It was in this context that I introduced the idea of dialogue journals, first in meetings with them individually and then, in January, in a follow-up discussion to clarify expectations and to respond to any concerns they might have about the process. For our January meeting, I selected an extract from a published journal (North York, 1991) to give them an idea about what might be involved. I also assured them that they were free to decide whether or not to become involved in the project. Of course, this presented me with something of a dilemma. I wanted the teachers to participate, but I wanted them to do so willingly and not from a feeling of obligation because of the authority position I held as researcher/vice-principal. Fortunately, all three teachers expressed willingness — though how far this was in order to accommodate me, I cannot say. In any event, agreement was reached to give the process a try.

The teachers and I decided to use the dialogue journal format to share reflections about current issues in teaching related to their growth plans. We were not quite sure at first just how things would proceed. The dialogue journal presents an opportunity for administrators to involve teachers in conducting their own action research in their classrooms. The three teachers with whom I worked all focused on enhancing the quality of instruction for the benefit of students' learning. Carol's growth plan was focused on changing teaching strategies to improve behavior management in the classroom; Linda was interested in the integration of special education pupils in her class; and Jane was concentrating on the evaluation of student progress in the area of literacy. They were each conducting their own action research in their classrooms as I conducted mine at the school level.

From the point of view of my research, it was important for me to discover how the teachers felt about the use of the dialogue journals. This was obviously a topic that might arise in the journal writing itself. But I was not willing to leave the matter to chance, so I explicitly asked the teachers to give me their reactions. This is how Jane reflected on the process:

> I had never really been involved in too many of them (journals) but I thought it was worth a try just to see if expressing my ideas on paper was any better a reflection of what I'm doing than carrying it around in my head all the time. I think for me it was useful, because it actually made me do it. Made me sit and reflect on my ideas, how what I'm doing affects the future. How all of what I'm doing — evaluation and everything — it gave me a focus of not just what I'm doing now, but what I intend to do. It was helpful for me.

Establishing and Maintaining the Conditions for Dialogue

Although my action research project focuses on the dialogue journal exchange, this was not our only means of communication. The three teachers and I also had many opportunities for face-to-face communication and discussion, not only about the journalling, but also about other things that were occurring in the school and about personal matters. Working in the same building, with the possibility of being able to converse and visit the journal partner both informally and formally, seemed to significantly facilitate the journal sharing process with the teachers; it gave an added sense of immediacy in the response — if not in writing, at least in passing conversations and contact.

Unfortunately, in the case where I shared a journal with Bill, we were at different schools and face-to-face contact was at a minimum. This, I am sure, affected the frequency of our exchanges which, in turn, had a considerable impact on the flow of the communication. I recall Bill writing to me after a two month period, "I no longer apologize for taking so long — it seems to just be a reality with open-ended deadlines in journalling."

Nevertheless, a sense of collegiality and bonding developed between Bill and me as we proceeded in sharing the journal, and so, although there might be long periods of silence, I never prompted Bill about his reply. In a way, I also did not want to have him feel pressured to respond within a time limit. The fact that we were involved in the process was enough for me. However, he often said that, after our meetings, he was spurred on to reignite the flame and get on with the writing. So it would seem that the personal contact does play a great part in facilitating the dialogue journal writing process.

This experience with Bill certainly influenced my thinking about when and how often to respond to Carol, Jane and Linda. I was anxious that they should not feel under any additional pressure because of their dialogue journal writing with me. Perhaps, as a result, I slowed down the exchanges unnecessarily. The teachers started the journal writing in January and we shared back and forth about once a month over a period of six months, resulting in three entries for each partner. The process ended when I left the school in June. I felt as though we had just started to get things under way when we had to stop. In light of the short time frame we had in sharing dialogue journals, and after talking with other teachers and administrators who have used this approach, it seems that six months is just long enough to give you a taste of the process. In order for further depth and growth for all of those involved, more time would be necessary to interact — time for teachers and administrator to grow together.

In beginning the process, I suggested that the teachers start the journal by writing an entry related to the objectives that they had set out and that we had discussed during the development of their individual growth plans. Therefore, the teachers were left with writing the first entry. Jane comments on her feelings about taking the first step in writing.

> [That] was the hardest thing to do. That was where all your feelings about well, why should I write? Not necessarily 'What did my partner want to hear?' No. That's not an appealing way for me to write. You get used to doing it.... It was a new experience for me actually to sit down and write. So, I guess it had to do with some of the courses that I was doing and to do with my areas of interest, so I sat and decided what to write the first time.

I was somewhat surprised by how the teachers chose to write. One chose to type her journal and the other two used a computer. This was unanticipated in that I expected that their journals would be handwritten in a booklet format, as mine was with Bill. The fact that the teachers initiated the writing enabled them to start off the journal sharing in the mode in which they were most comfortable. I shared my surprise with Bill and wrote the following in my dialogue journal,

> My work with staff in the area of dialogue journals continues. Something interesting occurred. The three teachers I work with use the computer to write their feelings. Last time I received the latest entry from each — almost a letter format. I then responded on my computer. (The first time I wrote back on the back of their sheet of paper.) This left me with a written sample of my response. I wonder if the change to individual pieces of paper may speed up the process. This way I could write to them without waiting for a journal to be returned — or could that be pushy? On an average, I guess we switch back and forth once a month — it seems like a long time but I don't believe one can push progress — the Supervision for Growth model is one of growth over time after all — is it not?

Writing on separate papers likened the process to letter writing and allowed for more flexibility in writing back and forth without having to wait for the booklet to return. Although we never tried this, Linda indicated that she would have liked more frequent feedback during the short time we had to share the journals. However, she was concerned about responding as an added pressure. I purposely chose to wait until I had received the written journal submission back from the teachers before responding so as not to pressure them into thinking they had to write back on demand. Tension at the school was high since each of the teachers I was working with was involved in a school program review being conducted by the board. In future, when I share dialogue journals with teachers, I will keep in mind to encourage more frequent responses — and not necessarily wait to get a reply before writing to my partner. The tendency to wait for a reply is also similar to waiting for a letter. In regard to the written format, another consideration would be to include the possibility of extending the writing to a computer network as a medium for the dialogue journal. However, this might be more appropriate for a small group of teachers involved in more of a peer coaching mode. Since trust is such a strong issue, I also wonder about the confidentiality factor with using a computer network.

As already mentioned, the effects of adding to an already full workload was a matter of concern for all of us. The time it takes to write and the length of time between responses were mentioned both in the journal and in the subsequent discussions. Carol, concerned about the extra work load, said

> I thought it would be more work. (laughing) I thought it would. I'm being totally honest. But it turned out that it wasn't. It turned out to be a good, a positive technique for me. But I think at the time I was like "Oh no! More work to do." But it did turn out to be better because it allowed me to get things organised, my thoughts down and you know, those things. It worked out a lot better than I thought.

On reflection about the timing aspect with the teachers at school, Linda said that she might have appreciated a time limit or a prompt to respond earlier:

> I think you have to set up something where it's a system where you have to hand it in... regularly at a specific time. Like the 15th. Not that if you missed the deadline it's a big problem. Then you feel pressure because you never know what might be going on that particular week. But just where it's a part of your routine. Because a teacher's life is so hectic that you forget — you have so many things on your mind as it is. But if you know it's done regularly, then you sit down and do it.

Bill also mentioned similar feelings about pressure and the hectic pace of teachers' lives in relation to the length of time between responses in his journal reply to me:

As you well know, the job of principal/v.p. is made up of hundreds of things happening at once. Multiple initiatives are being promoted and monitored simultaneously. Advance planning for future events is essential. Responding to immediate needs and issues of students, teachers and parents is ongoing. And teachers' jobs are no less demanding and challenging.

I was glad that I had left responding to the journal up to him.

Trust and Honesty

Establishing a climate of trust and confidentiality is an important priority in the dialogue journal process (Beatty and Diakiw, 1991). According to Fullan (1982), "It is what develops in minds and actions that count.... Change is a difficult personal and social process of unlearning old ways and learning new ones ... deeper and solid change must be born over time." The struggle for teachers and administrators involved in sharing dialogue journals is to take a risk in adapting to the new roles that are called for by the dialogue journal process. Such risk-taking is more likely to occur when a trusting environment has been established over time. It takes trust to enhance open communication and growth. Fortunately, I had known each of the teachers for a period of three years prior to the beginning of the project and, over this time, rapport had been established and a level of collegiality had evolved. However, the positive feeling of trust that already existed between administrator and teachers was further enhanced by the natural and informal language we used in communicating through the journals. As stated by Elliott (1990), "this knowledge of each other as persons [does] much to foster free, open and tolerant professional discourse" (p.6).

In their journals the teachers provided me with a broader perspective about what was happening in their classrooms. They also gave me important insights into how they really felt about what they were doing. The importance of trust was one of the issues that they commented on. Linda, for example, had the following to say about the need for trust in overcoming her worries about the risks involved in confiding in a superior:

> Well, I wouldn't have been honest with or trusted a new person so soon.... I was probably trying to work things in a quiet way too. Because the administrator is my boss. But I wasn't hiding anything. Whereas, if it was somebody I didn't know, and I didn't trust, then I'd probably not say some of the things that I did. That would be if I was having a problem. If everything was going smoothly, in what I'm writing about, then it wouldn't make any difference. But if I was venting

some frustration or opinion that might not be the opinion of other people, then it would be more difficult to say it to somebody that I didn't know.

... if they're that intimidated by the administrator then it wouldn't be the right thing. But if they felt comfortable with the administrator, and they just needed somebody to have some current education philosophy, or even organization — that type of thing — or new ideas, or how to cope with parents, or behavior problems, then that would be great....

The teachers also expressed their feelings about the importance of trust in general and Jane added her views about risk-taking:

I think if you and your partner are open communicators — I didn't feel that anybody was evaluating me in terms of my competence. It wasn't threatening at all.

But it was Carol who was most explicit about the importance of the quality of the relationship for the success of the dialogue. Reflecting on one particular exchange, she observed:

And there was another time also that I got a response that made me feel more comfortable. It was very honest, about how I react to the kids. How I get too involved and I was getting very honest responses.... The response was "You don't have to do it that way. You have to realize that you have to distance yourself and not get too involved." And I think that the fact that... my administrator could say that to me made me more willing to be able to say things to her. So I think it was a give and take.

Identifying Growth

It was this comment by Carol that appeared to make the greatest impact on her professional development. We talked about it at length after finishing the process. She told me that, although at first she was somewhat taken aback by one of my comments in particular, in retrospect what I said made sense to her. The class she had was one which included several students with significant difficulties. There was a need to get help from support services. In her April entry, Carol wrote about her increased involvement with her support resource personnel and the amount of team planning that they had done together. She wrote:

We have spent a lot of time reviewing class rules, procedures etc., and reviewing the needs of the class. Barbara [resource person] has also spent a lot of time in the class getting to know the children... We have discussed many forms of behavior management programs and have implemented one which seems to be working well for the time being. All of the children are on the program, and they receive individual points which are used towards both individual and class rewards. Interestingly, some children — no matter what type of program is used — don't seem to respond. I am finding it necessary to spend a lot of time trying to find out what will make a difference for some of these kids. Most of these children respond well, 90% of the time, to discipline — as many of them don't get much discipline at home. However, it is still, and it appears it will always be difficult to reach these children when they are not 'with the class,' due to personal problems — another reason why I'm almost glad that there are so many of these kids in one class. If one is having a bad day, no one seems to mind or notice much! ... I feel that overall progress is being made with the behavior problems in the class. However, one thing I've learned from Barbara — which I have to remember often — is that this is a process. It is important to keep that in mind when what seems like five or six months of work has been lost because of a child's problems. However, I hope that through this process the months aren't lost they are still there for the child to learn from and to give them support.

I had been working directly with Carol and through Barbara with Carol. I was aware of the kinds of tensions that she was struggling with regarding the students in her class. I felt that Carol was learning how to be more objective and professional in her dealings around very sensitive issues that involved her students. I was concerned about her ability to leave the school problems at school and develop her professional objectivity. I was not aware just how much my response to her in the journal jolted her until we discussed the process in June. I was pleased with the sensitivity of Carol's comments. I remember that, when I wrote my response, I had intended to be supportive of her work with colleagues and to encourage her to dialogue with other support services in a proactive manner. I was somewhat concerned, however, that all the pressures that she was experiencing should not overwhelm her, and so I wrote the following to her:

> I encourage you to remain open and congenial in your working together with such people as Barbara and the consultant in order to reflect on your growth and development as a teacher. Since we are inundated with such a flood of demands on our time, it would seem even more important that we should make opportunities to collaborate with other professionals in order to enhance the learning environment. I understand that you have also been concerned with the home environment of some of your students — and that's O.K. to a

point — the point being that you do the best you can within your limitations. When you seek out the advice of other experts in the field, such as Barbara, Children's Aid and others, you also enable yourself to grow. The time spent on such activities as setting class rules and even organising the room most effectively and displaying the rules and consequences with other strategies — as you say, it's the process that's important. The process also impacts on how you develop and change as a result of the coaching and mentoring you receive. Some day you may be in the mentor position when a novice teacher gets a surprise into the real world of teaching. Even if you reach one child — that could be a lot. The important thing is to keep trying and not give up. That's where the coaching and working collaboratively with your colleagues can be of great help. Don't forget, it is the attempts to provide the positive models within the five hour structured school day that some children have as their only means of gauging what is a 'norm.'

At the beginning of her career, Carol appeared reluctant to go to the support services for assistance. As Carol and I talked in regular school team meetings around critical issues, she stated that she was feeling more comfortable about working with the various support agencies. In this, her third year of teaching, it was most necessary for Carol to access and meet with support services. This was the beginning of an important development for Carol, as she will be bound to have continuing dealings with a number of different support services and learning how to interact and access them as a professional is vital to helping the students. I feel that now she may be more ready, willing and able to look into her own practice and to dialogue with her colleagues in order to explore the dialectic between practice and theory through collaborative inquiry. She has taken the first steps through this dialogue journal activity and her active interactions with support staff.

In my response to Carol in the journal, I recognized her suggestions and encouraged her to continue to collaborate with her peers. I wrote:

> I agree that a session for staff with Children's Aid Society is in order and have spoken to the counsellor informally. Remind me please to present the idea to staff for sometime in the June P.A. sessions. There are some programs and strategies that Barbara can share with you about how to set up the classroom not only now but also to consider for next September.

My request for her to remind me to present the idea to staff was intended to include Carol in presenting strategies to staff, based on her experiences during the year.

Finding the Key

Dewey (1963) explains that "the principle that development comes through interaction means that education is essentially a social process. This quality is realized in the degree to which individuals form a community group" (p.58). The partnership created within the dialogue journal sharing experience creates an opportunity for both partners, teacher and administrator, to collaborate and learn from each other.

The coaching strategies that Schön (1987) outlines may provide a model for administrators in their new roles within this paradigm shift to transformational leadership. Schön says that "an important part of a coach's artistry consists in his ability to draw on an extensive repertoire of media, languages, and methods of description in order to represent his ideas in many ways, searching for the images that will 'click'" (p.297). The dialogue journal process provided me with the opportunity to share thoughts and concerns with these teachers, and to become more of a resource and support in helping them reach their goals. I also became more aware of their needs and was better able to facilitate their access to resource personnel and materials. Journal writing was a key that opened the door to further dialogue and developed added insights.

Searching for images that would 'click' was part of making the most appropriate suggestions about support services and resources to the teachers. In her first entry in January, Jane expressed her interest in assessing the literacy skills of her students. In my response to her, I suggested a couple of resources, among which was the Ontario Assessment Instrument Pool (O.A.I.P.), which was in the school. In her final entry in June, Jane expressed confidence in her knowledge about the principles in the O.A.I.P., which had been given to her in the course she was taking. In this entry, she articulated some of the similarities and differences between the junior division model and the secondary model presented in her course. She commented as follows:

> Both documents (Junior and Secondary Ontario Assessment Instrument Pool [O.A.I.P.]) are based on on-going observation, or 'Kid Watching,' which can involve conferences as well as observing work and behavior. This is a great approach because it is 'ability' based, in large part, except for the sections on 'miscue analysis,' which focus on errors in prog-

ress.... Well, I must admit that my evening [with the guest speaker about the secondary program] was enlightening, however, it seems ironic that secondary schools are just getting into the kind of evaluation that elementary teachers have been working with for years. It was as if the movement away from summative evaluation to a more formative approach is something of a new philosophy, a philosophy that secondary teachers are ready to take credit for! Glad you [secondary teachers] could join us!

Reflections

Conscientious professionals seek ways to be positive and continuous learners. One way for educators to learn more about teaching and learning is to step back and reflect on our experiences. For we do not actually learn as much from experience as we do from reflecting on that experience. This notion is illustrated in the image of the teacher-as-learner and active decision-maker who uses information about the classroom and school life to fashion instruction, as reflected in the dialogues within the journals. When such observation is tied to informed reflection it becomes inquiry. Encouraging teachers to share and accept contributions from others, to reflect and inquire is ongoing within the dialogue journal process.

In contrast to Elmore's claim (1992) that educational research does not grow out of existing practice and, thus, has no necessary relationship to existing school organization, I have presented an overview of a study that grew out of the existing practice of using a dialogue journal to promote teacher growth and help principals and teachers adapt to new and challenging expectations of their changing roles. As previously stated, through the dialogue journals the teachers, too, were conducting their own action research inquiries.

Gordon Wells (1986) describes the problem of constructing meaning in conversation as a collaborative activity. This was certainly true of the conversations we had about using dialogue journals. Throughout the process, I felt that there was a search for a common language, among and between the journal partners, in which to express our goals and understandings. In this way, the dialogue journal process can be particularly beneficial in a school milieu where a shift is taking place from evaluation of teachers, to a growth-oriented model of supervision.

Jane commented on this as she reflected on the impact of sharing her feelings in writing:

> You do want to please your partner, because you're committed

to them, but after a while that sort of feeling goes away and you actually get personally involved with it. Because you're thinking of it in your own terms. "Well, what do I want to get out of it?" And I know that I have a copy of the journal and later I will probably look at it and say, "Well, how did I feel about this?" And, "What were my problems?" And maybe in five years from now, I'll probably still be struggling with some of the same things but I may be able to deal with it in a different way. If I keep it up with somebody else it would be interesting to see how it would go. It's fascinating. As I said, I've never really taken the time just to sit down and read it. I assumed that it was happening. But writing it is a different story.

I agree with Jane's account and will also have the journal to look back on to see how I responded to a situation, and how this might change in the future. In sharing journals with teachers another time, I feel that I would move the focus away from the mentorship aspect and try to focus more on the actual sharing of ideas. In the case of Jane and Carol, I felt that what was expected was more advice and direction. With Linda, however, I might have been more able to have an ongoing dialogue about other issues and trends.

The Dialogue Journal as a Communication Tool

The dialogue journal enabled me to address and clarify issues that otherwise might not have come to the forefront. For Carol the journal provided an added vehicle of communication.

> ...it (the dialogue journal process) gave me the opportunity to focus... I think it's in each individual person, how you respond to each other. It was worthwhile... for both. I think it's a good opportunity because also you don't always have that chance — you're busy and they're running and I think that's a good reason to have it also. To have it as a communication tool — which you might not necessarily have.

I had an opportunity to respond to Linda differently when she wrote about her concerns regarding the program review and how myopic a process this could be. My response was more to placate her than to share perceptions. Linda wrote:

> I was pleased that the (school) review was positive. However, I have to admit that I felt very pressured. I felt stressed when I found out that the Superintendent was coming into our class. I felt that we had 40 minutes to prove to this evaluator that our class was well adjusted. Prior to our first visit, one of

the students had been acting out I was afraid that he would 'explode' during the visit.

This is how I replied:

You are not alone in your concerns about a 40 minute visit being able to influence someone's decision about what's going on. Perception, however, is reality. People are constantly forming opinions based on few, if any, facts. Sometimes the consequences of jumping to conclusions are great.

The concern of having so much rest on two 40 minute visits has been expressed by teachers undergoing evaluation — you know how much fun that can be! One thing that really helps is when there is a pre-conference meeting. At this time the teacher can discuss any possible 'actors' or tenuous situations that might arise. As long as the observer is prepared with an explanation, it would/should eliminate — or at least diminish — any fears of 'what if — acts out?'

The pre-visit meeting is also a time to determine the purpose of the visit. During this time the teacher explains the main objective chosen for the specific lesson and time. Let's not forget that the supervisors are also educators. They are not here to merely pass judgment but to assist in clarifying the perceptions — it helps the school ascertain whether or not what is being attempted is being achieved — or to what degree. I see it as a microscopic view on what the school thinks is happening and a chance for the school to demonstrate the attempts that have been made towards a certain goal in relation to teaching and learning. The move to supervision for growth now is intended to give teachers more of an opportunity to dialogue with administrators in establishing growth plans intended to enhance teaching and learning from the point of view, interests, needs and abilities of the individual teacher. I hope it's working. It's not often that educators are awarded the opportunity to dialogue professionally or the time to reflect collaboratively on teaching and learning.

As it turned out the review team discerned just about what we expected. There was also a chance for the school to advertise the positive thrusts and initiatives that were going on. The positive exposure is important to the esteem or climate of the school. I'd say we've had enough of the negatives. It's time we celebrated our achievements and had them publicly acknowledged. In a community such as ours it might be even more important to let the parents in on the what, how, why, where and when of the decision-making in the school. They seem to react more positively when they are aware and have been briefed on the reasons behind the decision-making. I realise that this involvement is not always necessary or possible, but I think that the school can make a move in this direction — similar to the way we have been doing. I hope that I've been able to answer some of your concerns.

You've certainly given me an opportunity to think about evaluation again and the role it plays in the teaching and learning that goes on every day!

Rereading this response, I now see that it might read as more defensive and reactive than the proactive and supportive message I had intended. Linda did, however, inspire me to rethink the role of evaluation and supervision. Perhaps if we had shared the dialogue journal over a longer period of time, the mutual professional dialogue would have surfaced.

Role Changes

The role of the school administrator is changing in the nineties, in line with the changes that are taking place throughout society. The traditional role of the principal as the all-knowing and all-seeing evaluator has all but disappeared and is being replaced by one in which he or she counsels teachers and helps them to develop or improve a self-selected aspect of their teaching. This approach also gives a new role to teachers as participants in decision-making regarding the development of their goals to improve the teaching/learning process. Within this approach, the sharing of dialogue journals between practitioners and administrators can provide a refreshing and productive way of facilitating professional growth.

This is what is happening in our school. Through the use of dialogue journals in the context of 'Supervision for Growth,' the three teachers who have been involved in this approach have been encouraged to play a more agentive role in their own professional development. In their journal entries and in the responses they received, they have been led to examine the way in which the intellectual world of theory and objectives, as set out in their personal growth plans, affects the practical world of learning and teaching. By trying out and testing their plans and objectives, and by recording their perceptions of what was happening in their classrooms, they have been encouraged to question the extent to which their theory is being validated in practice and, where necessary, to make changes. The dialogue journals have thus provided a means for them to monitor and direct their own growth and development in their own specific areas of concern.

Carol, for example, shared in her journal that she felt, "overall,

progress is being made with the behavior problems in the class."
My experience corroborated this, for I noted that there were fewer
children from her room coming to the office with problems. Jane
followed through on all the readings and materials that I suggested, and discovered that the suggestions in the journal and the
input from the course she was taking overlapped. It made me feel
good to know that what I had suggested was also being validated
in her course. She also made the connection and felt proud to have
been aware of the resources before they were introduced in the
course. Linda took time to vent some of the frustrations she was
experiencing with the added pressure of the program review
going on in the school. Her final journal entry was the longest; in
it, she suggested ways of planning for strategies with her students next year.

This form of action research opens up exciting new possibilities
for school-based staff development, that of teachers planning and
carrying out inquiries to enhance instructional practices in their
own classrooms. Because it addresses real life problems encountered in schools, inquiry of this kind is practical in orientation —
geared to action, not to decontextualized knowledge. Conducted
by practitioners, it also provides a way for educators to investigate school issues through shared decision-making and to use
this information to effect appropriate changes.

However, although the teachers were involved in action research, I did not use the journal exchanges to explore this aspect
of their concerns as fully as I might have done. If I engage in
another project of this kind in the future, I shall certainly attempt
to encourage the teachers to become involved in their own action
research and to share the experience through dialogue journal
exchanges.

The concern which initially guided me in the journal sharing
process was to identify what was going on in relation to the
teachers' growth plans and the implementation of their objectives. However, as the experiment proceeded, and as I subsequently reflected on the experience, I found that my concern was
changing; from focusing mainly on what was happening with the
teachers, I began to include consideration of who I am as an
educational leader, and how I can better support the teachers.

Looking back on the experience, I can now see that my role, too,
has shifted. From being purely an administrator, I became
mentor, coach and confidante. As a partner in the dialogue, I too
was a learner, and worked collaboratively with the teachers, not
only in guiding them along their paths but also in expressing my
ideas and concerns. I was also able to be proactively supportive,
supplying them with resources, promoting and encouraging their

dialogue with colleagues, and offering support at critical moments.

Implications for the Future

I certainly hope to be in a position to use dialogue journals with teachers again. My goal as an administrator is to develop a culture of influence, which encourages teachers, as professionals, to express their concerns and ideas in a climate of trust, respect and mutual consideration. Dialogue journals seem to provide a particularly effective means for the attainment of this goal. In the future, however, I will pay much closer attention to when and how I respond and to what I single out for attention.

Having had an opportunity to reflect on the dialogue journal process, I can see that it provides an opportunity for the administrator to interact with teachers on a different level from that of routine organization. For example, if she knows, from reading a teacher's journal, what are the issues of concern to that person, the administrator can provide proactive support and encourage a mutual sharing of ideas and concerns that is responsive to the individual teacher's needs. I believe that, in the study I have reported, I was able to do this for Carol and Jane more than for Linda. For most of the six month period I saw my role chiefly in terms of mentoring. Having had this experience, and a subsequent period for reflection, I hope I would enter another similar situation more as a learner. In so doing, I might be better able to help the teachers to perceive themselves as learners as well.

I see this as part of the more general move towards a staff community in which all recognize the need to learn from each other. Another administrator told me that, during her first year of exchanging a dialogue journal with a teacher, she spent much time waiting for inspiration to strike before responding to her partner in writing. That certainly ties up the process and models a different attitude than the collaborative learning which I would now wish to encourage. However, in this my first experience I went through a similar process of discovering just what my role was and how best to play it out. Perhaps if we had continued into the next school year together, Carol, Jane and Linda and I would have revealed even more of ourselves. As Linda said of herself, after the process was over, "I was probably trying to work things in a quiet way too, because the administrator is my boss." Extending the process to allow for more time might help to overcome this feeling of "working things in a quiet way" and focusing too much on one's own role — as I tended to do.

The dialogue journal process provides such an opportunity for both teachers and administrators to become more active listeners and critics. It also allows us each to find a voice with which to become more involved in discussions about teaching and learning and, in the process, more open to self-revelation. As Jane so aptly put it:

> [It's important] for my voice to come out, something I'm not used to. If you write in a very dry traditional way — [the way] you're used to writing for courses — I think your own voice is not always clear.... My own voice and what I have now is not what comes out in writing other things. I think [what is important is] searching for my voice as teacher and [not] just as a person.

As I have discovered, the dialogue journal provides an opportunity for us to find our own voices. But this process takes time. I look forward to finding my voice and helping others to do the same in my next experience of dialogue journal sharing.

11

Watching Ourselves Grow

Gordon Wells

Last year, I received an invitation to teach a summer course at another university. My immediate inclination was to accept. At the same time, however, I recognized that I was taking on a new challenge. Because the course would be held during the summer months, both the students and I would be away from our normal places of work. How, then, could we make action research on our own teaching a central part of the course?

As I explained in the Introduction to this book, my overriding aim in working with teachers and administrators is to encourage them to take responsibility for creating the conditions that they judge to be optimal for their students' learning and development and to assist and support them as they attempt to make changes in their practice towards this goal. Over the years this has involved me in a variety of working relationships: as a consultant to action research projects initiated from within school districts; as a researcher working collaboratively with volunteer teachers on funded projects that I have initiated; and as a teacher of graduate level courses which require course members to carry out an action research project as a central part of their study. In all these situations, the inquiries have been carried out over the course of the school year in conjunction with the participants' normal activities. Under these conditions, there is no separation between research and practice, since it is some aspect of the practice itself which becomes the focus of inquiry.

In the summer months, however, an inquiry of this sort would not be possible. It was therefore with trepidation as well as enthusiasm that I accepted the teaching assignment, uncertain as I then was about how I should approach it. Could I find a way of organizing a university-based course that would, nevertheless, embody the principles that I had attempted to put into practice in the other situations I have described? In whatever way I solved the problem, however, one thing was certain: in planning, teaching and evaluating the course, I should, myself, adopt the stance of action researcher. Having made this decision, I realized that, by subsequently writing about this inquiry into my own teaching situation, I could contribute a chapter to this book on the same terms as the other authors. In the account that follows, therefore, I shall try to recreate some of the salient features of this learning and teaching experience, considering them from the perspective of a number of issues which remain, for me, both central and problematic. To a considerable extent, these issues are similar to those addressed by my fellow teacher-researchers in the preceding chapters of this book. They can be briefly stated as follows:

- How can the curriculum be reconceptualized with collaborative inquiry as the focus of learning and teaching?

- How can we gain greater recognition for the central role of discourse as the medium of learning and teaching?

- How can we help teachers to see that developing the understanding necessary for responsible social action should be the purpose of their own and indeed all students' learning?

- How can these issues be addressed through action and reflection on our own practice?

It was the attempt to find answers to these questions in collaboration with my students — I now realize in retrospect —that provided both the challenge and the satisfaction I experienced in teaching the course I am about to describe.

Planning for Inquiry: The Three Strands

One of the attractions of the invitation I received was that I was given complete freedom to choose what the course would be about. It did not take me long to decide. I would call it "Talk and Text: Learning and Teaching Across the Curriculum."

As a researcher in Bristol, England, I spent many years following a representative sample of children from before their first words until the end of their elementary education (Wells, 1986). From this attempt to understand how children learn to talk and use talk to learn, I have long been convinced that it is through interaction with others that they both master the language of their community and construct a mental model of the world in terms of the cultural categories that are encoded in that language. However, neither language nor mental model is an end in itself; rather, both are means for living and acting in a world shared with other people. They are semiotic (meaning-making) tools that we learn to use in order to participate in purposeful social and individual activity.

Such a functional view of language has been slow to win acceptance in education. Despite the efforts of proponents of 'whole language' and 'process writing,' it is still quite common for language to be treated as a separate subject — on a par with math, social studies, and science — itself fragmented into the separate 'skills' of reading, writing and spelling. Rarely, in such classrooms, are written texts used as tools for thinking and communicating or the activities of reading and writing seen as opportunities to engage in an ongoing dialogue the aim of which is to increase understanding. As for talk, it is not even mentioned; tolerated in small group activity, as long as not too loud, and taken for granted when directed by the teacher in whole class lessons, its central role in the constructing of 'common knowledge' (Edwards and Mercer, 1987) is simply not recognized.

An exploration of the mediating functions of talk and text in the co-construction of knowledge across all areas of the curriculum thus seemed one important focus for the course. This, then, would be the first of the three strands. Not that I thought that those enroling would be strangers to such a functional view of language. In fact, just the opposite. But, by creating a forum in which experience gained from practice could be brought into dialogue with knowledge of a more theoretical origin, I hoped we could all gain a greater understanding of this important topic.

My own understanding of the teaching-learning relationship and of the central role of discourse in its enactment owes much to the writings of Vygotsky and other sociocultural theorists. In contrast to the highly individualistic conceptions of learning and development which have dominated educational thinking for most of this century, their emphasis on the cultural provenance of individual knowledge and on the inherently social and transactional nature of the encounters in which learners take over this knowledge and make it their own provides a firm basis for a more collaborative approach to classroom practice. It is only recently, however, that Vygotsky's writings have been translated into English and so, as yet, they are still largely unfamiliar to the majority of educators. I therefore decided to make an exploration of the relevance of sociocultural theory for educational practice another theme for the course. This would be the second strand. Deciding on the content was the easy part of my initial planning. Much more difficult was to decide how to embed this content in a form of organization that would encourage course members to become inquirers into their own practice and agents of change amongst their colleagues when they returned to their teaching, advisory or administrative positions in the following year.

As I pondered on this problem, I began to think about the features that distinguish action research from other forms of professional development for teachers. Two seemed to be criterial. The first is the teacher's choice of the issue to be addressed and ownership of the ensuing investigation, and the second is the dialectic between practice and theory in the actual conduct of the investigation. Further reflection led me to wonder whether these are not also important features of any sustained learning endeavor. If so, could they not be built into the design of the course I was planning in such a way that they not only structured the learning experience but were themselves made the subject of reflective investigation? Re-reading Eleanor Duckworth's (1987) essays about teaching and learning gave me good reason for believing that such a plan was feasible. And so I decided to try to find a way of making students' own inquiries the focus for our exploration of learning and teaching. This would provide the third strand which, hopefully, would act as the warp on which to weave the overall design.

Stating my intentions in this way, however, gives a quite false impression of my actual thinking processes, which were much less sharply focused. As with many of the teacher inquiries that I have been involved in, the actual formulation of the organizing strands of the course and of the questions that I wanted to investigate occurred over many months and has only taken final shape in the writing of this chapter. Nevertheless, from the beginning, I was conscious of two very general issues that I needed to grapple with in my planning: the relationship between action and reflection in inquiry-based learning, and that between student initiative and choice on the one hand and teacher direction and instruction on the other. However, I was not thinking of the terms in these two pairings as opposed in any absolute sense. In each case, both needed to be treated as essential components of the experience as a whole. The issue was therefore not of choosing between them, nor even of attempting to achieve an optimal balance, but rather that of sustaining a dynamic interplay between them as the course developed.

As I thought about the problem of course design over the winter months, I was also carrying out collaborative investigations with two teachers on the role of language in the learning and teaching of science (Wells and Chang-Wells, 1992b; Wells,1993). As it happened, in both the grade three and the grade six classrooms, the topic under investigation was the theme of time and, in both classrooms, we were all involved in some interesting practical work on pendulums. It was this that suggested the solution to my initial problem. Since the course members would not be able to carry out investigations of learning and teaching in their own classrooms, we would take the theme of time and explore it as a topic worthy of investigation in its own right, while using the experience of so doing as a point of reference both for our study of Vygotskian ideas about learning and teaching and for our exploration of the place of texts and talk in the learning-and-teaching process. My hope was that, by interweaving the three strands — inquiry, discourse and sociocultural theory — we could, as a community of learners, gain a greater understanding of how best, as teachers, to provide learning opportunities for others.

A month before the course started, I sent the following letter to all those who were enroled, telling them about my plans for the course. (As will be seen, I still had some way to go in arriving at the metaphor of the three interwoven strands that I described in the preceding paragraphs.)

There are two basic ideas behind the course — hypotheses, if you prefer — that we shall be putting to the test during our weeks together. The first is that, to be more effective teachers, we need to attend to and reflect upon the total activity of learning-and-teaching, that is the transactions between the learner, the teacher, and the topic of their joint attention, in the context in which it occurs. One way to do this is by engaging in a learning-teaching enterprise about a topic that really engages us and simultaneously subjecting our experience to reflective scrutiny. This is why I have proposed that we devote a substantial part of our time together to an exploration of the theme of time.

The second idea, or hypothesis, is that the learning-teaching transaction is essentially a form of conversation — a dialogue that each learner has with other people, and with the texts that he or she composes and interprets, about his or her topic of inquiry. By attending carefully to the utterances and their sequels that make up these conversations, therefore, we should be able to understand better how we ourselves learn and so be better able to provide learning opportunities for others.

As well as reflecting on our own activities within the group, it will be helpful, I think, if we can also compare these with episodes of learning and teaching in schools. If you possibly can, therefore, I should like you to record (preferably on videotape) one or two episodes in your own classroom that you think it might be interesting for us to look at and discuss together. I shall have some recorded episodes to share, too, in some of which I tried to put my ideas into practice when working with junior-age children.

Since I got the idea of organizing a course of this kind from reading some of the essays in Eleanor Duckworth's book, *"The having of wonderful ideas" and other essays on teaching and learning*, I thought you might like to read one of them before we meet so that we shall have a shared experience as a basis for starting our conversations. I am enclosing a copy of the paper with this letter.[1]

Finally: the theme of 'time.' When did time begin? Do all cultures think about it in the same way? How do our varying experiences of the passage of time — depending on what we are doing — relate to real time? What is real time? You might like to start a list of questions about time that you find intriguing and think about how you might set about answering them. This will give us a flying start when we get together in July.

Having provided the students with what I hoped would be a helpful indication of the sort of learning experience I wanted the course to be, I set about making my own preparations. I gathered copies of papers that I thought would be relevant to each of the three strands and added a number of my own books to form the basis of a small class library. (Details of these papers and books are given in Appendix 1.) I also selected a number of excerpts from video recordings I had made of children working on science themes during the preceding months. Finally, I made my own personal selection of sonnets and other short poems on the theme of time and copied tape recordings of pieces of music that I found particularly interesting from the point of view of tempo and rhythm. These were to be my contribution to the resources on which we might want to draw during the weeks ahead; however, I expected that course members would also have resources that they wanted to contribute.

As it happens — and not entirely by chance — I was at this time reading Judith Newman's *Interwoven Conversations* (1991), in which she gives a reflective account of a summer institute she had taught. From it, I picked up a number of helpful suggestions concerning practical matters to attend to, such as ordering the video playback equipment we would need *ahead* of time and arranging for instruction in the use of the university computer for those who needed it. She also reminded me to make sure I had a brand-new notebook in which to record my reflections! This I packed in my carry-on bag, along with the lap-top computer on which I planned to write more extensively. With my video camera, audio recorder, and a plentiful supply of recording tapes, I was now ready to leave for the University of British Columbia, where, in the Department of Language Education, the course was to take place.

Opening Moves — Through Students' Eyes

In describing the way in which my intentions for the course gradually emerged, I have said nothing about detailed planning. This is because, beyond what was included in the letter, I did not have specific plans about what particular materials we might use nor about the precise way in which the three strands of the course might be interrelated. These were decisions that I hoped could be made collectively by the class as a whole, as individuals and groups decided on what topics they wanted to investigate and on how they wanted to proceed. However, I did have to decide on an agenda for the first meeting. And it was in thinking about this that I found Newman's book most helpful, particularly the chapter whose title I have borrowed for this section: 'Opening Moves.' This phrase captures very well my sense of teaching and learning being, as a whole, an ongoing conversation or, rather, a series of interwoven conversations. And, as in a game of chess, the opening moves are crucially important in setting up possibilities and constraints for what can happen later.

My chief concern for this first meeting was to establish the ambience that I wanted to prevail — that of a community of reflective inquirers who could pursue their own individual interests while providing support for, and learning from, the interests, expertise and experience of others. I planned, therefore, to spend a considerable portion of the afternoon in open-ended discussion so that people could begin to get to know one another in a relaxed and non-threatening atmosphere. First, we would meet as a whole group to talk about the questions that interested people in relation to the theme of time, and then we would meet in small groups to discuss one or more of the poems and pieces of music that I had selected. My intention was that these discussions would open up possibilities for the two types of 'project' that I wished them to undertake. These were to carry out an 'empirical' investigation into some aspect of time, and to create an 'aesthetic' response to the theme of time, in writing, music, art, dance or drama.

At the same time, I knew that the course members would want to know how I envisaged that the three strands of the course might be articulated in the twenty meetings that stretched before us, what my expectations were for the assignments that they would be required to complete, and how I would arrive at their final grades for the course.

First, we all introduced ourselves. There were 25 students in the group; three were experienced high school teachers, the others held teaching, advisory or teaching/administrative positions at the elementary level. Most lived and worked in the Greater Vancouver area, though some came from much further afield and were resident on campus for the duration of the course. Two members of the group were doctoral students; the remainder were taking the course as part of their M.Ed. program.

After these introductions, I took some time to outline my tentative plans, presenting the study of the theme of time as a challenge, which called for active inquiry; the other two strands of the course, I suggested, could be seen as providing theoretical perspectives on the first, which called for a more reflective kind of inquiry. Within this general framework, I emphasized the negotiability of each day's agenda, and the many opportunities there would be for them to set their own goals and to decide on their own ways of addressing them. As a way of stressing the reflective, inquiry orientation I hoped they would adopt, I explained that for me, too, this approach to teaching was experimental and that I intended to treat the course as an occasion for inquiring into my own practice through action research.

Apart from a few minor hitches, such as the failure of the cassette recorder which I had planned to use to play the musical selections, the afternoon appeared to go very much as I had hoped it would. From the beginning, we were able to establish a dialogic rather than a transmissional mode of interaction, and much of the orienting information that I wanted to provide was given in response to questions or comments rather than in straight lecture form. For example, the discovery that some students had not actually received the paper by Duckworth, that I had sent out in advance, provided an opportunity for me to explain again my reasons for wanting them to make a study of time; it also allowed us to explore what I meant by an 'empirical' investigation. In her paper, Duckworth describes how, on one occasion, she asked her class to carry out a systematic investigation into the behavior of the moon as a 'second-order' task that would enable them to study their own learning, and I suggested that this was the sort of reflective inquiry that I had in mind for our course. This led naturally into a discussion of my expectations for the final assignment, which, I explained, I wanted to be a reflection on their experiences as learners during the course and on how these had affected their thinking about the opportunities for learning that they provided for their students.

As I wrote my journal entry at the end of the day, I was feeling optimistic about the weeks ahead. "The big question at the moment," I wrote, "is what form this course is going to take. Can I succeed in weaving the three strands together, or will it remain fragmented? The key lies in the dual emphasis on product and process; on action and reflection; on practice and theory."

Had I remembered Swartz's questions and discoveries (chapter five), I should also have been concerned about what the students were thinking. What sense were they making of the expectations for the course that I had so enthusiastically described to them earlier that day?

The first hint that not everybody was as enthusiastic as I came when I talked to one of the teachers a few days later. This was made more explicit in her journal entry at the end of the week:

> The first week is over and I must confess to being somewhat confused. I'm really not sure where we're headed. What is the purpose of spending a considerable amount of our limited time working on the Time project?... Perhaps I am a product of my generation, but I would like more structure to our sessions.

Nor, apparently, was she the only one to feel disoriented, though I did not discover this until I read the final assignments for the course. This is how another member of the class wrote about that opening session:

> On the first day of class, Dr. Wells presented us with a large topic for which we were to brainstorm ideas. Having never encountered this approach before, the reaction in the class was mixed, ranging from acceptance and enthusiasm to antagonism and a wish to "show Dr. Wells how to teach."

Even more disturbing was the discovery, unfortunately also made only at the end of the month, that one of the course members had been offended by my describing the course as 'an experiment'; she really resented being cast in the role of one of the guinea pigs on whom the experiment was to be conducted. Thus, in various ways, I gradually discovered that my ideas about the organization of the course had not initially met with universal approval.

It is a fundamental principle of the sociocultural theory of learning-and-teaching — which I had chosen as one of the major themes of the course — that, to teach effectively, one must be responsive to the needs and concerns of the learners. In my enthusiasm to design the course as a challenge to the students to initiate and pursue their own inquiries, both individually and in collaboration with others and, in responding to the readings, to form their own interpretations and test them against their present and past experience, I had neglected to think about how my plan would be perceived by those whose prior experience led them to have different expectations.

In an early journal entry, Sophie revealed a much greater perceptiveness than I had shown:

> I admire your courage in applying your ideas about teaching and learning to your work with the adults in this course. Unfortunately, most of us are products of an education system that, above everything else, taught obedience. We're accomplished at doing what we're told, but feel uncomfortable and insecure when offered choices and a share in charting our own learning. These are barriers that haven't reached the same height in children. But I would say that our enthusiasm helps to compensate for our uncertainty. It will be exciting to watch ourselves grow.

However, by the time I learned about the consternation, and even in some cases resentment, that I had aroused by my unconventional approach, those who had initially reacted most negatively had come to appreciate the opportunities for learning that this approach provided. Nevertheless, that is no excuse for my insensitivity. Even though I would probably not have been willing to make major changes without clear evidence that my intended approach was proving unhelpful, I should have encouraged more open discussion, that first afternoon, about the match between my intentions and the students' expectations, and about my reasons for believing that they would indeed find it exciting to watch themselves grow.

I have certainly tried to learn from this experience. At the first meeting of my new class, a few weeks ago, I started by outlining my expectations for the course — including the importance I attached to the teachers planning and carrying out a small piece of action research on some aspect of literacy in their place of work. But, this time, I actively encouraged them to express their doubts and concerns so that we could, together, think about ways of addressing them. Several did raise problems, which seemed to get resolved in further talk. But there may still have been others who did not speak what was on their mind, for fear of the possible consequences.

I have since talked with a number of teacher-educators, who have experienced similar difficulties. The problem, as one of them put it, is that"open conversation doesn't come that fast — it takes time for teachers to trust that they can raise problems" (Newman, personal communication). However, by the time we got into the second week of the summer course, the problem seemed to have been largely overcome.

Community, Collaboration and Conversation

As Sophie had observed in her journal entry, teachers have often had little experience of working together collaboratively on an intellectually challenging problem of joint concern. In asking them to undertake an empirical investigation on some aspect of time, my intention was, at least in part, to give them the opportunity to discover, at first hand, how enriching an experience this can be. As Harste (in press) puts it, "collaboration, like conversation, means that others are involved in your inquiry and that others live in your text in intimate and connected ways." It is not simply that, when faced with a problem, two heads are better than one, but that, by struggling to make explicit to the other group members one's perception of the problem and one's tentative ideas for its solution, one clarifies and extends one's understanding of the problem as a whole — for oneself as well as for the others (Barnes, 1976).

This, in fact, was what people were discovering as the empirical inquiries got under way. As they struggled to identify the questions they wished to investigate and, still more, as they tried to make sense of the evidence that they were collecting, they found, like the student teachers with whom Kowal worked (chapter eight), that they were learning from, as well as with, each other. As the course progressed, this awareness of the value of working collaboratively with others became more and more prominent in journal entries and in reports in class of the progress that the different groups were making as they explored their chosen topics.

As I had hoped, this experience of learning with and from each other also helped them to understand the more theoretical papers I was asking them to read. Many of them had difficulty, on first encounter, with Vygotsky's claim that most of the knowledge we construct — and indeed even the mental activities of remembering, reasoning and hypothesizing that are involved in the construction process — are taken over from the culture in which we live in the course of engaging in joint activities (Vygotsky, 1978, 1981). To those whose beliefs about learning have been formed in a culture that emphasizes individual rather than community achievement, and competition rather than collaboration, the insistence by sociocultural theorists on the cultural provenance of our individual understandings and abilities, and on the inherently social nature of the learning process, is often difficult to accept. But as they reflected, in the context of the papers they were reading, on how they were learning as they tackled their projects on time, the validity of these theoretical claims was underscored by their personal and group experiences.

This validation was still further enhanced when reflection turned to these small group discussions themselves, for here too, as they struggled to make sense together of the papers they were reading, they realized, at first hand, how central a role spoken discourse plays in the appropriation and internalization of new ideas. But, for them as well as for me, it was the multiple connections that they found themselves making, as work progressed, among all three strands — their group inquiries, the texts by Vygotsky and others that they were reading, and the talk that occurred in the groups in which these activities were pursued — that was really exciting.

This sense of exhilaration is captured in the following excerpt from Rachel's journal.

> MAJOR EXCITEMENT, MAJOR SYNCHRONICITY. I've been noticing the difference between the talk on our projects and the talk on theory. Then yesterday in my group on Vygotsky, Courtney asked a real question about times when we'd experienced that excitement about learning that was in Gordon's account of the chicks in the classroom [Wells and Chang-Wells, 1992, Chapter 1]. Breakthrough! We were at another level, bringing experience, affect, anecdote into our discussions of Vygotsky…. I left for my project group thinking that the two kinds of talk were merging, each taking on aspects of the other.But then a level of communicative sharing opened up in my group that made much of that we'd done heretofore seem superficial by comparison. Perspectives are widening and deepening as we experience each other as learners, knowers, people who have had deep life experiences that have had considerable impact on our beliefs and theories. I'm interested if other groups are finding that, as they work and think together, the depths of their personalities are complicating and enriching the empirical/theoretic context from which you're working?"

Extending the Conversation through E-Mail

This journal entry — as it's final sentence suggests — was not written only as part of the writer's conversation with herself. It was also a contribution to the electronically mediated conversation that we had established in the class through the use of e-mail. This added another dimension to our exploration of the use and significance of talk and texts as tools for learning and teaching.

My decision to encourage all course members to learn to use e-mail was based, initially, on my need to collect data for the action research stance I was adopting. Electronic communication would allow me to keep a record of the interchanges that took place in dialogue journals without having to remember to photocopy the relevant pages before returning the journals to their writers. There were also two further reasons. I quickly realised that, with 25 members in the class, it would be impossible to read everything that each person wrote and make more than a cursory response. And, even then, there would inevitably be a considerable time delay between the initiation and the response. E-mail offered a solution to both these problems. I therefore asked course members to select from their personal journal entries the issue they would most like to discuss with me and to send it to me by e-mail; for my part, I undertook to send a response back within 24 hours.

This arrangement worked well and, over the course of the month, I was involved in a wide variety of dialogues that extended over many turns. Most of Raoul's messages, for example, arose from her personal responses to the readings in sociocultural theory, and particularly from her concern with the lack of explicit attention to affect in these writings. Others, like Christine, shared their deepening understanding of what the form of the course was enabling them to learn about themselves as learners and teachers. Sean and Igor both kept me posted on the progress that they were making with their empirical studies and in this way I was able to share the twists and turns of their ideas and actions. The following two messages from Igor give a flavor of the range of problems he and his group were grappling with.

> 9 July.
>
> The moon watching is going great. Will have to do some modifications of our sighting equipment — especially the one we use for sighting angle. I'm afraid it is not too accurate. I am thinking of building a scope to mount on it instead of just sighting down the top of a ruler edge.... I'll bounce the idea off the rest of the group.
>
> 14 July.
>
> Thought I'd give you an update on what I'm doing. I started on my Reflections paper last Sunday. I reviewed the articles you had given us to read and tried to relate them to our moon project.

Regarding the moon project, I have been observing some interesting things. For the second night in a row I have noticed that the moon seems to be going ever so slightly back in the sky. I mean that I see it in the SE sky and then later it seems to be moving more towards the East than towards the South. Could that be? When I first noted this I thought my measuring was incorrect. However when I noticed this again last night it caused me to think that it was an actual phenomenon. This moon watching is raising more perplexing problems every day.

But perhaps the most important benefit of using this medium was that I was able to give some time and thought to how best to respond, with tutorial support and guidance, to the concerns that individuals raised, and yet to do so without undue delay. Thus, by 6.30 in the evening I was able to reply as follows, to the message quoted on p. 245 above, which was sent at midday by the student who was feeling confused.

I understand your feelings and will try to reassure you if I can. As Eleanor Duckworth explains in her article, 'Teaching as Research,' we can only study learning and teaching if people are learning and teaching. The reason for studying time, therefore, is to have a real learning experience to think about. So, as well as making your empirical study of time and creating an 'aesthetic artifact' in relation to that theme, I want you to be thinking about how you are setting about these tasks, about what you are learning and how, and about the conditions that seem to facilitate or impede your learning and the satisfaction that comes from 'coming to understand.' If you are feeling a little frustrated, perhaps you should look at what you and your colleagues are doing. Does there need to be some re-vision? Can you define for yourself what sort of structure you think would be helpful and then try to create it? Let me know what you think about this.

E-mail also allowed me to send messages to everybody in the class that they could read and think about at their leisure. I found this useful when an idea that seemed important occurred to me as I reflected on the afternoon's discussions. Several times my messages led to further dialogue, as individuals responded in terms of their own experiences and awareness of their developing understanding. In the same spirit, some course members took the plunge and began to send messages to the whole class. Messages such as Rachel's, quoted above, even if they did not receive responses also addressed to the whole class, played an important part in widening and deepening our 'interwoven conversations.'

To some extent, these advantages of e-mail over more traditional means of communication were already familiar to me from my own experience as a regular participant on XLCHC, an e-mail network devoted to discussion of sociocultural theory and its applications to education.[2] During the course, I continued to participate in this world-wide discussion, but only as a reader. Then one day, when, as a group, we were struggling with the distinction between the concepts of learning and development as used by Vygotsky, I decided to send an e-mail message to Mike Cole, to ask for his opinion. Within hours, I received his reply, which I was immediately able to pass on, in the same medium, to all the members of the class. I also took his advice to reread Dewey's (1963) *Experience and Education* and, as a result, extracted several lengthy quotations, which, when passed on to the class, generated still further discussion. This was indeed the sort of interweaving of the strands of the course through talk and text that I had hoped would develop. It was also further evidence of Vygotsky's claim that we learn through discourse with peers and more knowledgeable others.

However, there was a further benefit that I had not anticipated. For quite a number of course members, the use of a computer as a tool for writing and thinking was totally new and, even for those who had computers of their own, the technicalities of using a computer as a communication device presented a considerable challenge. Two introductory classes were arranged in the first week, but these were not sufficient to sort out all the technical problems of those who, like me, wanted to send messages from home via a modem. A few decided the difficulties were insurmountable and simply used the terminals around the campus, as did those who did not have access to a computer of their own. But others persisted and, with advice from the staff of the computing centre, and from colleagues and friends, finally succeeded in establishing communication. By the second week, therefore, all but one or two members of the group were making use of e-mail, and some even established contact with Newman's summer students at Mount St. Vincent University. Thus, although I had not thought of it in this light, my request that they should learn to use e-mail was a challenging learning experience of a different kind that, once more, provided evidence in support of the theory we were studying.

Here is Marilyn's comment:

> I am testing your hypotheses 1) "reflection on learning and teaching" while I am trying to be successful in sending this e-mail. Believe me, much "reflective scrutiny" has transpired before I have been successful in sending this message. 2) "learning-teaching = dialogue." Yes, yes, much dialogue —

with at least four other persons over the course of two days. But oh the feeling of success!

Erin made still further connections and indirectly offered me more food for thought about the way in which I was still failing to practice the theory I was preaching. She was referring to a message I had sent about Vygotsky's notion of the 'zone of proximal development' (ZPD), which had contained the following sentence: "And the best way to discover any learner's ZPD is to engage in the task with him or her and to give the assistance that is necessary." She replied:

Gordon, I really enjoyed reading your message on the ZPD.... One thing I am trying to do is reflect on the interactions taking place in class and discover their relevance, if any, for working in the ZPD. I thought it was very interesting when Heidi asked something to the effect: "Could you give us a short biographical sketch of Vygotsky? Why are we studying him now?" It occurred to me that she was searching for the overriding concept or framework for our work. I think by providing students with the overriding concept/framework you can significantly extend their ZPD....

Take, for another example, learning MTS. Without understanding that it is an electronic mail system, with which you can send messages to one another through the computer, it would have been much harder to learn. The discrete bits of information would have been hard to integrate into some meaningful whole.

I guess this is nothing startling. When young children are learning to read we know it's much easier to help them if they understand the big concept of reading — i.e. what it's all about. But I'd never thought of it as a way of extending the ZPD.

In fact, I had not provided the 'overriding concept' in response to Heidi's question, believing that to do so would be to accept the responsibility that I was trying to get the course members to take on for themselves of constructing understanding of the significance of what we were engaged in doing. Although I think that this was appropriate as an overall strategy, I realized, when I read Erin's message, that I should have made an opportunity earlier to talk with Heidi about her request and about my reasons for not meeting it. And, although I did not do so, I should perhaps have done the same in my reply to Erin, as well as suggesting, as I did, that she post all or part of her message to the class as a whole.

As I hope these anecdotes have shown, the use of e-mail significantly enriched the possibilities for meaningful conversation within our community of learners. And now, reflecting on the benefits that accrued from this mode of communication, initially introduced mainly for my own convenience, I am determined to encourage students in future classes to give it a try, whenever this is feasible. In the past, I have tried to keep in touch with individual class members through dialogue journals written in a notebook which is handed in one week and returned the next. But, like Maher (chapter four) and Swartz (chapter five), I have found that this weekly exchange is too infrequent to encourage the development of true dialogue. However, as I thought about the preference of the teachers Keating worked with (chapter ten) for writing on loose sheets rather than in a book, I saw one possible explanation for the lack of dialogue that I and others had experienced. To be valuable to the participants, the written exchanges need to be responsive to the ebb and flow of their thoughts and feelings, flowing thick and fast at some times and not at all at others. From this point of view, the administratively convenient practice of collecting and returning book-size journals in alternate weeks fails to do justice to the purpose dialogue journals are intended to serve. E-mail communication, on the other hand, is ideally suited to the rhythms of action and reflection and, with more and more people buying their own personal computers, it can add a new, personal dimension to the relationship between teacher and students in university-based classes.

Looking to the Classroom

Like Erin, in the e-mail message quoted above, many course members were reflecting on their experiences with action, talk and text, as they collaborated with other members of their groups, and wondering how these experiences might be translated into similar opportunities for the students in their classrooms in the coming year. As the month progressed, this became a more explicit focus of attention as, in small group discussion and whole class meetings, we explored the connections between our own experiences during the course, the video tapes that they and I had brought of work in classrooms, and the papers that I had selected by writers who directly applied the ideas of sociocultural theory to the classroom.

Early on, I had asked them to read two papers about the power of self-motivated inquiry. The first, an unpublished paper by Antonio Bettencourt (1990) entitled 'On Understanding Science,' contains the following sentences:

> Understanding begins with a question. Not any question, but
> a real question.... A real question expresses a desire to know.
> This desire is what moves a questioner to pursue the question
> until an adequate answer has been made. Desiring to know
> opens ourselves to experiencing what is new as new and the
> already known as renewed under new aspects.

I remember how, on first reading this, I was struck by how accurately this captured my experience as a researcher and a writer. When I am working to make an answer to a question that I really care about, I am very reluctant to break off to attend to other matters that, by comparison, seem much less important. It also seemed to fit equally well the sustained engagement of some of the children that we saw at work in the videotapes that I had brought to show to the class (transcripts of these tapes are discussed in Wells and Chang-Wells, 1992 a and b; Wells, 1993).

Now, as they pursued the questions that they had formulated for themselves in carrying out their empirical investigations, this quotation became significant for them, too, and several made reference to it in their final papers. Here is Julia's account of the experience of the 'moon' group:

> ... our question became: 'What patterns of change can we see
> in the moon's phases and in its movements?'

> For the next three weeks our group lived 'moon.' With com-
> passes and crude home-made sextants, we were up at all
> hours of the night taking measurements intended to locate
> the moon in a consistent way. Our findings were recorded and
> compared, often to our dismay. More questions were being
> generated than were being resolved. We were to move deeper
> into the layers of the moon study than we had ever intended,
> drawn in by discrepancies that begged for resolution.

> One might think that enthusiasm would fail with the increase
> in the complexity and number of problems, but the reverse
> seemed to happen. People were driven to try to solve the moon
> mysteries. Later I would think back and realize that at least
> some of our motivation was due to our question.... It was a real
> question.

In the same paragraph, Julia also made reference to another paper we had read, by Carl Bereiter and Marlene Scardamalia (in press). In it, they reported a study carried out with grade five and six children, in which they compared the questions that the children generated about a given topic after reading a text or reference book with those that they generated about the same topic without any prior input. What they found was that the latter type of questions — what they called 'knowledge-based questions'— were the more powerful, both in arousing interest and in generating subsequent inquiry. Because the 'moon' group had formulated their question on the basis of what they knew and did not know, rather than on the basis of prior reading, it acted as a powerful spur to learning, driving them, as Iris commented, to far greater efforts than any question of mine could ever have done.

As we talked about ways of creating opportunities in schools for students to ask similarly generative questions, an issue that began to assume increasing importance was the affective climate of the classroom. Reporting on their projects to the rest of the class, several groups commented at length on how crucial it had been to feel able to take risks and how this, in turn, had been dependent on feeling they could trust the other members of the group to be supportive of their ideas and suggestions, however incomplete or inadequate these were in their first attempts at expressing them.

Looking back at the way in which she had met the challenge of making an aesthetic response to the theme of time, Peggy wrote, rather ruefully:

> In this case I chose an artefact that was fun but, on reflection, perhaps too safe. I have seen the incredible results of risk-taking — in the form of the presentations by fellow class-mates. I hope I will seize another opportunity to stretch my learning and, as a teacher, will encourage this in my students.

Janis also commented on this aspect of her experience during the course, recognizing her own initial reluctance to take a risk. Thinking about the implications of this for the way she will plan her classroom program in the future, she wrote:

> Now I think I shall have to be more aware of the needs of the non-riskers in my classroom. I would like to be able to provide them with the safety net that will give them the courage to take a risk, to know that it's OK to be wrong or not to know the answer. Affect has a great effect on learning and I should be aware of the worries of the more cautious children.... I would like to make sure that all the children in my class get a chance to try, and I would like them to feel confident about what they know.

Of Talk and Text

Running through all these reflections was the discovery of the importance for learning of the semiotic tools of written and spoken discourse. Messages on e-mail, responses to papers read, notes to share at group meetings with fellow-inquirers, charts, graphs and captions for the presentation of results, all provided occasions for extending understanding as the writers strove to make understanding intelligible to others. About the final assignment, Laura wrote: "I can't remember a writing project which has focused me to learn about its topic, as I was composing it, to the extent that this one has." From these experiences, course members looked to ways of encouraging a similar variety of functions for writing in their classrooms in all areas of the curriculum.

But it was about the importance of spoken discourse that the most important discoveries were made. As teachers, the course members were aware of the importance of talk for, inter alia, giving instructions, imparting information and checking on what had been learned. However, in the writings of Vygotsky and other sociocultural theorists, they were meeting a claim for a much greater role for talk.

> The very mechanism underlying higher mental functions is a copy from social interaction; all higher mental functions are internalized social relationships.... Even when we turn to mental [internal] processes, their nature remains quasi-social. In their own private sphere, human beings retain the functions of social interaction (Vygotsky, 1981, p.164).

In the process of appropriation, what forms the bridge between the social *(inter-mental)* and the individual *(intra-mental)* planes is the mediating tool of spoken discourse. By being formulated and refined in the talk that occurs in the course of purposeful activity with others, new ideas, and new ways of acting and thinking, are integrated into one's personal knowledge and internalized to become a resource for individual thinking and problem-solving in the discourse of inner speech.

Encountered initially only in solitary reading, Vygotsky's ideas might well have appeared too abstract to make much personal sense. However, because they were being experienced daily, as the groups made sense together, through talk, of their empirical inquiries and of the papers they were reading, they came to have a personal significance for themselves as learners that changed their thinking about the role of talk in the classroom.

Some were recognizing that, although they had thought they had valued talk in their classrooms, they had really paid little more than 'lip-service' to its importance. As Gail wrote in her final paper, "I *thought* I was as concerned about the processes as I was about the product but, reflecting on my actions, I see otherwise.... I recorded only their products." In fact, as she explains:

> More than half of the session passed before the significance of talk struck me profoundly. This revelation came as a result of Gordon requesting that all students transcribe a stretch of

talk. I began to do so by listening attentively to a recording which I made of my empirical study group when we were discussing our initial observations of the pendulums and the first trials we conducted in attempting to isolate variables....

Through this 'hands on, minds on, talk on' experience I learned not only more about pendulums but also more about learning.... As a result of transcribing and subsequently studying the text in print I could follow the path of learning which, reciprocally, emphasized to me how crucial it is to listen to the voices of the learners.

At one level, then, the course was developing successfully. The three strands were proving mutually reinforcing and, by actively working together to make sense of the various challenges I had posed, all participants were discovering, in practice as well as in theory, the value of community, collaboration and conversation.

Mutual Interdependence: Individual and Social

At the same time, the strong emphasis on learning through social interaction did not meet with universal acceptance. On the first afternoon, when most people, with varying degrees of enthusiasm, were forming groups around possible areas to explore for their empirical study of time, three individuals unostentatiously chose to work alone. I was a little disappointed at their decision but made no attempt to persuade them to change their minds, for freedom to choose both topic and method of working was one of the underlying principles that I had emphasized in presenting what Edwards and Mercer (1987) call the 'ground rules' of classroom activity.

As I met with each member of the class individually during the next few days, I was interested to discover whether there were any common attributes that distinguished these three from their apparently more socially inclined colleagues. As it turned out, there were: they all had fairly clear ideas, in advance, of the questions they wanted to pursue; all three were also secondary teachers with a background in English studies. Whether this latter commonality was really influential in determining their decision I do not know but, certainly, the questions that interested them were of a more literary and philosophical bent than those that were selected by the other groups.

Interestingly, however, even these three, who initially did not wish to work in a group, decided after a few days to form an 'umgroup,' each pursuing his or her own individual inquiry under the 'umbrella' theme of 'the distortion of time.' As the weeks went by, they found that they gained a great deal from sharing their experiences as well as their projects with each other (see Rachel's journal entry on p. 248 above) and, when it came to the final presentations, they rewarded us with a highly original and thought-provoking exploration of their theme, in a series of dramatic monologues spoken in the characters of the poet, the witch and the fool.

Nevertheless, at the outset, they all expressed a degree of scepticism about the value I attributed to collaborative intellectual activity and about Vygotsky's emphasis on the inherently social nature of learning. Kermit, in particular, was unwilling to relinquish what I saw as an unduly individualistic conception of knowledge construction. As he wrote in an e-mail message in the second week:

> I find the matter of knowledge acquisition difficult to come to grips with. This was behind the question we posed today: "What does the child bring to learning?" It seems to me that Vygotsky describes (quite convincingly) a process — but that description is of a process that doesn't 'require' anything of the child.... Rumelhart (for example) suggests, in schema theory, a valid process — restructuring — to account for an active contribution of the learner toward his/her own learning. By comparison, Vygotsky's process is almost 'done to' the child. Rumelhart and Norman say "Carrying over existing features of existing schemata allows us to make inferences about the new situation without explicit knowledge of the new situation." Can this be an individual (as opposed to a social) undertaking?

As I read this message, my first reaction was of wanting to 'correct' him, or at least to show him the intellectual error of his ways. He had clearly failed to understand what Vygotsky was saying! Fortunately, e-mail enforces a certain amount of time for second thoughts and the reply I actually sent was, I hope, a more dialogic rejoinder.

> I'm not sure that I understand why you think that V's account of interpersonal learning requires nothing of the child. In order to participate in the joint activity, the child has to draw upon (i.e., activate) a lot of knowledge. This is the basis on which s/he appropriates the new or, to use a different metaphor the basis on which the adult scaffolds further construction. Actual interactions with children (or transcripts of them) show them contributing a substantial amount. The Rumelhart and Norman account seems to me to fit quite neatly into the larger sociocultural framework.

With even further time for thought, I realised that Kermit's dissenting point of view needed to be discussed further. How indeed could Vygotsky's claim that "all higher mental functions are internalized social relationships" be reconciled with the conviction that several people had voiced that they did not need to be interacting with others in order to come up with new ideas? Or, more generally, if all knowledge is taken over from other members of the culture, how can there ever be advances in knowledge? In reacting against rampant individualism, wasn't Vygotsky's emphasis on the social origins of individual thinking going to the other extreme in undervaluing individual abilities and achievement?

Here was a 'real' question; so, not having any 'experts' on hand to provide a ready-made answer, I sat down at my computer to try to construct my own. The following message, sent to the whole class, was the outcome of my efforts.

One of the issues that seems to be causing some confusion is Vygotsky's claim that what is internal was first external — that is to say that the higher mental functions are first in the interpersonal domain before they become intrapersonal. By my understanding, this does not mean that all our ideas are encountered in face-to-face interaction. There are, I think, three points that need to be made:

1. Mental functions are based on sense-making capacities that are biologically given and which undergo maturation. This 'apparatus' is a prerequisite for intellectual development. However the mental activities we learn to perform, such as remembering in a systematic and strategic manner, reasoning according to 'logical' principles, carrying out the operations of arithmetic, etc. are all activities that are cultural in origin. They are appropriated from numerous situations in which they are enacted in a joint activity with a more mature member of the culture. So, for the individual, they were first in the interpersonal sphere and then internalized to become individual means of problem-solving, etc.

2. This does not mean that every solution we construct to a problem nor every idea we have has to derive immediately from face-to-face interaction. It is the strategies and tools we use (i.e., reasoning in inner speech, the use of diagrams to help us think) that were first social and now individual. And so individual mental activity has this 'quasi-social' character, as Vygotsky puts it. But, in actual fact, many of our ideas and solutions are social in a more obvious way. Although the 'eureka' may occur when we are alone, it emerges from a transaction with the problem situation to which we bring relevant knowledge that was constructed from social en-

counters with other members of the culture in the past.

3. A second way in which we need to extend the notion of 'social' beyond face-to-face interaction concerns our interaction with cultural artifacts, since they constitute cultural memories of solutions to past problems. Of these artifacts, the texts created by (admired) individuals represent an important subcategory. So reading, as a strategy to help us solve problems, make new meanings and generally come to understand, is also a form of social interaction.

As I sent this message, I couldn't help thinking that the composition of the text and its transmission by e-mail provided an excellent example of the complex dialectical interplay between intra-mental (individual) and inter-mental (social) that we were seeking to understand.

Both the message itself, and the manner in which I composed it, had a distinctively individual character. This is seen in the particular structure of the text, in the arguments I chose to put forward — based on *my* interpretation of the texts by Vygotsky and others that I have read and discussed with other readers — and in the choice of tone and style, realized in the selection of particular words and structures. Although not recoverable from the text as semiotic artifact, the manner in which I had composed it was also individual, involving a particular way of creating parts of the text, reading what was written, and making minor or substantial revisions as seemed called for in the light of my growing understanding of the meaning I was trying to communicate. In other words, both the composing event, and the text that resulted from it, were unique — the creative solution to a specific problem of meaning-construction, as I had formulated it for myself.

However, this individual act of composition and the resulting text are only meaningful — and indeed only possible — within a larger social context. First, the text, as a physical object, was created through my use of a cultural artifact (my computer linked by a modem to the university mainframe system) according to the conventions of the associated cultural practice (e-mail) which I had learned (i.e., appropriated and internalized) partly through reading other cultural artifacts (instruction manuals) and partly through actual participation in an e-mail network. The same sort of account goes for the text seen as a semiotic artifact. In composing it, I engaged in a different sort of cultural practice (communicating in the genre of exposition embedded within the genre of argument), again according to conventions learned through reading and through participation in previous instances of this practice which, in turn, were based on an ongoing appropriation of the resources of the language which I share with other speakers and writers of English (Bakhtin, 1986). Finally, as an act of communication, the text was created in response to messages from other members of our particular social group, and assumed a degree of shared familiarity with a range of other texts that we had all been reading. In all these ways, then, my individual behavior was 'quasi-social,' in that each of its many facets had a social origin and required, to be effective, a community of others with functionally equivalent knowledge of the relevant artifacts and practices.

There is, however, a further twist. Without individual creative acts of meaning-making, there would be no discourse. And, conversely, without discourse, there would be little occasion for anyone to make meaning through language and certainly no opportunity for learners, through participation in this social practice, to appropriate the semiotic tools that make meaning-making possible.

Whether Kermit would have been convinced by this lengthy exemplification of the point I was trying to make I do not know, for it is only now, in the writing of the preceding paragraphs, that I have thought out the argument in detail. At the time, however, he was not convinced, and the debate continued throughout the remainder of the course — and indeed beyond. For this I am doubly grateful, since the initial difference of opinion, and the dialogue that followed from it, led me to look critically at my assumptions on two important issues. First, as I have spelled out in some detail above, it caused me to think more deeply about the matter of our disagreement itself, resulting in my working out, in my message to the class, a deeper understanding of the nature of the interdependence of 'individual' and 'social.' But it also set me thinking again about the nature of the teaching-learning relationship.

In an article that I and many of my students have found helpful, Judith Newman (1987) encourages us to be open to being surprised by the events that happen in our classrooms, for it is by looking more closely at what surprises us that we can 'uncover our assumptions.' I was certainly surprised — and uncomfortably so — by my initial reaction to the scepticism that some course members expressed concerning the social origins of individual thinking. In contrast to my expressed commitment to reciprocity and to the validity of every individual's beliefs and opinions, my behavior on this occasion revealed the authoritarian pedagogue lurking embarrassingly close to the surface, convinced of the superior validity of my own opinion and ready, when given the chance, to use the advantages accorded by academic status to ensure its (apparent) acceptance by my students.

Whether this assumption of superiority was based simply on my status as teacher or on a presumed greater expertise resulting from extended study of the writings of sociocultural theorists is, in the last resort, unimportant. For the interactive effect of my behavior, had I acted upon my initial impulse, would have been the same: to signal that unquestioning acceptance of authority is what is expected of students, not a reciprocal dialogue in which all participants learn by attempting to formulate their current understandings in a way that makes them, and the grounds on which they are based, clear to co-participants and, thus, open to challenge and modification. Such 'progressive discourse,' as Bereiter (1992) has called it, must surely be the model for classroom interaction, rather than the unilateral transmission and attempted imposition of the beliefs of 'experts' or 'authorities.'

But, some will argue, how can those who are uninformed take part in such progressive discourse? Without having mastered the field and acquired the necessary social and intellectual skills, how can they develop a valid personal point of view or make an original contribution? To correct students when they fail to understand or make mistakes is properly part of a teacher's responsibility.

On the face of it, this objection has considerable plausibility, and it is on its apparent self-evident validity that most traditional education has been based. Indeed, it has even colored the interpretation that has been put upon the notion of 'apprenticeship,' a metaphor which has been much used by sociocultural researchers in recent years to describe the teaching-learning relationship (e.g., Rogoff, 1990; Wells, 1987, in press). Frequently, in using this metaphor — and the attendant metaphor of scaffolding (Wood, Bruner and Ross, 1976) — educators have tended to place the emphasis on mastering basic skills and concepts; that is to say they have interpreted it in terms of the induction of the individual into the ways of the culture.

However, to focus only on ensuring cultural reproduction and continuity is insufficient. The purpose of an apprenticeship is that the learner should become an independent master craftsman who creates new artifacts and adds to the cultural resources. By the same token, education must be equally concerned with cultural renewal and development, and with fostering the creativity and originality which make this possible.

The most important feature of an apprenticeship, however — at least as a metaphor for the teaching-learning relationship — is the manner in which the transactions between teacher and learner are conducted. In this mode, learning takes place in the context of purposeful activity, as learner and teacher work together to create a product that has its own intrinsic value. In doing so, they make use of a range of tools and task-related processes that have been developed within that craft community. Furthermore, it is from observing their use by others and attempting to use them on his or her own, that the learner gradually masters the craft, that is to say appropriates the practices and internalizes the associated knowledge and procedures. Certainly, in this process, the teacher offers guidance and instruction. However, this is given, not in the form of decontextualized abstractions, but when needed and in context, in order to enable the learner to carry out the task more effectively. When problems arise, as they inevitably do when new artifacts are being created or new situations encountered, the learner is encouraged to offer possible solutions and to test them out in practice (provided the cost of failure is not too great). For part of skilled craftsmanship is being able to invent new tools and techniques to solve emerging problems and to put existing ones to new uses. As the history of science and technology demonstrates or, equally, that of the creative arts, advances most often arise from this interplay between tradition and creativity.

The metaphor of apprenticeship is taken from the domain of skilled performance, of 'hands-on' activities which make use of physical tools. However, one of Vygotsky's most productive insights was to see that there are also mental tools — semiotic artifacts, such as numerical systems, diagrams, mnemonic strategies and reasoning procedures — which facilitate the performance of 'minds-on' activities. So, without much distortion, the metaphor of apprenticeship can be applied equally validly to the domain of mental work. Here, the tool of greatest importance is language, the preeminent joint activity that of discourse, and the purpose of the activity that of creating common knowledge and enhancing individual understanding.

So, to return to those who argue that progressive discourse is not possible until learners have acquired the prerequisite knowledge and skills, we can reply with some conviction that the very opposite is the case. That is to say, it is *only* by taking part in such discourse that learners can appropriate the necessary knowledge and skills and, in making them their own, become accepted members of the relevant discourse community who, by virtue of their own personal experience and understanding, also have valid individual contributions to make. In other words, worthwhile social interaction does not depend upon the prior development of individual participants; rather, it is through participation in social interaction that participants themselves develop as individuals.

Teaching: Judging When and How to Intervene

Metaphors are all very well for theoretical discussions of education. But what does the metaphor of apprenticeship look like when translated into practice? This was, in fact, the main purpose of my action research: to attempt to answer this question, by acting in accordance with this guiding metaphor, by simultaneously observing and reflecting on what actually transpired, and by encouraging course members to do the same.

I have already said quite a lot about the overall design of the course and shown how, at this level, the various strands were gradually interweaving in the students' experience to create what Gail described as 'hands-on, minds-on, talk-on' learning. As the weeks went by, more and more comments were made about the power of this combination, when linked with the opportunity for students to define their own goals for inquiry, both individually and in groups, under the 'umbrella' of the themes that I had proposed in advance of the first meeting.

This I see as the 'macro' level of teaching: creating a challenge that one hopes will interest the students and inviting them to engage with questions that stretch their capacities and lead them to extend and deepen their understanding of their chosen topics (Wells, 1993). As mentioned earlier, this challenge also needs to be one that encourages both action and reflection and, within the community of inquiry, sets expectations for collaborative group work, whole class sessions of various kinds, and occasions for individual meaning-making. Then, having set the process in motion, the teacher's task is to manage the pacing, adding or deleting elements according to expressed interests and time constraints, and making sure that adequate time is allowed for the various tasks to be brought to a satisfying completion. In the present case, I hoped that these decisions could be taken together and, to this end, I set part of each session aside to plan the short-term and long-term agenda. To a considerable degree, this strategy was successful. As groups became increasingly involved in their empirical projects, a daily pattern emerged: part of each afternoon was devoted to these projects, part to small-group discussion of the papers read, and part to a whole class session in which we followed up issues that had arisen in group work, or explored a topic suggested in advance by one or more of the students or by myself.

There were, however, a number of modifications to the pattern with which we started. Several students found that, by the end of the afternoon, they were too tired to participate fully in the whole class sessions and so, at their suggestion, we reorganized the daily agenda to bring this session earlier in the afternoon. A second modification, that happened imperceptibly for me, was the decision by many of the groups that had formed around the empirical inquiries to work together on their aesthetic responses as well. Space is too limited to describe these in detail, but it was clear that, here too, collaboration took many forms, ranging from everybody working on a common artifact to mutual support and critical response among members of a group who each had their own personal projects.

The third modification was one that I introduced, although without being aware at the time that that was what I was doing. About half way through the month, when the daily pattern had become well established, I began to be concerned about bringing the empirical inquiries to closure with enough time left to engage in reflection together on what we had been doing. So I proposed that we should schedule the dates for the group presentations and, as I thought, gained general agreement for the actual schedule that was negotiated. Once again, however, I had failed to give due attention to the expectations that had by then been established. As Trudie wrote in her final assignment:

> Until then, Dr. Wells had allowed the students to put forth their concerns and the class was very student-directed. However, at this point he imposed his own timetable on the students. The class's reaction was very interesting in that many resented the imposition. After having given the class so much freedom and choice, it was to a degree taken away and deadlines were established. Speculation ran rampant as to the cause of this.

My decision to 'establish deadlines' was, of course, taken in what I considered to be the interests of our joint endeavor. But, to use Erin's image (p. 252 above), I had failed adequately to explain "the big concept". I had reverted to the more traditional autocratic stance of 'teacher knows best' and, although I wasn't aware of it, the students certainly were — though of course they were too polite to say so at the time, or too used to being treated in this manner.

In addition to this macro level of course design and negotiation of the activities to be undertaken, there is also the 'micro' level of teaching. In Vygotskian terms, this can be described as 'working in the students' zones of proximal development' (or ZPD), which he defines as the zone with respect to any task between what the student can manage alone and what he or she can achieve with the assistance of a teacher or more knowledgeable peer. Since we were all relatively lacking in systematic knowledge about the theme of time and, at the same time, all teachers by profession, I assumed that a great deal of this responsive assistance would occur spontaneously within the groups. And, indeed, this was what occurred. Course members certainly learned from each other and, in the process, came to a fuller understanding of how they might create opportunities for their students to learn from each other in their own classrooms.

Insofar as I played a role over and above that of group members, it was with the intention of helping them both to succeed with their chosen tasks and to become more conscious of strategies that might help them to do so. Typically, when the class was working in groups, I moved around, staying for ten to fifteen minutes with each group. Most of this time I would spend in observing and listening in order to discover how the group had defined their task and what progress they were making with it. Then I might add an observation of my own or ask a question, either to encourage them to clarify or make more explicit an idea under discussion, to suggest an aspect of the topic that, in my view, deserved further attention, or, occasionally to challenge what seemed to me an inadequate solution. Sometimes, a question would be put to me, asking for background information or for my gloss on a term with which they were having difficulty.

This active listening has come to seem to me, over the years, to be one of the most important aspects of teaching for, as Moscoe points out (chapter three), it is absolutely essential if one's interventions are to be both responsive to the needs of learners and appropriately pitched within their ZPD. By paying close attention to the way in which the learner is contextualizing the task or text (Lemke, 1989) — that is to say, by noting what experience of other tasks or texts he or she considers relevant and by attending to the terms in which the relationships are expressed — one is better able to make a contribution to the ongoing conversation that focuses, builds upon or, where necessary, redirects the meaning that is being constructed.

At this micro level, then, I see teaching as being a form of dialogue — what Tharp and Gallimore (1988) call an 'instructional conversation,' or what I and my colleagues have called 'collaborative talk' (Wells and Chang-Wells, 1992a). Unlike the monologic presentation, or lecture — which certainly has a place in the overall design — this dialogue arises out of the student's current engagement in a particular task and has as its first function to facilitate the satisfactory completion of the task. In engaging in this dialogue, however, the teacher also has a second purpose in mind: strategically to introduce into the joint solving of the problem procedures and knowledge that are in some sense 'in advance' of the student's current mode of engagement so that, as their significance is understood in the intermental context of the current task, they may be appropriated and internalized to become an intramental resource for use by the student in similar tasks in the future.

At both macro and micro levels, then, the teaching-learning relationship is essentially dialogic. At the macro level, which involves the whole class, the teacher initiates with a challenge of some kind, to which the students respond by making sense of the challenge in terms of their existing resources. The teacher then follows up by making available resources that are relevant to the student response and by developing or modifying the overall scheme in the light of student uptake. However, the most important kind of follow-up, I am convinced, is the dialogue that I have described as constituting the micro level of teaching and learning. Here, as the teacher engages with small, task-based, groups or with individual students, it is the student's way of responding to the initial challenge that should provide the initiating move, with the teacher responding to that response in whatever way she or he judges will enable the student to gain greater control and understanding of the task in hand.

In the chapter that I asked course members to read before the start of the course, Duckworth (1987) offers a rather similar two level analysis of the teacher's role.

> In my view there are two aspects of teaching. The first is to put students into contact with phenomena related to the area to be studied — the real thing, not books or lectures about it — and to help them notice what is interesting; to engage them so they will continue to think and wonder about it. The second is to have the students try to explain the sense they are making and, instead of explaining things to students, to try to understand their sense. (p.123)

Influenced by Vygotsky, I have perhaps placed more emphasis than Duckworth would on the assistance and guidance that the teacher can offer, in the light of his or her understanding of the student's sense-making response. But about the importance of the student's response providing the point of departure for this dialogue there is no question. And it was this sort of dialogue that I was trying to engage in as I moved from group to group, met with individual students at their request, or conversed with them by e-mail.

But how far was I being successful? In order to obtain an answer to this question, I needed to hear the students' reflections on what had been going on. Rather than ask directly, however, I decided to adopt a more indirect approach.

Reflecting on Action; Reflecting in Action

From the beginning, it had been one of my aims to encourage a continuous dialectic between action and reflection, and I had made this intention explicit in describing my expectations for the final assignment. This assignment, I had explained, was an opportunity for them to reflect, in whatever way they chose, on their experience of the course in the light of their classroom practice and of the theory that they were encountering in the readings.

What this called for was retrospective reflection, or what Schön (1987) terms 'reflection-on-action.' However, a different kind of reflection is called for, he argues, to deal effectively with the surprises that occur in the course of action. This he terms 'reflection-in-action.'

> What distinguishes reflection-in-action from other kinds of reflection is its immediate significance for action. In reflection-in-action, the rethinking of some part of our knowing-in-action leads to on-the-spot experiment and further thinking that affects what we do — in the situation at hand and perhaps also in others we shall see as similar to it. (p.29)

Both kinds of reflection, of course, have a role to play in the continuing effort to improve one's practice as a teacher that characterizes action research in the classroom. But to become really skilful at that aspect of teaching which involves working with students in their zones of proximal development through dialogue that is responsive to their needs, one needs to become adept at dealing with the surprises that are inherent in any form of spontaneous discourse. In Schön's terms, one needs to become good at reflection-in-action. But how to provide occasions for the development of this reflective bent is something of a problem.

Before the course started, I came up with the idea of what I called a 'freeze': that is to say, calling for an interruption of the action for a few minutes, in order to notice and reflect on what is going on. However, as those I spoke to about the idea were not very convinced that it would be successful, I was somewhat hesitant about putting it to the test. But by the third week, as the discussion groups were obviously engaging in a considerable amount of reflection-on-action, I decided one afternoon to see what would result from trying my plan.

By that stage, I had already started video-taping some of our sessions and, on the afternoon in question, I had left the camera recording one of the group discussions. No further action was required on my part, therefore, to capture the group's reactions when I tried this new technique. Later, when I had the opportunity to review the tape, I wrote the following vignette.

"OK. Freeze! What's going on here?"

The seven teachers, who are just getting up to rejoin the rest of the class in the neighboring room, look at each other in surprise, wondering what is coming next. For the last hour they have been discussing their reactions to a group of papers they have read, each of which looked at learning and teaching in the classroom from the perspective of sociocultural theory.

"I want you to think back over the last little while, and take a few minutes to write about what you have been doing and thinking. Then, when you've finished writing, I'd like you to share what you've written with each other."

As they gather their thoughts and then start to write, I leave the room, having first checked that the video camera is still recording. As they are well aware, it has, in fact, recorded the whole of the preceding discussion.

Some minutes later, having finished writing, they begin to talk about their texts. Courtney suggests that one of them should read her account and the others should note any discrepancies. Anna starts. She tells how she feels she has a partial understanding of Vygotsky's ideas but needs to fit this into the larger picture. She feels good when others agree that one should start slowly in applying Vygotsky's ideas to the classroom. It is necessary, she insists, to build up the trust of children who have previously had different experiences. One must be consistent and, for this, theory must be understood.

"Was that it?" asks Courtney, in surprise.

Her account, which she proceeds to read, focuses on rather different matters. Describing the experience she has had in the other working group of which she is a member, she has written:

The evolution of [our] question through the group-process experience — how the language of the group has changed over the course of that experience. And how the reading, the talking and the thinking, and the thinking about the reading and talking and thinking, and all the reflections, ideas, etc. written on scraps of paper in my various journals and on the fridge — (she laughs) how all of those have come together — how the two journals have now almost become one ... and now my job is to put the two together.

Evidently, they have given very different accounts of what had been going on, so it is decided to continue round the circle. As the others read their reflections, it is clear that, although not overtly expressed in the immediately preceding discussion, they have each, in their unspoken thoughts, been making very individual connections between all the different activities in which they have been engaged and between these and the classroom activities that they have been involved in in the past and, more importantly, those that they are envisaging for the future.

The resulting discovery of how diverse their accounts are provokes further reflection, giving them an insight into how the co-construction of meaning that goes on in public conversation is enriched by, and in turn enriches, their own internal conversations, in which more personal connections are made. Quite unexpectedly, this sort of reflection-in-action has led them into thinking about thinking — "an enlightening experience," as one of them subsequently comments.

Then, as the discussion is drawing to a close, Trudie introduces a further idea. "Does anybody else feel that the process we just went through with the writing and then sharing it with each other was a form of closure in itself that helped us solidify our thinking of what we'd been doing before?"

"Yes", replies Rachel. "We should get all our kids to do it."

Obviously, then, the 'freeze' had been a significant further addition to the enactment of the dialectic between action and reflection that I had been trying to bring about, at what I called the 'macro' level. It had also suggested a further strategy for deepening students' understanding in their own classrooms. But what about the 'micro' level? Did their reflections cast any light on their perceptions of the way in which I had been interacting with them individually? A single phrase in one of the accounts revealed that they had been talking about this earlier in the session, so I decided to watch the videotape of the preceding discussion. It turned out that it was a discussion of when to intervene when working in the students' ZPD that had led to the comments about my way of teaching.

Courtney: Don't you think that's one of the elegant

things about what Gordon has done, though? Haven't you noticed that, throughout the course, he's been modelling every step of the way—everything, you know, the small groups, the individual, the 'pull the questions out of the air and shoot them in' and make you really frustrated so you can find the answer.

Trudie: That's exactly what he did with his paper.[3] I mean, why didn't he give us this right at the beginning?

Jackie: I know why: if I had read that at the beginning

Courtney: You'd have gone "Huh? Huh?"

Marilyn: We have a stake in it now.

               (many speak at once in agreement)

Trudie :   So that indicates that there is a right time to do these things.

Jackie: But if you notice the way the class has learned the awareness of where he's going. Gordon knows exactly where he's going.

Courtney: Oh sure he does.

Courtney then goes on to recount how, after listening to the members of the 'moon-group' talk about their progress to date, I had "thrown in a monkey-wrench" by asking how they were going to measure the moon's angle of inclination. This had apparently led to a whole rethinking of the issue. "The perfect question and it made me mad as hell," she adds.

Such appreciation was certainly gratifying — all the more because it wasn't expressed directly to me. But the perception of me as modelling, and of knowing exactly where I was going, surprised me. As I had told them at the beginning, to teach a graduate course in this way was a new experience for me; I certainly did not have the route mapped out in advance in the way they seemed to think. Neither was I acting with the conscious deliberation that, for me, is implied by the term 'modelling.' Where did their perception come from, then? To try to answer this question, I decided to do some 'reflecting-in-action' myself.

The next day, I made a deliberate attempt to think about what I was doing while I was actually doing it. As I had thought, I found I was not consciously acting with the intention that they should see my behavior as a demonstration of how to interact with learners in their ZPD. Instead, I was genuinely interested in what they were trying to do or understand and, when I intervened with a comment or a question, it was in the same spirit as other members of the group. That is to say, my intention was to assist them in solving their problem, but without imposing my idea of the correct solution.

To take the question I put to the 'moon-group' as an example: as I listened to their account of their first observations of the moon, I surmised that it would not be sufficient simply to record the direction of sighting at successive points during the evening. But instead of pointing this out, I asked how they were going to measure the angle above the horizon at each sighting. In this way, I raised what I thought was a pertinent issue, while leaving the group to decide whether they too thought it pertinent. If they did, it was their responsibility to find a solution. Or, to take another example, when I listened to the results of the group who were trying to discover whether balls of different mass, volume and surface texture took the same amount of time to roll down an inclined plane, I wondered whether changing the angle of inclination might make a difference, again leaving the group to decide whether this was a relevant issue to consider. Certainly, I intended my questions to be provocative of further thought and I asked them in the belief that, in considering them, the group might well make progress in their inquiry. But in intervening in this way it was not my intention deliberately to model my theory of teaching.

However, my students had been more perceptive than I. For what I came to realize was that, when I engaged *with* them in their inquiries, with the intention of helping them to make progress towards their chosen goals, I was in so doing also enacting my theory of teaching. And, although I was not self-consciously providing a demonstration for them to imitate, to the extent that they were reflectively aware of the effect of my interventions, they could see my behavior as an instantiation of that theory. This idea was captured very clearly by Julia, who commented:

> Observing what this professor did was as much a part of the lesson as the readings or group projects had been. The teacher had not just modelled the technique of teaching, he had modelled what he valued in the teaching-learning transaction.

Put more simply, modelling does not have to be deliberate to be effective. Provided the significance of another's behavior is apparent to the learner as contributing to the achievement of the goal of their jointly undertaken activity, that behavior can serve as a model to be appropriated and made part of his or her repertoire of strategies for achieving goals of a similar kind. This is, of course, inherent in Vygotsky's theory of learning through social interaction, but I had not, until this moment, seen how it applied to my own behavior as a teacher.

Conclusion

Obviously, in the space of one chapter it is impossible to describe every aspect of a month's work or even to mention all the important events that occurred. Much more could be said, in particular, about the various groups' presentations, each of which was as interesting for what group members had discovered about their own learning as for the results they reported from the investigation itself. Nevertheless, I hope that those events that I have chosen to describe in some detail will have been successful in conveying something of the substance of our daily meetings and in showing the many levels on which learning was occurring.

In selecting the events to describe I have also tried to include some that were, for me, what Newman (1987) calls 'critical incidents,' that is to say, occasions when something unexpected led me to look more closely at my assumptions and, by reflecting on what I was doing and why, to arrive at a deeper understanding of the complex of motives, beliefs and attitudes that influences my practice on particular occasions. As I have learned, it is only by subjecting one's present behavior to critical scrutiny, that one can hope to see clearly how it might be improved in the future. In the process, however, like the other authors whose inquiries are reported in this volume, I discovered that, if I am ready to learn, there is much that my students can teach me.

This, then, is the hallmark of an inquiry-oriented classroom: that "while the students learn, the teacher learns, too" (Duckworth, 1987, p.134). Indeed, as Gianotti shows (chapter two), when the students become involved in the teacher's inquiry and the teacher in the students,' together they create a community of inquiry in which all learn with and from each other. This was what I hoped would happen during our month together and, to a considerable extent, I believe it did.

But that was not my ultimate goal. Duckworth goes on to conclude her paper on 'Teaching as research' with the following vision:

> This kind of researcher would be a teacher in the sense of caring about some part of the world and how it works enough to want to make it accessible to others; he or she would be fascinated by the questions of how to engage people in it and how people make sense of it; would have time and resources

to pursue these questions to the depth of his or her interest, to write what he or she learned, and to contribute to the theoretical and pedagogical discussions on the nature and development of human learning. (p.140)

My hope was that, as a result of their experience of being part of a community of inquiry in our classroom at the university, some of the students in this summer course might wish to extend the experience to the community of colleagues with whom they worked during the rest of the year. For me, therefore, the strongest evidence of the value of this form of university-based learning experience was the number of course members who, at its conclusion, expressed their intention of embarking on an action research project in the coming year, particularly those who planned to work collaboratively with their colleagues.

Perhaps one factor contributing to their decision to try action research for themselves was their participation in what came to be, not simply my, but *our,* joint inquiry. As students in the course, it is true, they were initially given no choice in the matter (and at least one course member was actively, but silently, opposed to the idea — see above); however, the attitude of reflective inquiry that I had proposed in my introductory letter was adopted, at first tentatively and then enthusiastically, by the majority of the participants. In this context, the discussions in which we shared our reflections on our learning and teaching came to be as significant for them as they were for me, and figured as centrally in their final papers as in mine. Since, in this way, they were already fulfilling part of Duckworth's vision of the teacher-researcher, it was perhaps quite natural that many should have been contemplating ways of carrying over this stance to their professional roles as educators.

In writing about this summer course, I, too, have been attempting to act as a teacher-researcher. By presenting some of the events that, at the time or in retrospect, I experienced as problematic, and by using writing as a tool for exploring their significance, I have tried to arrive at a fuller understanding of those issues that currently most concern me in my role as a teacher-educator. Introduced in question form, at the beginning of this chapter, they are concerned with the relationship between inquiry, discourse and purpose in learning and teaching, and with the dialectic of action and reflection, of practice and theory, in the attempt to bring about improvement in the learning opportunities that, as teachers, we create for our students. To a considerable extent, these same issues have been addressed by my fellow-contributors to this volume. And, although working in very different contexts, we have tended to follow similar routes and arrive at similar conclusions. For all of us, inquiry has been the means of achieving a deeper understanding of our own practice; we have also discovered how powerful inquiry is in motivating and sustaining our students' learning. For all of us, too, conversation through talk and written dialogue has been of prime importance, both as the medium of learning and teaching that we have tried to foster, and as a focus of our own inquiries. As Mayer (chapter seven) and Bernard and Konjevic (chapter nine), in particular, emphasize, we have also appreciated the conversations with colleagues and among ourselves that have helped us make sense of what we were learning through those inquiries. But just as important, we have come to recognize the crucial role played by the talk that has surrounded the writing and revising of the texts in which these inquiries are reported. Finally, we have shared a similar purpose. As action researchers, the goal of our inquiries has been to integrate our developing understanding of theory and practice in order to become better educators.

As efforts have been made to find more effective alternatives to the traditional forms of teacher development, increasing emphasis has been given to reflection. But, despite its value in promoting self-knowledge, reflection by itself is not sufficient. To bring about improvements in practice that really benefit our students, teachers' reflections need to lead to specific plans for change that are put into action and then subjected to observation and further reflection. If the goal of reflection is understanding, the purpose of understanding is improvement in action. It is through engaging in this ongoing cycle of action research that we can best hope to change schools from within.

Notes

1. The paper I enclosed is entitled 'Teaching as research' (Duckworth, 1987).

2. This network is organized by Michael Cole at the University of California, SanDiego.

3. 'What have you learned?': Coconstructing the meaning of time' (Wells and Chang-Wells, 1992b).

Appendix

The following are the texts that were read and discussed by all course members in relation to the strands of sociocultural theory and talk and texts. Individual students also read additional texts in relation to their personal inquiries.

Bettencourt, A. (1991). On understanding science. Michigan State University: Unpublished paper.

Confrey, J. (1991). Steering a course between Vygotsky and Piaget. *Educational Researcher,* November 1991: 28-32.

Duckworth, E. (1987). Teaching as research. In *'The having of wonderful ideas' and other essays on teaching and learning.* New York: Teachers College Press.

Edwards, D. (1990). Discourse and the development of understanding in the classroom. In O. Boyd-Barrett and E. Scanlon (Eds.), *Computers and learning.* Reading, MA: Addison-Wesley.

Gianotti, M.A. (1992). Moving between worlds: Talk during writing workshop. Chapter 2, this volume.

Heap, J. (1985). Discourse and the production of classroom knowledge: Reading lessons. *Curriculum Inquiry, 15 (3):* 245-279.

Lemke, J.L. (1989). Social semiotics: A new model for literacy education. In D. Bloome (Ed.) *Classrooms and literacy.* Norwood, NJ: Ablex.

Moscoe, T. (1992), Conferences: Planned transactions. Chapter 3, this volume.

Newman, D., Griffin, P. and Cole, M. (1989). How the West was won. In *The construction zone: Working for cognitive change in school*. Cambridge: Cambridge University Press.

Nystrand, M. and Gamoran, A. (1991). Student engagement: When recitation becomes conversation. In H.C. Waxman and H.J. Walberg (Eds.) *Effective teaching: Current research*. Berkeley, CA: McCutchan Publishing Corp.

Scardamalia, M. and Bereiter, C. (in press). Text-based and knowledge-based questioning by children. *Cognition and Instruction*.

Vygotsky, L.S. (1978). Interaction between learning and development. In *Mind and Society*. Cambridge, MA: Harvard University Press.

Vygotsky, L.S. (1981). The genesis of higher mental functions. In J.V. Wertsch (Ed.) *The concept of activity in Soviet psychology*. Armonk, NY: Sharpe.

Wells, G. (1992). Introduction. In G. Wells and G.L. Chang-Wells, *Constructing knowledge together*. Portsmouth, NH: Heinemann Educational Books.

Wells, G. (1992). Talk for learning and teaching. In G. Wells and G.L. Chang-Wells, *Constructing knowledge together*. Portsmouth, NH: Heinemann Educational Books.

Wells, G. (1993). Working with a teacher in the ZPD: Action research in the learning and teaching of science. *Journal of the Society for Accelerated Learning*.

Wells, G., Chang, G.L. and Maher, A. (1990). Creating classroom communities of literate thinkers. In S. Sharan (ed.) *Cooperative learning: Theory and research*. Reprinted in G. Wells and G.L. Chang-Wells, *Constructing knowledge together*. Portsmouth, NH: Heinemann Educational Books.

Wells, G. and Chang-Wells, G.L. (1992). 'What have you learned?': Co-constructing the meaning of time.

Wertsch, J.V. (1985). The social origins of mental functions. In *Vygotsky and the social formation of mind*. Cambridge, MA: Harvard University Press.

Wertsch, J.V. (1991). The heterogeneity of voices. In *Voices of the mind*. Cambridge, MA: Harvard University Press.

Wertsch, J.V. and Stone, A. (1985). The concept of internalization in Vygotsky's account of the genesis of higher mental functions. In J.V. Wertsch (Ed.) *Culture, communication, and cognition: Vygotskian perspectives*. Cambridge: Cambridge University Press.

References

Allen, K. and Albert, M. (1987). Asking questions: a researcher-teacher collaboration. *Language Arts, 64 (7):* 722-726.

Applebee, A. (1987). Musings ... Teachers and the process of research. *Research in the Teaching of English, 21:* 5-7.

Ashforth, M. (1988). *Blessed with bilingual brains.* British Columbia: Pacific Educational Press.

Atkin, M. (1991). Teaching as research. Invited address to the American Educational Research Association, Chicago, 3-7 April, 1991.

Atwell, N. (1987). Building a dining room table: Dialogue journals about reading. In *In the middle: Writing and reading and learning with adolescents.* Upper Montclair, NJ: Boynton/ Cook, pp.190-197.

Atwell, Nancie (1992). The thoughtful practioner. In *Side by side.* Portsmouth, NH: Heinemann Educational Books.

Baird, W. (1992). Literate thinking in the classroom. In W. Baird and G. Wells, Language and learning: *Learners, teachers and researchers at work.* Vol. 1 *Description and evaluation.* Toronto: OISE, Joint Centre for Teacher Development.

Bakhtin, M.M. (1986). *Speech genres and other late essays.* Austin,TX: University of Texas Press.

Barnes, D. (1976). *From communication to curriculum.* Harmondsworth, UK: Penguin.

Barton, B. and Booth, D. (1990). *Stories in the classroom.* Toronto: Pembroke Publishers.

Barth, R. S.(1990). *Improving schools from within.* San Francisco: Jossey Bass.

Beatty, N. and Diakiw, J. (1991). A superintendent and a principal write to each other. *Educational Leadership, 48, (6)*: 47-50.

Bereiter, C., (1985). Toward a solution of the learning paradox. *Review of Educational Research, 55 (2)*: 201-226.

Bereiter, C. (1992). Implications of postmodernism for science education: Science as progressive discourse. Toronto: OISE, Centre for Applied Cognitive Science: Unpublished paper.

Bettencourt, A. (1991). On understanding science. Michigan State University: Unpublished paper.

Bissex, G.L. (1986). On becoming teacher experts: What's a teacher-researcher? *Language Arts, 63 (5)*: 482-484.

Bissex, G.L. (1988). On learning and not learning from teaching. *Language Arts, 65 (8)*: 771-775.

Bissex, G.L. and Bullock, R.H. (Eds.) (1987). *Seeing for ourselves: Case study research by teachers of writing.* Portsmouth, NH: Heinemann Educational Books.

Booth, D. and Thornley-Hall, C. (Eds.) (1991). *Classroom talk.* Portsmouth, NH: Heinemann.

Brissenden, T. (1988). *Talking about mathematics.* Oxford: Basil Blackwell.

Bunting, E., illus. Hamler, R. (1990). *The wall.* New York: Clairon Books.

Burningham, J. (1974). *The snow.* London: Jonathan Cape.

Calkins, L.M. (1983) *Lessons from a child: On the teaching and learning of writing.* Portsmouth, NH: Heinemann Educational Books.

Calkins, L.M. (1986). *The art of teaching writing.* Portsmouth, NH: Heinemann Educational Books.

Calkins, L.M. (1991). *Living between the lines.* Portsmouth, NH: Heinemann Educational Books.

Carr, W. and Kemmis, S. (1986). *Becoming critical.* London and Philadelphia: Falmer Press.

Chambers, A. (1985). *Booktalk: Occasional writing on literature and children.* London: The Bodley Head.

Chang, G.L.(1990). Teachers as learners: Researching our practice. *Let's Talk: Newsletter, 2 (2).* Peel Board of Education (April 1990)

Chang, G.L., and Wells, G. (1988). The literate potential of collaborative talk. In M. MacLure, T. Phillips and A. Wilkinson (Eds.) *Oracy matters.* Milton Keynes, UK: Open University Press. Reprinted in G. Wells and G.L.Chang-Wells (1992a), *Constructing knowledge together.* Portsmouth, NH: Heinemann.

Clay, Marie (1989). Involving teachers in classroom research. In G.S. Pinnell and M.L. Matlin (Eds.) *Teachers and research: Language learning in the classroom.* Newark, DE: International Reading Association, (pp.29-46).

Connelly, F.M. and Clandinin, D.J. (1988). *Teachers as curriculum planners: Narratives of experience.* New York: Teachers College Press.

Cummins, J. (1984). *Bilingualism and special education: Issues in assessment and pedagogy.* Clevedon, UK: Multilingual Matters.

Cummins, J. (1989). *Empowering minority students.* Sacramento: California Association for Bilingual Education.

Cummins, J. and Swain, M. (1986). *Bilingualism in education.* London: Longman.

Delpit, L. D. (1988). The silenced dialogue: Power and pedagogy in educating other people's children. *Harvard Educational Review, 58 (3):* 280-298.

Dewey, J. (1963). *Experience and education.* New York: Collier Books.

Dodson, C. J. (1983). Living with two languages. *Journal of Multilingual and Multicultural Development, 6 (5).*

Donaldson, M. (1978). *Children's minds.* London: Fontana.

Duckworth, E. (1987). *'The having of wonderful ideas' and other essays on teaching and learning.* New York: Teachers College Press.

Dwyer, J. (Ed.). (1989). *A sea of talk.* Rozelle, NSW, Australia: Primary English Teaching Association.

Dyson, Anne Haas (1989). *Multiple worlds of child writers: Friends learning to write.* Columbia University, New York: Teachers College Press.

Edwards, D. and Mercer, N. (1987). *Common knowledge: the development of understanding in the classroom.* London: Methuen.

Elley, W. and Mangubhai, F. (1983). The impact of reading on second language learning. *Reading Research Quarterly, 19 (1).*

Elliott, J. (1990). *Action research for educational change.* Milton Keynes, UK: Open University Press.

Elmore, R.F. (1992). Why restructuring alone won't improve teaching. *Educational Leadership, 49 (7):* 44-48.

Fosnot, C.T. (1989). *Enquiring teachers, enquiring learners: A constructivist approach for teaching.* New York: Teachers College Press.

Fullan, M. (1982). *The meaning of educational change.* Toronto: OISE Press.

Glass, G. (1993). E-mail message to "Educational Research List," 7 Jan 1993.

Goodman, K.S. (1986). *What's whole in whole language.* Portsmouth, NH: Heinemann Educational Books.

Goodman, Y.M. and Goodman, K.S. (1990). Vygotsky in a whole language perspective. In L.C. Moll (Ed.) *Vygotsky and education: Instructional implications and applications of sociohistorical psychology.* Cambridge: Cambridge University Press.

Gordon, K.A. (1990). The role of staff development in teacher growth: Promoting involvement in professional activities. Toronto: OISE, unpublished paper.

Goswami, D. and Stillman, P. R. (Eds.) (1987). *Reclaiming the classroom: Teacher research as an agency for change.* Upper Monclair, NJ: Boynton Cook Publishers, Inc.

Graves, D. (1983). *Writing: Teachers and children at work.* Portsmouth, NH: Heinemann Educational Books.

Graves, D. (1989). *Experiment with fiction.* Portsmouth, NH: Heinemann Educational Books.

Grimmett, P.P., Erickson, G.L., MacKinnon, A., Riecken, T.J. (1990). Reflective practice in teacher education. In P. Clift et al. (Eds.) *Encouraging reflective practice in education.* New York: Teachers College Press.

Hancock, J. and Hill, S. (1987). *Literature-based reading programs at work.* Richmond Hill, ONT: Scholastic.

Harste, J. (1991). The inquiry-based curriculum. Presented at the 'Reading for the Love of It' Conference, Toronto.

Harste, J. (in press). Literacy as curricular conversations about knowledge, inquiry and morality. In M.R. Ruddell and R.B. Ruddell (Eds.) *Theoretical models and processes of reading. (4th edition)*

Heald-Taylor, G. (1986). *Whole language strategies for ESL Primary students.* Toronto: OISE Press.

Heath, S.B. (1983). *Ways with words.* Cambridge: Cambridge University Press.

Hodges, R.E. (1981). *Learning to spell.* Urbana, IL: National Council of Teachers of English.

Hollis, L.Y., and Houston, W.R. Recruiting mature adults as teachers. *Teacher Education and Practice, 6 (2):* 29-36.

Jacobs, M. and Roderick, J. (1988). Diary of a singular season: Reflecting on dilemmas in teaching writing. *Language Arts, 65 (7):* 642-651.

Jaggar, A.M. (1989). Teacher as learner: Implications for staff development. In G.S. Pinnell and M.L. Matlin (Eds.) *Teachers and research: Language learning in the classroom.* Newark, DE: International Reading Association.

Lampert, M., (1985). *How do teachers manage to teach?* Harvard Educational Review, 55 (2): 178-194.

Lemke, J.L. (1989). Social semiotics: a new model for literacy education. In D. Bloome (Ed.) *Classrooms and literacy.* Norwood, NJ: Ablex.

Lotman, Y.M. (1988). Text within a text. *Soviet Psychology, 26 (3):* 32-51.

Lyons, N. (1990). Dilemmas of knowing: Ethical and epistemological dimensions of teachers' work and development. *Harvard Educational Review, 61 (3):* 112-118.

Moores, D.F. (1987). *Educating the Deaf: Psychology, principles and practices.* Boston: Houghton Mifflin.

Newman, J. (1987). Learning to teach by uncovering our assumptions. *Language Arts, 64 (7):* 727-37.

Newman, J. (Ed.) (1989). *Finding our own way.* Portsmouth, NH: Heinemann Educational Books.

Newman, J. (1991). *Interwoven conversations.* Toronto: OISE Press and Heinemann Educational Books.

Norris, D and Boucher, J. (1980). *Observing children.* Toronto: The Board of Education for the City of Toronto.

North York Board of Education (1991). *Supervision for growth: Pathways to professional growth.* North York, ON: North York Board of Education.

Ontario Teachers' Federation (1992). Ontario teachers break new ground in education reform. *Teachers in Charge, 1 (1):* 1-2.

Phillips, T. (1988). On a related matter: why 'successful' small-group talk depends upon not keeping to the point. In M. Maclure, T. Phillips, A. Wilkinson (Eds.), *Oracy matters.* Milton Keynes, UK and Philadelphia: Open University Press, 69-81.

Pontecorvo, C. and Zuccermaglio, C. (1990). A passage to literacy: learning in a social context. In Goodman, Y. (Ed.) *How children construct literacy.* Newark, DE: International Reading Association.

Probst, R.E. (1988). *Response and analysis: Teaching literature in Junior and Senior High School.* Portsmouth, NH: Heinemann Educational Books.

Quigley, S.P. and Paul, P.V. (1990). *Education and deafness.* New York: Longman.

Rich, S. (1983). On becoming teacher experts: Teacher-researchers. *Language Arts, 6 (7):* 892-894.

Rigg, P. and Enright, D.S. (Eds.) (1986). *Children and ESL: Integrating perspectives.* Teachers of English to Speakers of Other Languages.

Rogoff, B. (1990). *Apprenticeship in thinking.* New York: Oxford University Press.

Rosenblatt, L.M. (1975). *Literature as exploration.* New York: Noble and Noble.

Rosenblatt, L.M. (1988). *Writing and reading: The transactional theory.* Center for the Study of Writing, Technical Report No. 13. University of California, Berkeley and Carnegie Mellon University.

Scardamalia, M. and Bereiter, C. (in press). Text-based and knowledge-based questioning by children. *Cognition and Instruction.*

Schaefer, R.J. (1967). *The school as a center of inquiry.* New York: Harper and Row.

Schön, D. (1987). *Educating the reflective practitioner.* San Francisco: Jossey Bass.

Schulman, L.S. (1987). Knowledge and teaching: Foundations of the new reform. *Harvard Educational Review, 57 (1):* 1-22.

Siu-Runyan Y. Learning from students: an important aspect of classroom organization. *Language Arts, 68: (2):*100-107.

Skinner, D. (1985). Access to meaning: The anatomy of the language learning connection, Parts I & II. *Journal of Multilingual and Multicultural Development, 6 (2) & 6 (5).*

Smith, F. (1986). *Insult to intelligence: The bureaucratic invasion of our classroom.* New York: Arbor House.

Stenhouse, L. (1975). *An introduction to curriculum research and development.* London: Heinemann.

Stevenson, J. (1989). *July.* New York: Greenwillow.

Street, B.V. (1987). Literacy and social change: The significance of social contect in the development of literacy programmes. In D.A. Wagner (Ed.) *The future of literacy in a changing world.* New York: Pergamon Press.

Strickland, D.S. (1988). The teacher as researcher: Toward the extended professional. *Language Arts, 65 (8):* 754-764.

Sydor, S., Hunt, G., (1991). Option five: Partners in developing professional expertise. University of Toronto Faculty of Education: Unpublished Option Statement.

Tashlik, P. (1987). I hear voices: The text, the journal and me. In T. Fulwiler (Ed.) *The journal book.* Portsmouth, NH: Boynton/Cook, 171-178.

Tharp, R. and Gallimore, R. (1988). *Rousing minds to life.* Cambridge: Cambridge University Press.

Thomson, J. (1987). *Understanding teenagers' reading: Reading processes and the teaching of literature.* New York: Nichols.

Torbe, M. and Medway, P. (1981). *The climate for learning.* Upper Montclair, NJ: Boynton/Cook.

Vygotsky, L. (1962). *Thought and language.* Cambridge: M.I.T. Press.

Vygotsky, L.S. (1978). *Mind and Society.* Cambridge, MA: Harvard University Press.

Vygotsky, L.S. (1981). The genesis of higher mental functions. In J.V. Wertsch (Ed.) *The concept of activity in Soviet psychology.* Armonk, NY: Sharpe.

Wells, G. (1985). *Language development in the pre-school years.* Cambridge: Cambridge University Press.

Wells, G. (1986). *The meaning makers: Children learning language and using language to learn.* Portsmouth, NH: Heinemann Educational Books.

Wells, G. (1987). Apprenticeship in literacy. *Interchange, 18 (1/2):* 109-123.

Wells, G., (1990a). Talk about text: Where literacy is learned and taught. *Curriculum Inquiry, 20 (4):* 369-404. Reprinted in G. Wells and G.L.Chang-Wells (1992), Constructing knowledge together. Portsmouth, NH: Heinemann.

Wells, G., (1990b). Intersubjectivity and the construction of knowledge. Paper presented at the conference on "Social Interaction and the Acquisition of Knowledge," Universita di Roma, "la Sapienza", Rome, 4-7 December.

Wells, G., (1992). Some reflections on action research. In Wells, G., Chang G.L. and Blake, M. (eds.) *Language and learning: Learners, teachers, and researchers at work. Vol. 4. Collaborative research.* Toronto: OISE, Joint Centre for Teacher Development.

Wells, G. (1993). Working with a teacher in the ZPD: Action research in the learning and teaching of science. *Journal of the Society for Accelerative Learning and Teaching. 18 (1/2):* 127-272.

Wells, G. (in press) Language and the inquiry-oriented curriculum. *Curriculum Inquiry.*

Wells, G. and Chang-Wells, G.L. (1992a). *Constructing knowledge together.* Portsmouth, NH: Heinemann Educational Books.

Wells, G. and Chang-Wells, G.L. (1992b). 'What have you learned?': Co-constructing the meaning of time. OISE: Joint Centre for Teacher Development. Unpublished paper.

Wells, G., Chang, G.L., and Maher, A., (1990). Creating classroom communities of literate thinkers. In S. Sharan (Ed.) *Cooperative learning: Theory and research.* New York: Praeger.

Wertsch, J.V. (1985). *Vygotsky and the social formation of mind.* Cambridge, MA: Harvard University Press.

White, C. (1989). *Jevon doesn't sit at the back anymore.* Toronto, ON: Scholastic.

Wilbur, R.B. (1977). An explanation of deaf children's difficulty with certain syntactic structures. *Volta Review, 79:* 85-92.

Wood, D., Bruner, J.S. and Ross, G. (1976). The role of tutoring in problem-solving. *Journal of Child Psychology and Psychiatry, 17:* 89-100.

Yonemura, M., (1982). Teacher conversations: A potential source of their own professional growth. *Curriculum Inquiry, 12 (3):* 239.

York Region Board of Education. (1991). *Evaluation of supervision and instruction of program.*

Zeichner, K.M., Liston, D.P. (1987). Teaching student teachers to reflect. *Harvard Educational Review, 57 (1):* 23-48.